Places to Go
with Children
IN
NEW ENGLAND

Places to Go with Children

IN

NEW ENGLAND

Diane Bair
Pamela Wright

Chronicle Books ▪ San Francisco

Printed in the United States of America.

Library of Congress Cataloging in Publication Data
Bair, Diane.
  Places to go with children in New England / Diane Bair, Pamela Wright.
     p.   cm.
  ISBN 0-87701-706-9
  1. Family recreation—New England—Guide-books.   2. New England—Description and travel—1981—Guide-books.   I. Wright, Pamela, 1953–   .   II. Title.
GV182.8.B35   1990
790.1′91′0974—dc20   89-27864
                                                                                    CIP

Editing: Julie Pechilis
Book design: Seventeenth Street Studios
Cover design: Brenda Rae Eno
Cover photograph: © 1989 Greg Nikas
Composition: Another Point, Inc.

10 9 8 7 6 5 4 3 2

Chronicle Books
275 Fifth Street
San Francisco, CA 94103

 *printed on recycled paper*

For Charlotte, Sadie, and Jared

Contents

Introduction

The person who said "Getting there is half the fun" never traveled with children.

As any parent can attest, "getting there" can be horrendous, especially if you run short of juice boxes, travel games, and/or restroom facilities. All this after spending hours—or days—packing favorite toys, food, and 300 changes of clothing. "This had better be worth it," you mutter, as your mood—and theirs—deteriorates.

This book is full of places that are worth it.

You'll find just-for-kids museums with exciting hands-on exhibits, boat cruises on which you can trap lobsters or explore islands in the Atlantic, centuries-old caves and medieval castles to visit, and special spots to pan for gold, hear ghost stories, make grave-rubbings, and see dinosaur tracks. We could go on and on. And we do.

Of course, you'll need to eat along the way, so we've included lists of family-friendly restaurants. The emphasis is on great locations—lots of waterfront spots—and menus that offer the best of New England dining, from freshly-caught seafood to regional ethnic specialties. Comfortable places where families eat out together.

And, because New England has more than its fair share of natural beauty, you'll find plenty of ways to enjoy the outdoors. Family hikes, ski resorts, wildlife areas, and spectacular mountaintop drives—often just minutes away from cities—are waiting to be explored. This book will tell you where to find them and how to make the most of them.

The pure pleasure of watching the children you love explore the world, try new things, and simply play—with you and each other—is unbeatable. This book was written in that spirit.

New England's city parks and gardens offer the chance to run and play or buy a balloon or just relax and watch the world go by.

Massachusetts

Boston

Steeped in tradition, yet pulsing with the beat of a modern city, Boston is one of the most popular tourist destinations in the world. Stroll the cobblestone streets of Beacon Hill or hop on the "T" (what the locals call their subway system) and you'll immediately notice the color and diversity that make Boston unique. Savor high tea at the Ritz, or slurp oysters at a raw bar in Quincy market. Take the children for a relaxing ride on a swan boat, or brave the bargain-hungry throngs at Filene's Basement. You'll soon learn why Bostonians love their city. Just listen to some of the locals: "Even though I grew up here, walking the Freedom Trail always stirs my imagination. It conjures up visions of Paul Revere's ride, the Boston Tea Party, the Revolution—it makes you feel a part of history." "Boston is a visual, sensory treat. Nothing feels as wonderful as walking down Marlborough Street surrounded by beautiful brownstones and dogwoods in bloom."

You've heard the phrase "Pahk your cah in Hahvahd yahd?" Forget it. Boston's maze of narrow, one-way streets is best navigated by foot, trolley, or subway—not by car. Don your sneakers (don't worry about fitting in—Bostonians wear them even with their pin-striped suits) and start walking. When little feet get tired, board the "T;" Boston's subway system is clean and modern and takes you to all major points of interest in the city.

Downtown

Museum of Science
Science Park; (617) 723-2500. Mon.–Sun., 9–5; Fri., 9–9. Adults, $6; 4–14, $4. Omni admission: adults, $5; 4–14, $3. Combination ticket: $7.50 and $5. Planetarium admission: $5 and $3.50. Combination ticket: $9 and $6.50.

You won't want to miss this world-renowned museum containing more than 400 participatory exhibits. Walk beside a three-story-high tyrannosaurus, see live animal and physical science demonstrations, or test your wits in the computer center. The centerpiece of the museum's new wing is an Omnimax theater—the only theater of its kind in New England and one of only 12 in the country—featuring the world's largest projection system and a dome screen 76 feet in diameter. The special multi-image theater presentations will dazzle you. Also housed in the new wing are the Hayden Planetarium, stages for Science Theater presentations, a three-story atrium with exhibits, and a computer arcade. Young or old, you'll leave wanting to come back.

Museum of Fine Arts

465 Huntington Ave.; (617) 267-9300. Tues.–Sun., 10–5; Wed., 10–10; Thurs. and Fri., West Wing and Evans Wing, 10–10. Adults, $5 during hours when entire museum is open, $4 during hours when only the West wing is open; 16 and under free; Sat., 10–noon, free to everyone.
Comprehensive collections of Chinese, Japanese, Indian, Egyptian, Greek, Roman, European, and American art, plus period rooms and musical instruments may be found here. The West Wing houses changing exhibits, restaurants, and the museum shop. The museum often hosts special children's exhibits with hands-on arts and crafts demonstrations. The kids can have fun—and learn too—while you survey some of the world's finest art.

Faneuil Hall Marketplace

Merchants Row; (617) 242-5642.
More than a million people every month visit this bright, bustling center of activity. Here, along cobblestone streets, you're likely to encounter clowns and mimes, harpists and guitarists, a regularly scheduled event, or a spontaneous rendition. The marketplace consists of four refurbished buildings containing more than 170 shops and restaurants. This colorful, festive area has become a model for the restoration and conversion of older urban sections into exciting centers for shopping, dining, and entertainment. It's crowded, noisy, and fun.

The Boston Common

Bounded by Beacon, Charles, Boylston, Tremont, and Park streets.
This is the oldest public park in the United States, occupying 48 acres in the city's busy downtown area. In colonial days the area was pastureland for animals and training ground for the militia. Today you'll find street

Youngsters learn scientific principles
while playing games at the Museum of
Science in Boston.

musicians, art-in-the park exhibits, theater groups, food vendors, and major outdoor events, concerts, and demonstrations. Pick up maps and information at the Visitor Information Center located on the hilly east side. This is also the starting point for Boston's Freedom Trail.

The Freedom Trail

If you really want to see downtown Boston, put on comfortable shoes and follow the red-brick road. Boston's Freedom Trail is a self-guided, 2.5-mile walking tour of 16 historic sites. A bold red stripe on the sidewalks, beginning at the Boston Common Visitor Information Center, leads visitors through the downtown financial/shopping district to Faneuil Hall, through the North End, and into Charlestown. Depending on how fast you walk, how many sites you see, and how long you stay at each site, the Trail can take anywhere from two hours to a full day to complete. Maps can be found at Visitor Information Centers located throughout the city. Freedom Trail Sites include: the State House, Park Street Church, Granary Burying Ground, King's Chapel, Ben Franklin's statue and the site of the first public school, the Old Corner Bookstore, Old South Meeting House, Old State House, the Boston Massacre Site, Faneuil Hall, the Paul Revere House, Old North Church, Copp's Hill Burial Ground, the U.S.S. Constitution, and Bunker Hill Monument. You might want to pick and choose sites along the tour to tailor it to your family's interest in history and architecture.

Boston-By-Little-Feet

Starts at the statue of Samuel Adams in front of Faneuil Hall (Congress St. side) on Sundays at 2 throughout the summer. (617) 367-2345. $4 per person.

This hour-long guided tour is especially designed for children aged 6 through 12. It takes them, accompanied by their adult friends, to some of the major sites in the city and teaches them about history, architecture, and people along the way. Each child gets a colorful map to follow and take home as a souvenir. A great way to introduce kids to the city of Boston.

Downtown Crossing

Adjacent to Boston Common.

Street vendors, flower carts and newspaper stands, musicians and mimes, restaurants and stores galore—all these and more add up to the hustle and bustle of Downtown Crossing. Bounded by Chinatown and the financial district, Downtown Crossing is closed to all traffic—and is a bargain hunter's dream come true. Here is where you'll find Filene's Basement, one of the most famous discount stores in the country. If you have a shopper or two in your group, you won't want to miss it. The area is colorful enough to keep the non-shoppers in the family easily entertained too.

Boston Public Garden

An oasis of tranquility in the middle of the bustling city, the Public Garden is a wonderful place to relax and catch your breath before the next stop on your agenda. Be sure to take a ride on the Swan Boats. This is the venue of McCloskey's *Make Way For Ducklings*, the all-time children's favorite tale of a mallard family looking for a home.

Wheelock Family Theater

180 The Riverway; (617) 734-5203. Evening performances Fri. and Sat., 7:30; matinees Sat. and Sun., 3. Tickets, $7.

Catch a performance of "Androcles and the Lion" or whatever child-pleasing production is playing here. This theater, run by Wheelock College, is a great place to introduce children, aged three and up, to the magic of the stage.

It's a sure sign that spring has arrived in Boston when the swanboats open for business.

Waterfront

Boston Tea Party Ship and Museum
Congress Street Bridge; (617) 338-1773. Daily, 9–7. Adults, $3.75; 5–14, $2.75.

Relive one of the most colorful chapters in our country's history. Kids will love tossing a bundle of tea in the harbor below (and pulling it back up again) as they relive the notorious rebellion aboard the Beaver II, a full-size reproduction of one of the famous Tea Party ships. The adjacent museum contains colonial exhibits and shows.

Children's Museum of Boston
Museum Wharf, 300 Congress St.; (617) 426-6500. Tues.–Sun., 10–5; closed Mon. except holidays. Adults, $5; 2–15, $4.

This is one of the largest and best hands-on children's museums in the country. You'll find a wonderland of interactive exhibits designed for youngsters from toddler to teen. Explore a castle, appear on T.V., blow giant bubbles, make friends with a computer, or pretend to be a dentist, a mechanic, a grocer . . . the activities are endless. You won't be able to do everything in one visit; families return again and again.

Computer Museum
Museum Wharf, 300 Congress St.; (617) 423-6758. Tues.–Sun., 10–5; Fri., 10–9; closed Mon. except holidays. Adults, $5; 5–17, $4. Fri. after 5, admission half price.

Right next door to the Children's Museum, the Computer Museum is a user-friendly spot with enough activity to keep children happy and enough gee-whiz technology to impress the most jaded adult. Hold a conversation with a computer, change the look of your face, design a new car . . . you'll find the latest in computer technology here, as well as some of the earliest vintage computers.

New England Aquarium
Central Wharf; (617) 973-5200. Mon.–Thurs., 9–5; Fri., 9–8; Sat. and Sun., 9–6. Adults, $7; 4–15, $3.50.

The world's largest circular, glass-enclosed tank brings sharks, turtles, and hundreds of underwater creatures inches from your face. If your children are like most, they'll get a real thrill out of walking through the tunnel of sharks at feeding time or hand-dunking for crabs, shells, and starfish at the Tidal Pool. Visit Discovery, the floating pavilion next to the Aquarium

*There are plenty of sea creatures to
touch—if you dare—at the New England
Aquarium.*

(admission is included in your aquarium ticket), for dolphin and sea lion
shows.

Boston Harbor Islands

If it's a sunny, warm day and you're tired of city sounds and sights, consider
a short ferry trip to one or more of the islands that make up the Boston
Harbor Island State Park. Spend a day exploring an old fort or swimming in
an ocean cove. There are lots of nice walks on the islands, as well as opportunities for boating and fishing. Several cruise companies leaving the waterfront piers will get you to Georges Island—from there take a free water taxi
to the other islands.

Back Bay

John Hancock Observatory

Copley Square; (617) 572-6000. Mon.–Sat., 9–11; Sun., 10–11. Adults,

$2.75; 5–15, $1.50.
New England's tallest building offers sweeping views from on high. A multimedia presentation gives a helicopter tour of the city.

The Skywalk
Prudential Center, 50th Floor, 800 Boylston St.; (617) 236-3318. Mon.–Sat., 10–10; Sun., 12–10. Adults, $2.50; 5–15, $1.50.
Get a 360-degree view of Boston and beyond from this 52-story building.

Where's Boston?
Copley Place, 100 Huntington Ave.; (617) 267-4949. Daily, shows on the hour.
This multimedia show gives a quick, all-around introduction to the city's sights, sounds, and people. Stop in before you begin your visit to Boston.

Institute of Contemporary Art
955 Boylston St.; (617) 266-5152. Wed.–Sun., 11–5; Thurs., Fri., and Sat., 11–8. Adults, $4; 16 and under, $1.50. Fri., 5–8, free.
Weird, wild, and wonderful art displays are here. Your children might get a kick out of the often-featured video and performance-as-art shows. Call ahead to see what's showing.

Beacon Hill

The State House
Beacon St., Mon.–Fri., 10–4. Free.
Samuel Adams laid the cornerstone for this gold-domed Boston landmark. Sitting atop Beacon Hill, the State House is now the seat of Massachusetts government. Two tours are given here: older children might enjoy the Legislative Process tour that explains how laws are made; a historical/architectural tour features the Hall of Flags and House and Senate rooms. Be sure to pick up the special booklet for children at the tour desk.

Granary Burying Ground
Tremont St., next to Park Street Church; (617) 542-3071. Daily, 8–4. Free.
Step back into history and recall the lives and times of our American heroes. This is the final resting place of John Hancock, Samuel Adams,

Robert Paine, and the parents of Ben Franklin and Paul Revere. Some say the grave of Mother Goose is also here.

Black Heritage Trail

This walking tour commemorates the history of Boston's 19th-century black community, which settled in this part of Beacon Hill. The trail begins at the African Meeting House (8 Smith Center), the oldest black church building still standing in the United States, and continues through Beacon Hill with stops at the Smith Court Residences, Abiel Smith School, the George Middleton House, the Robert Gould Show and the 54th Regiment Memorial, the Phillips School, the home of John J. Smith, the Charles Street Meeting House, the Lewis and Harriet Hayden House, and the Coburn's Gaming House. Pick up maps and information at Visitors Information Centers throughout the city.

North End

Paul Revere House

19 North Square; (617) 523-1676. Daily, 9:30–5:15; closed Mon., Jan.–Mar. Adults, $2; 5–17, 50¢.
The famous patriot Paul Revere was living in this house when he took his famous ride, shouting "The British are coming!" This house is the oldest building in Boston (built around 1680) and contains many original furnishings.

Haymarket Square

Haymarket St. (adjacent to Quincy Marketplace, behind the Bostonian Hotel). Fri.–Sat., dawn to dusk.
If you're near the North End of Boston on Friday or Saturday, you won't be able to miss this open-air farmer's market. Push your way through the crowds and endure the brisk, terse talk of the vendors to see a colorful menagerie of people, food, and flowers. Fresh fish and produce abound. If you like oysters, buy them fresh, on the half shell, for 25 cents apiece.

Feasts, Fairs, and Celebrations

North End (Hanover, Salem, and Prince streets), weekends throughout the summer.
The narrow streets of the North End come alive with celebration every

weekend throughout the summer. The statues are decorated and the streets blocked off to make way for pushcarts laden with Italian pizza, sausages, pasta, and pastries. Add parades, music, and song and you have a colorful, lively outdoor festival. Walk over and join the fun.

Scenic Stroll—Harborwalk
This is a self-guided tour along the Boston waterfront. Brochures (pick them up at Visitor Centers or major hotels) explain Boston's maritime history. A nice stroll and a great way to get to or from the New England Aquarium, Children's Museum, or Boston Tea Party Ship.

Scenic Stroll—Newbury Street
Newbury Street, from Arlington Avenue to Massachusetts Avenue, is lined with antique shops, fashion boutiques, exclusive stores, and fine restaurants. Sit at an outdoor cafe, roam through an art gallery, window shop, or people-watch. If you have a little time, meander down brownstone-lined Marlborough Street (especially beautiful in spring when the dogwoods are in bloom); stroll down Commonwealth Avenue, a tree-lined promenade of parks; or walk over to Copley Square, where you'll see beautiful Trinity Church and the Copley Square fountain.

Scenic Stroll—Beacon Hill
There's no other place in the country quite like Beacon Hill. The very first Bostonians resided here, and today it's still regarded as a highly desirable residential location. This is a neighborhood of charm and antiquity, full of 18th- and 19th-century town houses, narrow cobblestone streets, courtyard gardens, brick walkways, and gas-lit lanterns. The best way to see Beacon Hill? Wear comfortable walking shoes (most of it is uphill), start at Charles and Beacon streets, and meander.

Boat Cruises
Call A.C. Cruise Line, (617) 426-8419; Bay State Cruises, (617) 723-7800; Boston By Sail, (617) 742-3313; Boston Harbor Cruises, (617) 227-4320; Massachusetts Bay Lines, (617) 749-4500; The Spirit of Boston, (617) 542-2974.
Cruise to find a humpback whale playground, visit neighboring islands, or board a ship that will take you down to the tip of Cape Cod and back. A number of cruise companies offer a variety of itineraries for those who want a view of Boston from the water. Call ahead to discuss options, costs, and hours. All depart from points along Boston waterfront piers.

Tours
An old-fashioned trolley ride or horse-and-carriage tour are big hits with visiting children and (travel-weary) adults. Most allow you to get on and off along the way and feature narration on major points of interest. Regularly scheduled tours are offered by Beantown Trolley, (617) 287-1900; Boston Trolley Tours, (617) 427-TOUR; Old Town Trolley Tours of Boston, (617) 269-7010; Horse and Carriage Tours, (617) 523-5256.

Just Outside Boston

John F. Kennedy Library
Morrissey Blvd., Dorchester; (617) 929-4523. Daily, 9–5. Adults, $3.50; under 16, free.
This museum/library, the nation's memorial to President Kennedy, features audio-visual presentations, view clips, and a 30-minute film chronicling Kennedy's life. A collection of personal items, letters, and family photographs are displayed. The assassination is handled gently but matter-

Boston's Public Garden is a great place for picnicking, people-watching, and serious strolling.

of-factly. You'll enjoy the site, right on the ocean, and the impressive I.M. Pei-designed building.

Bunker Hill Monument
Monument Ave., Charlestown; (617) 242-5641. Daily, 9:30–5. Free.
This towering obelisk marks the site of the first battle of the American Revolution. Poised on the summit of Breed's Hill, this 220-foot monument was built to honor those who died on June 17, 1775. Children love climbing the 294 steps to the top; join them, and you'll be rewarded with a great view of Boston (not to mention a good workout).

U.S.S. Constitution and Museum
Constitution Plaza, Charlestown; (617) 426-1812. Year-round, daily, 9–4:30. U.S.S. Constitution is free. Admission to museum: adults, $2.50; 6–12, $1.50.
A visit to "Old Ironsides" can be an intriguing learning experience for the whole family. The ship, originally launched in Boston in 1797, is the oldest commissioned warship afloat in the world. Climb aboard for a tour, guided by one of the ship's active-duty sailors, and you'll learn about life at sea. Kids will love peeking into the nooks and crannies and climbing the ladderlike steps. The U.S.S. Constitution Museum offers an even greater opportunity for children to play sailor-for-a-day: there are several interactive exhibits—even a computer simulator that allows you to be ship's captain. Try your hand at nautical knot-tying.

Bunker Hill Pavilion
Constitution Plaza, Charlestown; (617) 241-7575. Year-round, daily, 9:30–4. Adults, $3; 16 and under, $1.50.
During your visit to Constitution Plaza, stop by the Bunker Hill Pavilion. You won't want to miss "The Whites of Their Eyes," one of the liveliest half-hour history lessons you're likely to encounter. This multimedia presentation on the Battle of Bunker Hill is both entertaining and informative. You'll find yourself rooting for the badly outnumbered colonists, who fought bravely until the ammunition was gone—a profound example of stubborn Yankee pride.

Museum of Transportation and Lars Anderson Park
15 Newton St., Brookline; (617) 522-6140. Park open year-round. Museum: early Apr.–Aug., Wed.–Sun., 10–5; Sept.–Feb., weekends only, 10–5. Adults, $4; 12 and under, $2.
The Lars Anderson Park, located about 15 minutes west of Boston, is a

lovely urban oasis where you'll always find children somersaulting on the vast lawn or skipping rocks on the pond. In winter the rolling hills are a favorite sledding spot for locals, and you'll get a great view of the Boston skyline in the distance. Don't leave without a visit to the Transportation Museum located on the grounds. Kids can climb on cars and motorcycles, try their wits at the scavenger hunt auto quiz, or climb into the hayloft to see the collection of antique bicycles. Sundays, in the summer, there are special outdoor exhibits, like the Model T Convention, British Car Day, or Ferrari Fun Day.

Puppet Showplace Theater
32 Station St., Brookline; (617) 731-6400. Sept.–June, Sat.–Sun., 1 and 3, July–Aug., performances also on Wed. and Thurs. at 1. Admission, $4.
Fairies, folk tales, fun, and fantasy all await you at Puppet Showplace Theater in Brookline (a short "T" ride from Boston.) Shows are designed for children aged five and up, and the 3:00 show on the third Saturday of each month is sign-language interpreted.

Blue Hills State Reservation
Rte. 138 (10 miles south of Boston), Milton; (617) 698-5840.
Just south of Boston, this unique area boasts a series of massive granite domes (monadnocks) rising more than 635 feet. A network of trails leads to a panoramic overlook on Great Blue Hill. Some parts of these trails are rugged; if your group includes young children or inexperienced hikers, stick to the lowlands of this large area. Houghton's Pond is a popular swimming spot, while Ponkapoag Pond is best for fishing. A trailside museum, operated by the Massachusetts Audubon Society, features native animals of the Blue Hills, including hawks, snakes, and foxes. Cross-country skiing in winter.

Boston Sports

There's hardly a kid alive who wouldn't enjoy an afternoon cheering the Red Sox at Fenway Park, hot dog in one hand and scorecard in the other. Or pick your favorite spectator sport . . . Beantown is well known for its championship teams. For tickets and information call the following numbers: Boston Red Sox, Fenway Park, (617) 267-1700; Boston Celtics, Boston Garden, (617) 523-3030 (If the Celtics are your team, good luck; tickets are hard to come by.); Boston Bruins, Boston Garden, (617) 523-3223; and New England Patriots, Sullivan Stadium in Foxboro, (508) 543-1776.

New England Sports Museum
Herter Park, 1175 Soldiers Field Rd.; (617) 787-2691. Year-round, Mon.–Sat., 10–6; Sun., noon–6. Adults, $2; under 6, $1.
Diehards in your family might enjoy a visit to the New England Sports Museum. You'll relive some of the greatest moments in New England sports history as you tour this museum located in the Christian Herter Park along the Charles River. Watch the magic of Bob Cousy's fast-break and Ted Williams' perfect swing on rare old sports films. Or play the video jukebox to see some of the best classic sports moments.

Restaurants

Quincy Market
Faneuil Hall Marketplace, Merchants Row; (617) 242-5642. Daily 'til 10.
Noisy, fast, and crowded, you can get just about anything you want here. There are food stands, specialty stores, and fine restaurants of every kind. Perfect if everyone in the family has a taste for something different. Grab a table, if you can, or sit outside on benches.

Durgin Park
Faneuil Hall Marketplace; (617) 227-2038. Mon.–Sat., 11:30–10; Sun., noon–9.
This is a Boston landmark. You'll get real Yankee cooking here—pot roast, succotash, and Indian pudding—all served family-style. Don't be shy; you'll be seated at long, picnic-type tables next to other friendly diners, and the waiters will give you a hard time if you don't finish your vegetables.

Serendipity
Faneuil Hall Marketplace; (617) 523-2339. Mon.-Fri., 11–1 a.m.; Sat.–Sun., 10:30–midnight.
You'll have fun here—and are sure to enjoy the crazy, eclectic menu of burgers, sandwiches, and finger food. Climb to the second floor of the South Market building at Faneuil Hall Marketplace and relax in the Victorian-style setting. Save room for dessert: Serendipity is well known for its fabulous ice cream sundaes and other sinful goodies.

Imperial Tea House
70 Beach St.; (617) 426-8543. Daily, 9–2 a.m.
For children who love finger food, this airy restaurant in the heart of
Chinatown is a fun experience. The Imperial House is known for its dim
sum, served at lunch.

Hood Milk Bottle
Museum Wharf. Seasonal, hours vary.
Shaped, indeed, like a giant milk bottle, this place is just the sort of oddity
children love. Plus you can eat outside on benches, dining on sandwiches,
hot dogs, and the like.

Jimmy's Harborside
242 Northern Ave.; (617) 423-1000. Mon.–Sat., 11:30–9:30.
Right on the water, with all the seafood specialties you'd expect. This place
is large enough and noisy enough that no one will notice if your children
are less than charming.

Ye Olde Union Oyster House
*41 Union St. (down the street from Faneuil Hall Marketplace). Sun.–Thurs.,
11–9:30; Fri.–Sat., 11–10.*
Boston's oldest restaurant; features New England seafood.

La Piccola Venezia
Salem St., North End.
It's tiny, homey, authentic, and the staff will treat you like family. What
better way to get into the spirit of the North End? You'll find some southern
Italian specialities on the menu, like tripe soup and calamari, as well as
"macaroni and gravy" (pasta and sauce) in several varieties. Order
anything—it's all delicious.

Pizzeria Regina
*11½ Thatcher; (617) 227-0765. Mon.–Thurs., 11–9; Fri.–Sat., 11:30–
midnight; Sun., 2–11.*
More than a pizza place, this is a Boston landmark. Families have been
coming here for about 40 years to enjoy the thin-crust pizza and soft drinks
by-the-pitcher. Regina's has become a chain of restaurants, but locals agree
that this is the only real Regina's, by far the best of the bunch. Noisy,
crowded, and fun.

Worth a Trip

Higgins Armory Museum
Barber Ave. (Rte. 12N off I-190, Exit 1), Worcester; (508) 853-6015. Year-round, Sat.–Sun., 12–4; Sept.–June, Tues.–Fri., 9–4; July–Aug., Mon.–Fri., 9–4. Adults, $4; 5–18, $2.75.
Worcester is located about 50 miles west of Boston, off the Massachusetts Turnpike. Its Higgins Armory Museum may be the only place in the country where your dreams of being a knight in shining armor can come true. At this one-of-a-kind museum, kids (adults too!) can try on an authentic suit of armor in the Participatory Gallery. The museum includes demonstrations of arms and armor, games, crafts, sound and light shows, and special events. The collections of medieval and renaissance armory and related artifacts are fascinating.

New England Science Center
22 Harrington St. (off Rte. 9) Worcester; (508) 791-9211. Year-round, Mon.–Sat., 10–5; Sun., 12–5. Adults, $4.50; 3–16, $3.50.
Don't leave the Worcester area without a visit to the New England Science Center. The three-story museum sits on 59 acres and includes hands-on exhibits, indoor and outdoor zoos, an omnisphere, and an observatory.

Worth a Trip

Lowell Heritage State Park and National Historical Park
Market Mills, Lowell; (508) 937-9300. Daily, 8:30–5.
Travel a maze of canalways on river barges or hop an antique trolley to the great 19th-century mill complexes as you learn about life during the American Industrial Revolution. As you tour the restored textile mills, you'll meet the mill girls and canal workers who first set the revolution in motion. (The American Industrial Revolution was born when Frances Cabot Lowell secretly brought the power loom design to the United States from England. Situated on the Merrimack River at Pawtucket Falls, Lowell had enough waterpower to create a cloth manufacturing industry.) Walk the Esplanade along the river, stop by Market Mills with its changing displays and shops, or attend the many special family programs held throughout the summer. It's an interesting, fun way to spend the afternoon.

Lexington/Concord Area

Prepare to soak up some 1775 spirit—and lots of history—when you retrace Paul Revere's famous ride. This is where the American Revolution began. As you stand on the North Bridge, it seems you can still hear that first "shot heard 'round the world," and as you walk Battle Creek, you're likely to feel some spine-tingling pride.

The historical landmarks are the big attractions in this area. But when children tire of history lessons, there are plenty of other things to do. Visit the top-notch Children's Discovery Museums in nearby Acton, hike to Thoreau's cabin on lovely Walden Pond, or canoe the calm waters of the Concord River. A visit to this area is a popular day-trip from Boston. But, coming from that direction, try to avoid morning and evening rush hour traffic as it can be murderous. In fact, locals joke that if Paul Revere were to make the ride today, he'd probably get stuck in traffic and opt to call John Hancock and Samuel Adams from his car phone, instead. ("Sam? Hi, it's me, Paul. Yeah, I'm calling from my car. The British are coming!")

Minuteman Statue/Battle Green

This is the spot where it all began in the early morning of April 19, 1775. The mounting tension between the British occupiers and the independence-seeking rebels finally erupted at a place now known as Battle Green. Leading the Minutemen onto the green was Captain John Parker, immortalized by the Minuteman Statue. Captain Parker's rallying cry: "Stand your ground, don't fire unless fired upon; but if they mean to have a war, let it begin here!"

Lexington Center

□ Buckman Tavern

1 Bedford St., Lexington; (617) 861-0928. Mid-Apr.–Oct., daily. Adults, $2; 6–15, 50¢.

Facing the Green is Buckman Tavern, where the Minutemen gathered before the battle. Of the many historic buildings in the area, this one is a favorite with children. Restored to its original state, the Tavern has period furniture, a display of colonial clothing, and signs limiting travelers to four in a bed.

□ Museum of Our National Heritage

33 Marrett Rd. (Rtes. 2A and 4), Lexington; (617) 861-6560. Mon.–Sat., 10–5; Sun., 1–5. Free.

The focus here is on the development of the United States, with changing exhibits and films that feature the dramatic events and turning points that shaped our history.

□ Minuteman National Historical Park

Off Rte. 2A, (508) 369-6944. April–Dec., daily. Free.

This 750-acre park spans three towns: Lexington, Lincoln, and Concord. Stop wherever you like—there are several visitor's centers in the park, each with maps and helpful staff to guide you. (A good place to start is Battle Road Visitor's Center, run by the National Park Service, with exhibits and films.) Be sure to visit the reconstructed North Bridge, where the "shot heard 'round the world" was fired.

The Wayside

455 Lexington Rd., Concord; (508) 369-6957. Fri.–Tues., 8:30–5. Adults, $1; 6 and under, free.

Follow Battle Road (Route 2A) into Concord, and you'll see a number of historic houses. Young readers will enjoy visiting The Wayside, the 19th-century home of Nathaniel Hawthorne, the Alcotts, and Margaret Sidney, author of the *Five Little Peppers* series. In nearby Orchard House, Louisa May Alcott wrote *Little Women*.

Sleepy Hollow Cemetery

Rte. 62, Bedford Street, Concord.

It is said that this is where the famous "headless horseman" rode many years ago. You'll also see the gravesites of famous people, with some heavy hitters buried along Author's Ridge: they include Thoreau, Emerson, Hawthorne, and the Alcotts.

Walden Pond

Rte. 126, Concord.

Combine your trip to the Lexington/Concord area with a stop at lovely Walden Pond. At the north end of the pond, you'll find a wooded walking path that will lead you to the site of Henry David Thoreau's cabin. This is where Thoreau lived and wrote from 1845 to 1847. Pack a lunch and bring your bathing suits—directly across the lake in the 150-acre Walden Pond State Reservation is a large picnic area and swimming beach.

Canoeing

Rte. 62 (Main Street), Concord; (508) 369-9438. Weekdays, $5.70/hour or $25/day; weekends, $6.95/hour or $35/day.

The calm, flat waters of the Concord River and its tributary, the Sudbury, are favorites for family canoeing. Stop by the put-in spot at Southbridge Boat House in Concord, where you can rent canoes by the hour or day.

The Discovery Museums

177 Main St., Acton; (508) 264-4200. School year: Tues., Thurs., Fri., 1–4:30; Wed., Sat., Sun., 9–4:30. Summer: Tues.–Sun., 9–4:30. $4.50 per person; both museums same day, $8 per person.

There are two wonderful hands-on museums for children of all ages, right next to each other in the nearby town of Acton. The cozy Children's Discovery Museum, especially for children ages one through eight, is in a 100-year-old Victorian house. Everywhere you look—in rooms, hallways, even closets—you'll find creative hands-on exhibits to explore. Tots will enjoy climbing aboard the Discovery Ship, building in the wall-to-wall Legos room, setting off a roomful of chain reactions, or listening to the sounds of the humpback whale. There are 10 exhibit areas in all—an afternoon's-worth of fun and learning.

Located behind the Children's Discovery Museum is the architecturally acclaimed Science Discovery Museum, especially for children ages six and up. The spacious, colorful building is full of interactive science exhibits. Build dams and waterfalls in the Water Discovery Room, make patterns with sound waves, shout in the echo tube . . . there are literally hundreds of things to explore. The kids will have so much fun they won't realize how much they're learning about science and technology.

Restaurants

Michael's

208 Fitchburg Tpke., Concord; (508) 371-1114. Daily, 11:30–10.

This small, busy Italian restaurant serves a variety of pasta dishes—the mixed grill and chicken-broccoli ziti are popular choices—along with steaks, chicken, and salads. No children's menu, but portions are large enough for sharing. Entrée prices start at $7.

Rossini's
Nineacre Corner (off Rte. 2), Concord; (508) 371-3280. Mon.–Sat., 11–10; Sun., noon–10.
In the mood for a more casual meal? Visit Rossini's Pizzeria, next door to Michael's, for pizza, calzones (highly recommended), and other Italian specialties.

Worth a Trip

Toy Cupboard Theatre and Museums
57 East George Hill Rd. (off Main St.), South Lancaster; (508) 365-9519. Admission 90¢.
For some creative, homespun entertainment, go visit Herbert Hosmer and his friendly gang of hand puppets and marionettes. For nearly 50 years, Herbert, a retired school teacher, has been running the Toy Cupboard Puppet Theatre and delighting young audiences with his renditions of favorite fairy tales and children's stories. It's a toss-up as to who enjoys the show the most—Herbert or his audiences. Whether there's a crowd of 2 or 52, the shows go on year-round the first and last Saturday (11am) and the last Sunday (2pm) of each month, September through June. In July and August, there are also shows every Wednesday and Thursday at 2. After the show, visit Herbert's collection of doll houses and toys (more than 40 furnished houses of all periods).

North Shore

Beautiful beaches, picturesque seaside towns, a colorful history—these elements make the North Shore a popular destination for families. Of course, some people drive 30 miles from Boston just to sample the delectable Ipswich clams.

Many visitors are attracted by Salem, the Witch City. If you're among them, you won't have to look hard to find traces of Salem's grim past. (Even its high school athletic teams are called the Salem Witches.) Salem has an official witch, Laurie Cabot, and museums that recount the events of the "Witch Hysteria" of 1692 in vivid detail.

Venture beyond Salem, and you'll find nautical Marblehead (Yachting Capital of the East), artistic Bearskin Neck in Rockport (home of the most-painted scene in America), and some of the best beaches in New England (not to mention two very different castles—and lots of magic).

Le Grand David and His Own Spectacular Magic Company

Cabot St., Beverly; (508) 927-3677. Year-round, shows every Sun. at 3 (doors open at 2:15). Adults, $7; 11 and under, $5.

Enter the beautifully-restored Cabot Street Cinema Theater and leave reality behind. Le Grand David, Marco the Magi, and troupe will delight you with comedy, pageantry, and fast-paced fun. The 2.5-hour show will be a bit long for the very young, but school-aged children will enjoy figuring out how to pluck rabbits from the air and how to make someone levitate. (Sit up front if you can.) More nice surprises: a hand-painted puppet theater with performing puppets, magicians' props on display, and clowns bearing goodies.

Whale-Watching

Cape Ann Whale Watch, 126 Clarendon St., Gloucester; (508) 283-5110. Capt. Bill's Whale Watch, 9 Traverse St., Gloucester, (508) 283-6995.

A whale-watching cruise can be a pleasant way to get out on the water and learn about these gentle giants. Although the whales don't always cooperate, local cruise companies claim sighting records of over 90 percent in recent years. On-board naturalists provide narration. Children—always the first to spot a whale's tail in the distance—squeal with delight as playful humpbacks leap into the air or pass near the boat. You'll want to bring a pair of binoculars, as well as sweaters or light jackets. Wear sneakers or rubber-soled shoes. Cruises leave daily from downtown Gloucester.

Hammond Castle Museum

80 Hesperus Ave., Gloucester; (508) 282-2080. Daily, 9–5; July–Aug., Wed. 'til 9. Adults, $4; 6–12, $2.50.

Like a fairy tale come to life, Hammond Castle has a moat and drawbridge, parapets and turrets . . . even an indoor reflecting pool. This recreated version was built as the home of inventor John Hayes Hammond, Jr., and houses his unique collection of Roman, medieval, and renaissance art, as well as a huge, working pipe organ. Children especially enjoy the tiny suits of armor and winding passageways. (Not stroller-accessible, so bring a backpack for baby.) Visit on a rainy day for an added element of spookiness.

Located on the Atlantic Ocean, the Castle hosts medieval fairs and celebrations, concerts, and performances especially for children. Call for a schedule of events. Guided tours, gift shop, café.

New England Alive

163 High St. (Rtes. 1A and 133), Ipswich; (508) 356-7013. Daily, May–Oct., Mon.–Fri., 10–5, Sat.–Sun., 9:30–6. Adults, $4; 3–12, $2.

Stroke a scaly snake, nuzzle a baby chick, or feed a kid goat from the palm of your hand. This small petting farm is a favorite with local children and a fun destination for a picnic. Meet native New England wildlife, including a bobcat, a red fox, a coyote, Yogi the black bear, and more. There's also a collection of native and exotic snakes. Most of the animals here were found injured and were brought to owner Lyle Jensen to be nursed back to health. Jensen gives informational shows first thing each morning, and will happily chat about any of the residents here.

Goodale Orchards

Argilla Road, Ipswich; (508) 356-5366. Mid-June–Dec., daily. Free.

A trip to Ipswich wouldn't be complete without a visit to Goodale's. Besides selling one of the world's best treats (a fresh cider donut with a cup of just-pressed cider), Goodale Orchards offers pick-your-own possibilities. Plan to pick your own strawberries from mid-June through July. Raspberries are ready to be picked in July, and blueberries are ripe from mid-July through mid-August (dates vary due to weather and crop conditions). In the fall, plan to pick a peck of apples and select a potential jack-o'-lantern from the pile of pumpkins. You can also watch cider being pressed in the old-fashioned cider mill or take a hayride through the orchard (rides are free). Children will love meeting the farm's animals, including horses, goats, and pigs. You'll love checking out the goodies in Goodale's store, a barn that features farm-grown produce, cider, preserves, cheese, and delicious, fresh-baked pies.

Salem Witch Museum

Washington Square, North Salem; (508) 744-1692. Sept.–June, daily, 10–5; July–Aug., 10–7. Adults, $3; 6–14, $1.75.

This multi-sensory presentation recreates the witch hysteria of 1692 with 13 stage sets, eerie music, and voice-overs. It draws no conclusions about the grim events, but asks visitors to "be the judge." Outside the museum, you'll notice a large statue that looks like a witch. It's not—it's Roger Conant, one of the first settlers of Salem, garbed in a flowing cape. Nonetheless, most kids prefer to think of him as a witch and to pose for

*At New England Alive, a personal
encounter with a boa constrictor adds to
the excitement.*

pictures beside him. (Also a popular souvenir: buttons that read "Salem Witch Museum. Stop in for a spell.")

Witch Dungeon Museum
16 Lynde St., Salem; (508) 744-9812. May–Nov., daily, 10–5. Adults, $2.75; 5–12, $1.75.
Featured here are a live reenactment of a witch trial and a guided tour of a recreated dungeon. Chilling, not a good idea for small children.

House of Seven Gables
54 Turner St., Salem; (508) 744-0991. July–Labor Day, daily, 9:30–5:00; rest of the year, daily, 10–4:30. Garden Coffee Shop open May–Oct. Adults, $5.00; 6–17, $2.50.
Of interest to older children and adults who have read Nathaniel Hawthorne's classic novel, this tour includes several houses: the "Gables" (c.1668), Hawthorne's birthplace (c.1750), Hathaway House (c.1682), Retire Beckett House (c.1655), and period gardens. A museum shop and coffee shop are also on the grounds (not stroller-accessible; bring a backpack for baby).

Salem Willows
173 Fort Ave., Salem; (508) 745-0251. Mon.–Sat., 10–9; Sun., 11–9; April–Sept., Free.
Visit this old-fashioned amusement park and enjoy one of the North Shore's guiltier pleasures. It's crowded and noisy, with a carnival-type charm. You can play Skee-ball in the Arcade, have your fortune told by a mechanical Gypsy, or take a ferry ride around Salem Harbor. There are kiddie rides for small fry, including flying horses and a century-old carousel. And then there's the food. Shrug off all your healthful habits here, and dig into fried clams, saltwater taffy, cotton candy, or—for the truly daring—a chop suey sandwich. Or stake out a picnic table and indulge in some classic New England cuisine: a lobster roll and onion rings, washed down with a raspberry-lime rickey. The people-watching is free.

Salem Trolley
Catch it at the Information Booth in Riley Plaza (in front of Salem Post Office). Every hour from 10–4. Adults, $6; 12 and under, $2.
Hop the trolley for a one-hour tour of the city's attractions. Salem Trolley stops at a number of them, including museums, the House of Seven Gables, and Pickering Wharf, where you can get off if you want and reboard an hour later. Get off and on as often as you like.

Myopia Polo

Rte. 1A (Exit 20N off Rte. 128 North), Hamilton; (508) 468-7956. Late May–Oct., Sun., 3, (grounds open at 1 for picknickers). Adults, $5; 12 and under, free.

Bring the kids to a polo match? Absolutely. While polo's image is genteel, the sport itself is a rough-and-tumble competition in which bumping is allowed and players traverse the field atop 1,000-pound horses traveling at 30 miles an hour. There's plenty of action, and the horses (called ponies) are beautiful. To get into the spirit, bring along an elegant picnic (this isn't the place for fast-food boxes) and cheer the Myopia team from the grassy sidelines. At half-time, go out on the field and help tromp down the divots of turf kicked up by the horses (kids love to do this). A different—and elegant—way to spend a Sunday afternoon.

Wenham Museum

132 Main St. (Rte. 1A), Wenham; (508) 468-2377. Daily, 11–4; Sun., 2–5. Adults, $2; 6–14, 75¢.

This gem of a museum—actually the Claflin-Richards House (c.1660) and connected buildings—houses some exhibits of special interest to children. These include a world-famous doll collection, toys, and incredibly intricate doll houses. A parade of teddy bears was recently featured. Telephone ahead for exhibit information.

Crane's Beach

Off Rte. 1A, Ipswich; (508) 356-4354.

With 1,400 acres and more than five miles of white sand, Crane's Beach is considered by many to be the North Shore's best beach. Swaying sea oats, graceful dunes, and sailboats bobbing in the distance are just a few of the features that make Crane's Beach so popular. Although the water never seems to get warm, children (and stout-hearted adults) don't seem to mind. But you will mind the dreaded greenhead, a pesky fly that often infests the area in mid-summer. The Crane Reservation Staff posts a greenhead warning at the gate if the flies are bad—once you pay the non-refundable parking fee on those days, you take your chances. Bathhouses, a snack bar, and lifeguards are on the premises. (Special note: Up on the hill you'll see Castle Hill, a 59-room English Stuart-style mansion built for plumbing magnate Richard T. Crane in 1927. Cultural events, including lots of July 4th happenings, are held at the castle. Call (508) 356-4070 for details.)

Wingaersheek Beach

Exit 13 off Rte. 128, Gloucester; (508) 283-1601. Memorial Day–Labor Day.

Summary is a season of celebrations at Crane Castle on Castle Hill, a North Shore landmark.

A perfect beach for children, Wingaersheek has sand bars and warm, shallow inlets. Small children will be content to plop right down in the warm water, while older ones will enjoy rock-climbing and swimming in the calm waters. Arrive early (by 9 on summer weekends) to secure a parking space. Expect to pay for parking. Beach food available at the snack bar.

Other beaches in Gloucester: Good Harbor Beach and Stage Fort Park. The latter has a small beach, but offers a playground area.

Bradley Palmer State Park
Rte. 1, Topsfield; (508) 887-5931.
Take a respite from the beach at this pleasant, relatively undeveloped state park. Hike along woodsy trails and enjoy a picnic among the pines. In summer, a giant fountain provides kids a place to splash and play. Adults watch the action on the grassy slope nearby. This is a popular site for cross-country skiing in winter.

Willowdale State Forest
Linebrook Rd., Ipswich. Canoes may be rented from Foote Bros. Canoe Rentals, Topsfield Rd., Ipswich; (508) 356-9771.

This 2,400-acre forest has hiking trails, both marked and unma
canoeing on the Ipswich River.

Scenic Drive—Atlantic Coast

From Boston, take Rte., 128 North to exit 20-S (Rte. 1A South) in Beverly,
Rte. 1A South to Cabot St., Cabot St. to Hale St., Hale St. to Rte. 127.
One of the North Shore's special pleasures—and it's free—is a drive along
the Atlantic Coast via Route 127 (Hale Street). This meandering road will
take you past colleges, private homes, and estates, and through Beverly,
Pride's Crossing, Beverly Farms, Manchester, and Magnolia. Notable
neighbors include author John Updike and Boston Celtics star Larry Bird.
Of course, you'll need some refreshment along the way. Our favorite spot:
Dick and June's Ice Cream, 642 Hale Street, Beverly Farms. Try one of the
devilishly good "gourmet flavors" (everything is homemade, even the cones)
and/or mix in bits of candy or nuts. Your journey will end in Gloucester at
Fisherman's Statue, facing Gloucester Harbor. "The Man at the Wheel" was
commissioned in 1923, in celebration of the seaport's 300th anniversary.

Scenic Stroll—Marblehead Harbor

Marblehead's scenic harbor is a sightseer's delight. Park your car in the
waterfront lot on Front Street and explore the winding streets of quaint Old
Town. Crocker Park, off Front Street, offers a great view of Marblehead
Harbor. On the weekends, watch sailing regattas from Castle Rock. Marble-
headers so love to sail that some continue to do so all winter; the sport is
appropriately called "frostbiting."

Scenic Stroll—Bearskin Neck

Rockport was a sleepy fishing village until artists discovered it after the
Civil War. Today Rockport's Bearskin Neck area is a thriving arts center.
Even if you've never visited Bearskin Neck before it may look familiar: The
fisherman's shanty overlooking Rockport Harbor, called Motif #1, has sup-
posedly been depicted by artists more often than any other building in the
United States. Plan to have dinner in one of the casual-but-good seafood
restaurants overlooking the harbor.

Restaurants

Woodman's
121 Main St. (Rte. 133), Essex; (508) 768-6451. Mon.–Thurs., 11–9; Fri.–Sun., 11–10.
Just as Filene's Basement is famous for shopping, Woodman's is famous for Ipswich clams. Billing itself as the birthplace of the fried clam, Woodman's also offers steamers, lobster-in-the-rough, chowder, and other (mostly fried) seafood. Noisy, rustic, and self-serve, this is the place most North Shore newborns go for their first restaurant meal (prop the car seat on the table). One steamer clam can keep baby amused for hours.

Prince Restaurant
517 Broadway (Rte. 1), Saugus; (617) 233-9950. Sun.–Thurs., 11–11; Fri.–Sat., 11–midnight.
Located on Route 1 heading north from Boston to the North Shore, the Prince is hard to miss—its facade features a giant leaning tower. (Route 1 is not a highway for understatement.) Inside, the place is massive, as are the servings of pasta and made-to-order pizzas. Children's shows featuring Calvin the Clown are held on Thursday nights and Saturday and Sunday afternoons. Calvin also shows up every day during school vacation weeks. Reservations are required.

Putnam Pantry
Pickering Wharf, Rte. 1A, Salem; (508) 774-2383. Sun.–Thurs., 11–9:30; Fri.–Sat., 11–10.
This is the home of the ice cream smorgasbord, a concept that was surely invented by a child. Pick your favorite ice cream flavors, syrups, and toppings (the choices are numerous), and create your own fantasy sundae (large or small dishes available). Then walk it off by strolling Pickering Wharf, home of unusual specialty shops and the Salem Maritime National Historic Site.

South Shore

Why make a stop when you're halfway to Cape Cod from Boston? For most families, the answer is Plymouth Rock. Sooner or later nearly every child is carted to the spot where, in the autumn of 1620, the pilgrims first set foot in the New World.

Unfortunately, not much remains of this rock that seems giant-sized in the minds of school children. Indeed, it once was—over 3,000 pounds of Plymouth Rock have been chipped away by tourists. Today the rock is protected, and much of it remains underground.

There's more to Plymouth than the rock. Plimoth Plantation is a favorite of visiting families, and the Mayflower II awaits. Set aside time to visit nearby attractions, too. Ride a steam locomotive through the cranberry bogs at Edaville Railroad, climb aboard a whaling ship at the Whaling Museum, or tour a tiny town filled with 2,000 toy trains at A&D Toy-Train Village.

At Plimoth Plantation, role-players play the part of actual Pilgrims, chatting about their lives with young visitors.

Plimoth Plantation

Rte. 3A, Plymouth; (508) 746-1622. Pilgrim Village open April–Nov., daily 9–5; Plimouth Wampahoag Campsite open May–Oct., daily, 9–5. Plantation only: adults, $12; 5–8, $8. Plantation and Mayflower II: adults, $15; 5–12, $10.

If you jumped into a time machine and set the dial to "Plymouth Colony, 17th Century," you'd be zapped to a place like this. Plimoth Plantation is no cutesy Pilgrim Theme Park—it's a living museum, peopled by folks posing as real Pilgrims to recreate life in Plymouth Colony. Portraying characters based on actual Pilgrims—each carefully researched by the Plantation—the Pilgrims perform the chores of everyday life in 1627. As in real life, chores change with the seasons. Busy as they are, the Pilgrims will take time to chat with visitors. Children will especially enjoy hearing their questions answered in "Pilgrimese." Remember, at Plimoth Plantation it's always 1627.

Also on the grounds is the Wampahoag Summer Campsite, where you'll see Indians (portrayed by Native Americans) perform their daily tasks in a recreated setting. Seeing these two very different cultures presented side by side provides a history lesson your children won't forget. Don't miss the museum shop, with a good selection of children's books, craft kits, and Pilgrim paraphernalia.

Mayflower II

State Pier, Plymouth Harbor; (508) 746-1622. Apr.–Nov., daily, 9–5. Mayflower II only: adults, $5; 5–12, $3.25.

Berthed at the State Pier in Plimoth, the Mayflower II is Plimoth Plantation's full-scale reproduction of the ship that carried the Pilgrims in 1620. Climb aboard the gangway and you'll meet the Mayflower passengers, realistically portrayed by Plimoth Plantation staff members. The stories they tell about the hardships of the voyage will capture your attention and will make history lessons come alive for your kids.

Plymouth National Wax Museum

16 Carver St., Plymouth (across the street from Plymouth Rock). Mar.–Nov., daily, 9–5:30. Adults, $4; 5–12, $2.00.

Wax museums tend to be a little creepy—maybe it's the deathly pallor of the characters' faces—and this one is no exception. But it is educational, depicting the Pilgrim story through 27 life-like scenes. Special lighting, sound effects, and animation add to the experience.

Cranberry World Visitors Center

Water St., Plymouth; (508) 747-1000. Apr.–Nov., Mon.–Fri., 8:30–4:30. Free.

Sponsored by Ocean Spray Cranberries, Inc., Cranberry World is filled with exhibits tracing the history and development of the cranberry industry. You'll see antique and modern harvesting tools and machinery and learn everything you ever wanted to know about this native American fruit. Children will enjoy sampling the numerous cranberry beverage combinations.

Edaville Railroad

Rte. 38, S. Carver; (508) 866-4526. June–Sept., daily, 10–5; May–June, weekends only, noon–5. Adults, $9.50; 3–16, $6.50.

This is one of the more unusual family fun parks you're likely to encounter—a curious blend of nostalgia, kiddie rides, and cranberries. Built on the grounds of an 1,800-acre cranberry plantation (still in operation), its major feature is a steam locomotive. You'll enjoy taking the train ride through the sprawling plantation (a 5.5-mile trip). Your kids will have fun hitching a ride on the antique fire engine. Other vehicles at Edaville include a horse-drawn trolley and miniature Model T's. Young children will like the Petting Zoo and Marionette Theater shows; older kids will enjoy the paddle-wheel steamboat and Edaville's Museum of New

A train ride through the scarlet cranberry bogs is the highlight of a visit to Edaville Railroad.

England Heritage. Plan to picnic at Cranberry Lake Park, or order lunch at the Barbecue Pavilion.

A&D Toy-Train Village
49 Plymouth St., Middleborough; (508) 947-5303. Year-round, daily, 10–6. Christmas Festival from mid-Nov. through the first week in Jan. Adults, $4; 5–12, $2.50.

There's a certain magic about toy trains; they bring out the child in everyone. This charming, family-run museum celebrates the toy train, with more than 2,000 on exhibit. Some are strictly for looking, including toy trains made of candy, china, and lead crystal. Others—more than 50—operate along 4,200 square feet of track. Children will love pushing the buttons (a number of trains are visitor-activated) to make the toy trains come to life. Plan to spend an hour or so here, with a stop at the gift shop. Special children's days and theme weekends are scheduled; call ahead for information. If you're bringing a toddler, ask if the "little tykes" train will be available for rides.

Whaling Museum
18 Johnny Cake Hill, New Bedford; (508) 997-0046. Daily, 9–5; Sun., 1–5. Adults, $3.50; 6–14, $2.50.

In *Moby Dick*, Herman Melville describes a city of "patrician-like" houses and "opulent" parks and gardens. "All these brave houses and flowery gardens came up from the Atlantic, Pacific, and Indian Oceans. One and all they were harpooned and dragged up hither from the bottom of the sea," Melville wrote. The city he's describing—New Bedford, Massachusetts—was the center of the prosperous whaling industry in the 19th century. Although the idea of killing whales is repugnant today, the Whaling Museum recalls New Bedford's exotic past. Children will enjoy climbing aboard the Lagoda, a half-scale replica of a square-rigged whaling ship (at 89 feet long, it's the largest ship model in the world). The museum also has a large collection of scrimshaw. You'll marvel at the intricate detail of these designs, engraved on the teeth of sperm whales or on pieces of whalebone. Whalemen usually whittled these as gifts for their mothers, wives, or sweethearts. The museum's "Windows on Centre Street" will point you toward other whaling-related sites along the waterfront area if you're interested in taking a walk through historic New Bedford.

The Children's Museum
276 Gulf Rd. (Exit 12 South off I-95), South Dartmouth; (508) 993-3361. Tues.–Sat., 10–5; Sun., 1–5. Open first Friday every month 'til 8. Closed

The whale ship Lagoda—on display at the Whaling Museum in New Bedford— beckons toddlers and others to climb aboard.

*Monday except during school vacations, holidays, and early Sept.
Admission, $3; children under 1, free. Free, first Friday every month, 5–8.*
A little out of the way, but worth a visit if there are toddlers and young
children in your group. Tots will head straight for the rigged Beetlecat
sailboat, where they can climb inside, don a life jacket, and "catch" plastic
fish and lobsters. The animal petting area is also popular—children can pet
rabbits, ferrets, a frog, and even a boa constrictor. Animals are housed in
cages, but museum staff members will bring them out to visit. Other
features include a 70-gallon saltwater aquarium and a toddler area. Outside
you'll find a playground area and trails to explore. The museum owns 60
acres of sanctuary land, made up of salt marsh, meadows, and forest.

Myles Standish State Forest
Rtes. 3, 44, and 58, South Carver; (508) 866-2526.
This is a beautiful spot for a picnic. Enjoy an after-lunch hike or swim, or—
provided you bring the gear—go fishing or camping.

Wompatrick State Reservation
Rte. 228, Hingham; (508) 749-7160.
This 3,000-acre state park offers hiking, fishing, and camping. Don't be
surprised if you share the trails with horses—this is a popular place for
horseback riding.

Boat Cruises
Catch a codfish, spot a whale, or just relax aboard one of the boats that
cruise out of Plymouth Harbor. Capt. John Boats offers deep-sea fishing
trips. Rent a rod and reel (Capt. John supplies the bait) and spend four
hours at sea trying to hook a big one. Snack bar and rest rooms on board.
Or go whale-watching aboard one of Capt. John's boats. About four to five
hours in length, these trips feature a slide show and a naturalist on board to
answer questions. Cruises depart from Town Wharf, Plymouth; (508) 746-
2643. Atlantic Clipper Cruise Lines offers narrated, 40-minute cruises of
the Plymouth Harbor area, as well as 90-minute sunset cruises. Food and
bar service; rest rooms. Cruises depart from Mayflower State Pier (adjacent
to Plymouth Rock); (508) 747-2400.

Restaurants

Freestones
41 William St., New Bedford; (508) 993-7477. Daily, 11–11.
This is a rare find—a fun, funky restaurant that likes kids. While the older children and adults in your party are enjoying the contemporary artwork here (note the brass monkey), the little ones will be busy playing connect-the-dots on their menus (small fry receive a mug of crayons and a take-home kid's menu as soon as you're seated). The kids' menu features the usual burger/hot dog/tunafish line-up, served with fresh fruit, if you like. Adults have lots of choices; just be sure to save room for the pumpkin-praline pie.

Muldoon's
140 Philip's Rd., New Bedford; (508) 995-6478. Daily, 11–midnight.
This low-key Irish restaurant/saloon offers a reasonably-priced menu and some nice touches for families. First, each high chair sports a balloon, helpful for amusing tots before the food arrives. Second, the children's menu offers a beef stew that's not bad at all. For adults, there are sandwiches, burgers, quiches, seafood, and Irish dishes. The meat pie and restaurant-baked beans are specialties.

Worth a Visit

The Hull Lifesaving Museum
1117 Nantasket Ave., Hull; (617) 925-5433. Year-round, daily, noon–5, except July–Aug., Wed.–Sun. only. Adults, $2; 5–17, $1.
Hurry, put on a Coast Guard uniform and hop in the dinghy to rescue your friends. At this hands-on museum, kids will learn what rescuers did when ships and boats were in trouble off the shores of Hull. Children can climb to the loft and talk to each other using telegraph keys in the radio room, maneuver boats and blocks over a floor map of Boston Harbor, or make signal code flags out of construction paper. Throughout the year special demonstrations are held—children might be asked to go for a mock rescue ride or to pull the ropes in on a safety buoy.

Springfield Area

The Springfield area of Central Massachusetts may lack ocean views, but visiting families don't seem to care. They're too busy enjoying the museums, parks, and attractions here. Where else can you spend one day in a re-created 1830s village and the next testing your jump shot at the Basketball Hall of Fame? And if there's a dinosaur fan in your group, you'll want to put the Springfield Science Museum and South Hadley's Dinosaur Land on your hit list. For outdoor enthusiasts, there are mountains to hike, boats to paddle, and plenty of ponds and streams. Spend some time poking around Springfield, Holyoke, and Sturbridge, and take advantage of one of Massachusetts' best-kept travel secrets.

Springfield Science Museum
State and Chestnut Sts., Springfield; (413) 733-1194. Year-round, Tues.– Sun., 12–5. Suggested donation: adults, $2; children, $1.
Part of a quadrangle of museums, Springfield's lively Science Museum was designed with families in mind. At the hands-on Exploration Center, for example, visitors learn to identify wildlife by playing games and responding to audio clues. At the Turtle Pond, turtles "talk" to you (on audio tape) as you look through eye-level portholes and watch them swim. Other areas include Dinosaur Hall (where you visit Tyrannosaurus Rex and can walk inside a giant dinosaur footprint), African Hall, and a planetarium.

Holyoke Children's Museum
444 Dwight St., Holyoke; (413) 536-5437. Tues.–Sat., 10–5; Sun., 12–5. Admission, $2.50; 2 and under, free.
This engaging museum has several neat features. One of the most unusual is a bumper tree made up of colorful, vertically-hanging tubes to tunnel through. Other favorites are the echo tunnel and a room equipped with marbles and wooden tracks. Kids who like water pistols (and what child doesn't?) will love shooting at targets with the high-powered blasters they'll find here. If there's a toddler in your group, you'll appreciate the TOT LOT. It's a separate area where the little ones can play without encountering rambunctious older kids. There's also a small eatery in the building, along with the Volleyball Hall of Fame. Across the street you'll find Holyoke Heritage State Park.

Holyoke Heritage State Park and Railroad

I-91 North to Rte. 202N to park signs, Holyoke; (413) 534-1723. Park open daily, 9–4:30, Thurs. 'til 9. Free. Train runs mid-June–Aug., Sat. and Sun., departures at 1, 2, and 3. Adults, $3; 12 and under, $1.50.

Tour the exhibits at the park's Visitor Center, and you'll get a glimpse of Holyoke's history. The exhibits are well-conceived; older kids will be most interested in the interactive water-power exhibit and examples of paper-making machinery. For younger kids, the lure here is the train ride, a five-mile, 45-minute round trip in restored 1915 and 1924 railroad cars. It's a bumpity ride—just the kind kids like—past mills and a canal. The volunteer conductors are especially good with children and will likely regale your kids with train stories in addition to answering questions. Special programs are often run, with many geared to children. Call ahead for a schedule.

Dinosaur Land

Amherst Rd. (off Rte. 116), South Hadley; (413) 467-9566. Year-round, daily, 8:30–5. Adults, $2.50; 12 and under, $1.50.

Dinophiles in your group? Visit this interesting quarry of dinosaur tracks made by prehistoric animals who once roamed these riverbanks and cliffs north of Springfield. Over 500 footprints have been quarried here. The oldest item is a 500-million-year-old trilobite fossil. An indoor museum features a collection of fossils, footprints, and historic artifacts.

Scenic Drive—Mount Holyoke Summit

Take Route 47 from the town of South Hadley to the Mountain Road. The road leads through the narrow Pass of Thermopylae, under an unusual rock formation called Titan's Piazza. Continue up the Mountain Road to the summit of Mount Holyoke, then return to Route 47 for a breathtaking view of Western Massachusetts from the summit house picnic area.

Mount Tom State Reservation

I-91 North to Exit 17 West, Rte. 141 West to park entrance, Holyoke; (413) 527-4805. Reservation open year-round; museum open Memorial Day–Labor Day.

Just minutes from downtown Holyoke, this area is worth exploring. Hiking trails abound, as do good spots to picnic. The Reservation Headquarters has trail maps. You'll also find a small nature museum—with collections of rocks, insects, butterflies, and birds—and a playground. Cross-country skiing and ice skating (on Lake Bray) in winter.

Forest Park

Summer Ave., Springfield; (413) 787-6440 (park), (413) 733-2251 (zoo). Park open daily 'til dusk. Zoo open Apr.–Oct., Tues.–Sat., 10–4; Sun. and holidays, 10–5; Nov.–Mar., Wed.–Sun., 10–3. 6 and up, $1.50; 5 and under, 75¢.

This delightful city park boasts two special features. You can rent two extra-special paddle boats and pedal your way around Porter Lake, duckling-style; then pay a visit to the Children's Zoo in the middle of the park to see wild and domestic animals from New England woods and farmyards.

Erving State Forest

Off Rte. 2, Erving; (508) 544-3939.

Swim in pretty Laurel Lake or fish for trout in the lake or streams. You'll also find a two-mile hiking trail and a half-mile nature walk, both marked. Cross-country skiing in winter.

Brimfield State Forest

Rte. 20, Brimfield; (413) 245-9966.

This hilly forest is a great place for energetic families to go hiking, with lovely views from several points along Mount Waddaquadduck. Cool off with a dip in the pond or fish for trout in fast-flowing streams.

Mount Tom

Off Rte. 5, Holyoke; (413) 536-0416. June and Sept., weekends only, 12–6; July–Aug., daily, 10–10. Adults, $11.95 ($9.95 after 5); under 7, $9.95 ($7.95 after 5).

During the winter, Mount Tom is a downhill and cross-country ski resort favored by local families. In summer, the attractions include a 4,000-foot Alpine slide (the longest in southern New England), a water slide, and wave pools, guaranteed to provide plenty of thrills for kids young and old. The brave can try the wet and wild "Flash Flood" water slide.

McCray's Country Creamery Petting Zoo

14 Alvord St., S. Hadley; (413) 533-0775. Year-round, daily, 9–9.

This working farm is the home of two child-pleasing attractions: a petting zoo and an ice cream shop. Meet horses, goats, sheep, pigs, and other domestic animals, along with peacocks and a llama. Then sit at a picnic table and enjoy a homemade, double-dip ice cream cone (inside tables, too.)

Basketball Hall of Fame

Rte. 5, Springfield; (413) 781-6500. Sept.–June, daily, 9–5; July–Labor Day, 9–6. Adults, $5; 9–15, $3.

Don't expect hushed voices and "do not touch" exhibits at *this* Hall of Fame. When you enter the door, you join the great American game of basketball. Participation is the key to this fun-filled sports museum. Visit the "How High Is Up" exhibit, where you can test your leaping ability as you try to hit panels hung from the ceiling. Try your skill at basket scoring in the Spalding Shoot Out—the most popular attraction at the Hall of Fame— where budding hoopsters shoot at baskets of varying heights while on a moving sidewalk. There's lots more, including video highlights of the great games, a special-effects motion picture that puts viewers in the middle of a game, and a peek at what some of today's famous NBA players keep in their lockers.

Old Sturbridge Village

Rte. 20 West, Sturbridge; (508) 347-3362. Year-round, daily, 9-5. Adults, $12; 6–15, $6.

What was it like to be a child growing up in rural New England more than 150 years ago? Children will have a great time mulling it over at Old

At Old Sturbridge Village, a recreated 19th-century rural community, the chores and activities change with the seasons.

Sturbridge Village, a living history museum which recreates life in a rural New England town of the 1830s. The Village includes residences, craft shops, meeting houses, mills, and a working farm. What makes this a living museum is the fact that costumed interpreters are busily engaged in early 19th-century chores and pursuits. You'll see a printer, blacksmith, tinsmith, and many other crafts people at work. They ply their trades in authentically-restored buildings which were transported to the Village from throughout New England. Visit the Freeman Farm, where you'll see how much work—and teamwork—was involved in raising crops and livestock, and in simply preparing meals for the family.

Since this is a rural community, many of the activities you'll see will change with the seasons. Spring brings sheep shearing, for example, and autumn means a turkey shoot and an early 19th-century Thanksgiving. If you can, plan your visit to coincide with one of the special participatory weekends scheduled throughout the year. Parades, musket shoots, children's activities—these will make your trip to Old Sturbridge Village more involving and more fun.

Restaurants

T. D. Smith's
57 Taylor St., Springfield; (413) 737-5317. Daily, 11–11.
Get a taste of the Caribbean without leaving downtown Springfield. From Caribbean cuisine to burgers, served in a tropical setting. Children's menu, too.

Gramp's
216 Lyman St., Holyoke; (413) 534-1996. Mon.–Fri., 7–3.
This local favorite features great sandwiches and serves breakfast all day long. Try a Roast Beef Melt or a Reuben, along with soup or a salad. No children's menu here, but most kids opt for a stack of Gramp's pancakes.

Red Rose Pizzeria
1060 Main St., Springfield; (413) 739-8510. Tues.–Sat., 11–midnight; Sun. 'til 11.
Try the best pizza in Springfield—and watch it being made right in front of you. Kids love watching Red Rose pizzamakers toss dough into the air in Red Rose's open kitchen. You can also get pasta specialties, grinders, and

eggplant dishes (the eggplant Parmesan is superb). No children's menu, but the folks at Red Rose don't mind if you order, say, a plate of ziti and split it.

The Berkshires

The far western region of Massachusetts, called the Berkshires (short for Berkshire Hills), is an area as graceful as its name implies. Blessed with beautiful countryside and charming Main Streets, the Berkshire offers a wealth of cultural and recreational activity. Plan to take it slow and savor the pleasures here. Enjoy a picnic on the lawn of Tanglewood as the Boston Symphony Orchestra provides background music. Visit a magnificent natural marble bridge with "graffiti" dating back to 1740. Or ride horseback through a forest of brilliant fall foliage. Even if you take a wrong turn along the way (and you probably will), so what? You're bound to discover something special around the next curve in the road.

Hancock Shaker Village
Rte. 20, Pittsfield; (413) 443-0188. Memorial Day–Oct., daily, 10–3. Adults, $5.50; 6–12, $1.50.
Hancock was one of 18 communities founded by the Shaker sect in the 18th century. Although the last of the Hancock Shakers left the Church family in 1960, this museum is a permanent memorial to the Shaker way of life. Twenty buildings have been restored on the site, including an unusual (but amazingly practical) round stone barn. You'll see farm animals, herb gardens, and craft demonstrations. You might be treated to a Shaker music program—children especially enjoy the dance demonstrations, with which everyone joins in. Guided tours are scheduled daily; plan to spend about two hours here, depending on the ages and attention spans of the children in your party. Light meals and snacks are available.

Natural Bridge State Park
Rte. 8, North Adams (.5 miles from town center); (413) 663-6392. Weekends, May–Oct., 10–6; weekdays 'til 8. Parking fee, $3.
The highlight of this tiny state park is a natural marble bridge, the only one of its kind in the nation. The bridge was formed when flowing water and

There is natural beauty everywhere you
look in the Berkshires, especially during
fall foliage season.

ice gradually eroded the many layers of rock covering the marble, at the rate of one foot every 2,500 years. Now deep, marble chasms are sculpted into the rock. Some of the walls of the chasms sport graffiti dating back to 1740. Picnic tables and rest rooms available.

Albert Schweitzer Center

Hurlburt Rd., Great Barrington; (413) 528-3124. Tues.–Sat., 10–4; Sun., noon–4. Donations accepted.

Dr. Albert Schweitzer devoted his remarkable career—as a medical missionary, ecologist, and philosopher—to preserving and maintaining the quality of life of people, plants, and animals. This "educational museum," set in a 150-year-old farmhouse, was founded to honor and sustain Dr. Schweitzer's humanitarian philosophy. Take a walk through the Center's wildlife preserve, and visit the Universal Children's Garden. Here children learn about herbs, beneficial weeds, natural healing, and how to deal gently and nonviolently with nature. Special programs for children are designed to foster a reverence for life through photography, film, puppetry, music, dance, and environmental awareness. (Contact the Center prior to your visit for specific information.) Conclude your visit by ringing the large steeple bell in the barn. This signifies that you, too, pledge to respect all life.

Talbot Stables

Foxhollow Resort, Lenox; (413) 637-2996.

If your feet are starting to feel the effects of too much museum-hopping, give them a break and go horseback riding. Talbot Stables offers guided trail rides for both Western and English riders of the grown-up persuasion, plus pony rides for children. Located on the grounds of Foxhollow Resort, this could be the perfect place for a child's first pony ride. Call ahead to reserve (hours are flexible here) so that nobody's disappointed.

Berkshire Museum

Rte. 7, Pittsfield; (413) 443-7171. Sept.–June, Tues.–Sat., 10–5; Sun., 1–5. July–Aug., open 7 days, 10–5; Sun., 1–5. Free.

If Jennifer likes science museums, but Christopher prefers painting, while mom and dad are history buffs, you've found the perfect museum. This one has something for everybody, and an aquarium to boot. Young children will be absorbed by the "Animals of the World in Miniature" exhibit. Special tours for children.

Tanglewood
Rte. 183 (West St.), Lenox; (413) 637-1940. Mid-June–Aug. Call in advance for ticket information.

This 210-acre estate is world-famous as the summer home of the Boston Symphony Orchestra. Bring a picnic and spread out on a blanket to enjoy the music under a star-filled sky. Or go earlier in the day and catch the BSO's rehearsal—a good option for families with young children, and the least costly way to go.

Western Gateway Heritage State Park
Rte. 8, North Adams; (413) 663-8059. Daily. Free.

This collection of historical attractions, specialty shops, and restaurants is located in a restored railroad freightyard. Admittedly it's a pleasant place to stroll around in, but we're including it in the book for a more specific reason: "The Tunnel Experience." This intriguing display, located inside a set of railroad boxcars, has lots of kid-appeal. Through sight-and-sound effects, visitors learn what it was like to dig the Hoosaic Tunnel during the mid-1800s. Explosions, dripping water, and the rapping of pickaxes against stone all recreate the drama of this undertaking. Nearly 200 workers died while digging this tunnel, which eventually linked the East, the Great Lakes, and the West. Tales of train wrecks and ghosts add to the experience. Junior conductors will enjoy taking a ride through the park on the Tot Train.

Mount Greylock
Mount Greylock, North Adams; (413) 743-1591.

The pinnacle of Massachusetts, Mount Greylock, can be reached by car. If you're visiting the Berkshires during fall foliage season, you won't want to miss it. At the top of the mountain, the Appalachian Mountain Club offers hikes, sunset walks, slide shows, special displays, and evening campfires. (You can spend the night at Bascom Lodge, run by the Club.) Meals and snacks are also available.

Jiminy Peak
Rte. 7, Hancock; (413) 738-5500. Weekends only, May–June, 10:30–9; daily, July–Sept., 10:30–9. Single ride: $3.75; 1.5 hours of ups and down, $9.25.

Lots of chills and thrills here. During winter months, Jiminy Peak is a ski resort, but during summer and fall you can ride up the chairlift and enjoy panoramic views of the Berkshires. Even better, the Alpine Slide will zip you down again. An hour-and-a-half of this, and your children will be blissfully exhausted.

Beartown State Forest
Blue Hill Rd. (5 miles east on Route 23), Monterey; (413) 528-0904.
Beartown Mountain is the major feature here (a group of wooded peaks).
Follow the signs to Laura Tower or the Alcott Trail lookout for scenic views.
Hike along the Appalachian Trail, fish for bass, or swim in Benedict Pond.
In winter, cross-country ski along 10 miles of marked trails.

Pittsfield State Forest
Cascade St., Pittsfield; (413) 442-8992.
This mountainous area offers plenty to see and explore, including caves,
waterfalls, and cascades. Many species of mammals live here . . .
occasionally a black bear or coyote is spotted. There are 30 miles of hiking
trails—several short ones. Drop a line in Berry Pond (stocked) or swim in
the stream at Lulu Brook picnic area. Ten miles of cross-country ski trails
are open in winter.

Pleasant Valley Sanctuary
472 West Mountain Rd., Lenox; (413) 637-0320.
Hike along the nature trail here and you'll see beaver ponds and lodges,
with muskrats sometimes sharing the living quarters. Visit the Trailside
Museum and you'll encounter live and stuffed animals, as well as electronic
nature games—a fun way for kids to learn about the environment. Fourteen
miles of hiking trails cross the area; traverse them on cross-country skis in
winter.

Restaurants

Cheesecake Charlies
83 Church St., Lenox; (413) 637-9779. Daily, 8–5.
Cheesecake lovers, rejoice! This little place, tucked away in downtown
Lenox, serves 30 varieties of the delectable dessert. Those who don't wish
to make a meal of cheesecake can choose from other items, including fresh
seafood. Open for breakfast, lunch, and dinner.

Dakota Restaurant
*1035 South St., Pittsfield; (413) 499-7900. Sun.–Thurs., 5–10; Fri.–Sat.,
4:30–11.*

This wild-West themed restaurant is a great place to take the kids—even little ones—for dinner. They'll enjoy watching the crustaceans in the large lobster tank and selecting their favorite nibbles from the extensive salad bar. The kids' menu, shaped like a steer, provides further proof that children are welcomed here.

Shaker Mill Tavern
Albany Rd. (off Main), West Stockbridge; (413) 232-8565. Daily, 11:30– "late at night."
Cozy up by the fire at this rustic restaurant/pub and enjoy pasta specialties, artichoke and red onion pizza, or perhaps a "Berkshire Burger." While there is no children's menu as such, the Shaker Mill offers several child-pleasing options, including "stix" (kabobs) and half-orders of pasta.

Cape Cod

More than four million people each year visit Cape Cod and its two tiny sister islands below it. It's said that there are more people on this small elbow of sand on a summer day than there are in the entire city of Boston. Why do vacationers continue to flock to the Cape? Why do they endure the legendary Cape Cod bottleneck, waiting sometimes nearly three hours to cross the Sagamore Bridge? Despite the summertime rush, Cape Cod has an allure that few can resist. Vacationers endure the traffic and summer crowds because they know what awaits them: miles of sandy, white beaches, wide open salt marshes and clam flats, scenic harbors, lighthouses, and picturesque, historic sea captains' homes and cedar-shaked beach cottages.

Families will enjoy the casual seaside atmosphere here, where lobster-in-the-rough and steamers fresh from local shellfish beds are daily fare. You'll find hiking, sailing, windsurfing, fishing, swimming, sightseeing, and any ol' amusement your family desires. There are animal petting zoos, water slides, video arcades, boat trips, train rides, aquariums, touch pools, museums, and more.

If your family likes a lot of action, you won't be disappointed. The bustling resort towns of Hyannis and Provincetown sizzle with energy during the summer months.

The best amusements are often the simplest ones, like a visit to a park with a great playground.

If you prefer more quiet pleasures, they are here, as well—tucked down the back roads of Falmouth, atop one of the striking cliffs in Truro, on a hike along one of the spectacular beaches of the National Seashore, clam digging in Wellfleet. . . . Nearly everywhere, despite the summer rush, you can get away to enjoy the Cape's beauty. A local's best advice is to "get lost" (said with a bit of tongue in cheek!). Meander the back roads, where you are sure to get confused, to discover some of the finest getaway spots on the Cape. But first you have to get there. Some words of advice:

1. Consider visiting the Cape off-season, during spring or fall;
2. Avoid weekend traffic; don't try to get to the Cape on Fridays between 4 and 9 or leave it on Sundays between noon and 9;
3. If you find yourself trapped in the infamous Cape Cod congestion, don't despair. In just three or four hours you'll be eating some of the best, freshest seafood in the world on some of the most spectacular beaches in the country.

Upper Cape
(Includes Sandwich, Falmouth, Bourne)

Heritage Plantation
Grove and Pine streets, Sandwich; (508) 888-3300. May–late Oct. Adults, $7; 5–12, $3.
A mixed bag of Americana spread throughout a beautifully landscaped, 76-acre site, the Heritage Plantation has a little something for everyone. It's particularly enjoyable on a warm, sunny day when children can skip along on any of a dozen native trails winding through plant displays, flower beds, wood groves (all are labeled), and along the shore of Upper Shawme Lake. But Heritage is not just a horticultural experience. A unique, Shaker-designed round barn houses an impressive collection of antique cars (a special one is set aside for the kids to climb on). Other buildings house collections of Indian artifacts, antique military miniatures, firearms, early tools, and folk art. Don't miss the working antique wooden carousel.

Thornton Burgess Museum
4 Water St. (on edge of Shawme Pond), Sandwich; (508) 888-6870. Apr.– Dec., daily; Jan.–Mar., Tues.–Sat. Admission by donation.
This is a favorite family spot among local Cape Codders. This quiet getaway is a memorial to Burgess, author of more than 15,000 children's stories,

including the famous Peter Rabbit and Mother West Wind. The museum was established in 1976 to "inspire in youth a reverence for wildlife and a concern for the environment." On warm summer afternoons, join the group of parents and children as they gather under a tree for Story Hour, often illustrated with live animals (July and August, every day at 1:30). Tour the small museum that contains Burgess memorabilia and an interactive hands-on children's exhibit (this changes regularly to reflect current museum themes). Or simply take a pleasant walk down one of the nature trails. The museum sponsors many wonderful special events and children's activities throughout the summer. Call for a schedule.

Green Briar Nature Center and Jam Kitchen
6 Discovery Hill Rd., Sandwich; (508) 888-6870. Admission by donation.
Jams and jellies are made here in an old-fashioned kitchen by turn-of-the-century cooking methods. Next door you can take a mile-long hike down historic Old Briar Patch trail.

Yesteryear Doll Museum
Old Main St., Sandwich; (508) 888-2788. May 15–Oct., Mon.–Sat., 10–4; Sun., 1–4. Adults, $2.50; under 12, $1.50.
If you like dolls, you'll love this museum. Here you'll see a worldly collection of rare, old dolls and doll houses. All are meticulously furnished in the style of days gone by. If you have an injured doll, bring her/him along—this is the best doll hospital around. Between May and October, about 200 dolls are treated for injuries ranging from broken limbs to torn neck sockets to missing parts.

Let's Go! Theater
Quaker Meeting House Rd., East Sandwich; (508) 888-5300.
If you're in the upper Cape area for long, check out the Sandwich Community School. Emphasis here is on children, and performances are fun for the entire family.

Beaches
Beaches on the upper Cape include Scusset Beach (Scusset Beach Road, near Sagamore Rotary, Sandwich), a state-run beach on Cape Cod Canal. Town Beach (bay side, off Route 6A and Tupper Road, Sandwich), has pretty views (it's a favorite spot of local photographers and artists) and good swimming. There's a nice hike along the boardwalk across Mill Creek. Bourne Scenic Park (Route 6, Buzzards Bay on Cape Cod Canal, Sandwich) has 70 acres of hiking, fishing, swimming, and playgrounds. Take a dip in

Cape Cod's beaches are among the most wild and beautiful in the world.

the unique sea-level pool—it changes with the tide. Other fine beaches include Surf Drive Beach (on Vineyard Sound, off Surf Drive, Falmouth), Old Silver Beach (on Buzzards Bay, off Bay Shore Drive, North Falmouth), and Menauhant Beach (on Vineyard Sound, off Menauhant Road, East Falmouth).

Beebe Woods
Off Depot Rd. in Falmouth Center.
Nearly 400 acres offer an abundance of hiking trails, from novice to expert. Intricate stone fences throughout remind you that you're in New England.

Shining Sea Bikeway
This nearly three-mile bike trail runs from Falmouth Center to Woods Hole along the shore line. Stop and watch the local activity at busy marinas along the way. Pick up the path on Locust Street in Falmouth; you'll end up at the Steamship Authority dock in Woods Hole.

Restaurants

Grandma's Restaurant and Pie Shop
On the Bourne Rotary, Buzzards Bay; (508) 759-2526. Pie Shop open at 9; restaurant open Sun.–Thurs., 11–9; Fri. and Sat., 'til 10.
This large, cheery restaurant serves everything from "Lazy Man's Lobster" to franks-and-beans. Even small fry have some better-than-usual options here, including fried chicken, fried clams, and chopped sirloin. If you're too stuffed to order dessert, you can get a pie to go from the pie shop (try the Swiss Chocolate Almond for a slice of pastry heaven).

Black Duck
Rte. 28 (follow signs to Woods Hole from Falmouth), Woods Hole; (508) 548-9165. Mid-May–Sept., daily, 10–10.
Lots of family-appeal here. You can eat outside, facing Eel Pond, and watch the drawbridge go up and down (indoor seating, too). Kids can feed the ducks—the restaurant supplies the duck food—while the grown-ups relax and enjoy the view. No kids' menu, but lots of possibilities, including pizza by the slice, fruit cups, and homemade soups. The Bahamian mussel stew is a local favorite.

Horizons on Cape Cod Bay

Town Neck Rd. (off Tupper Rd.), Sandwich; (508) 888-6160. Daily, Apr.–Nov., 11:30–10; Fri. and Sat. 'til 11.

The location can't be beat, and there are ocean views at most tables here. The town beach is steps away. Eat indoors or out, soaking up the beauty of the bay, then stroll along the shore after your meal. The food can't compete with the view, but it's not bad—sandwiches, salads, seafood, and beef. The only item designated for kids is a coney dog—you might do better with a chowder-salad combo or (after 5) a six-inch pizza.

Sandwich's Sandwiches

Route 6A and Jarves St., Sandwich Village; (508) 888-1221. Mon.–Sat., 10–4.

For a great beach picnic, head to Sandwich's and create your own sandwiches to go. Good salads, too. Bonus: an ice cream parlor and a candy shop next door.

Mid-Cape
(Includes Hyannis, Barnstable, Yarmouth, Dennis)

Cape Cod and Hyannis Railroad

252 Main St., Hyannis; (508) 771-1145. Mid-May–Oct., daily.

Board a refurbished 1920's parlor car and take a scenic tour of undiscovered Cape Cod. You'll see beautiful shorelines, salt marshes, cranberry bogs, and more. You won't have to give up your creature comforts, either—the train has first-class parlor cars and coaches and offers dining and snacking along the way. The railroad offers a variety of trips and scenic tours: take the train to Heritage Plantation or tie in with island and harbor boat cruises.

Cape Cod Potato Chip Tour

Breed's Hill Rd., Hyannis; (508) 775-3358. Weekdays, 9–5.

Watch potato chips being made on a free, self-guided tour of the factory. Free samples, too.

Sailing, Cruising, and Fishing

The Hyannis area offers just about anything sea-lovers and boaters can want—take a sunset island cruise aboard a luxury liner; sail the ocean in a

40-foot sloop or 1800s gaff-rigged ketch; go whale-watching or deep-sea fishing; or view the Kennedy Compound.

Boats leave from Hyannis or Barnstable and companies include Cape Cod Custom Tours (36 Ocean St., Hyannis; (508) 778-6933), Hy-Line Harbor Cruises, (Ocean St. Dock, Hyannis; (508) 775-7185), Windjammer Spray (10 Ocean St., Hyannis; (508) 775-1630; replica of 1800's gaff-rigged ketch), Hyannis Whale Watcher Cruises (leaves from Barnstable Harbor, (508) 775-1622) and The Wanderview (Hyannis Harbor; (508) 775-7361; deep-sea fishing).

Aqua Circus and Petting Zoo

Rte. 28, W. Yarmouth; (508) 775-8883. Daily, 9:30–5. Adults, $6.75; under 10, $3.75.
Many a road-weary family trapped in traffic along busy Route 28 has sought brief refuge at the Aqua Circus and Petting Zoo. You'll pass lots of motels, restaurants, miniature golf courses, amusement centers, and video arcades before pulling into this attraction. Small children will delight in the always-popular petting zoo, pony rides, and sea lion and dolphin shows. There's a small picnic area to catch your breath in.

Cape Cod Rail Trail

Trail begins in South Dennis off Rte. 134, across from the Hall Oil Company (you can rent bikes here).
For the energetic, this 11-mile trail takes you from Dennis to Eastham, where you connect with the National Seashore bike path. Take your swimsuits; you'll end up at Coast Guard Beach. You share the path with fellow bikers, walkers, and horseback riders through woods and bogs, around lakes and ocean shores.

Sea View Playland

Lower County Rd., Dennisport; (508) 398-9084.
This is pure honky-tonk fun. Skeeball, miniature golf, pitch and pull, and an old barn filled with nearly 100 different amusements provide a rainy-day paradise. You'll find the newest—and oldest—coin-operated games. Ask anyone in the area for directions to the Barn of Fun—they'll be able to tell you.

Bass Hole Beach

Center St. (off Rte. 6A), Yarmouth.
Also known as Gray's Neck Beach, this small, scenic beach is great for walking and picture-taking. A boardwalk takes you across marshlands.

There's swimming in Chase Garden Creek. Watch out for greenhead flies in July.

Sea Gull Beach
Off South Sea Ave., Yarmouth.
On Nantucket Sound, with snack bar and picnic area, Sea Gull is the best public beach for swimming in the Yarmouth area. It's calm and sandy; arrive early on hot summer days for a parking space.

Sandy Neck Beach
Sandy Neck Rd. (off Rte. 6A), Barnstable.
One of the best public beaches on Cape Cod. It's easy to spend a summer day here, sunning, swimming, and exploring the surrounding dunes and marshlands. For a spectacular view of the unspoiled Cape, take one of the many trails along Sandy Neck. Walk quietly, and you'll likely spot a number of rare birds and wildlife; you can also search for relics in hidden dunes along the way and wade in the water along the magnificent stretch of beaches. Be sure to return to the main entrance before dusk, where musicians, storytellers, and mimes perform around a campfire.

Restaurants

Barby Ann's
120 Airport Rd., Hyannis; (508) 775-9795. Daily, 11:30–10; Sun., 12–10.
You'll get served good, home-style cooking at this popular family restaurant. Try the seafood stew—the locals' favorite—or barbecued ribs. A special $3.95 children's menu is offered with all the kid favorites: chicken fingers, fish 'n' chips, hot dogs, and hamburgers.

Baxter's Fish & Chips
177 Pleasant St., Hyannis; (508) 775-4490. Tues.–Sun., 11:30–8:30.
Right on the harbor, this casual restaurant serves some of the freshest fried seafood and fish. Go outside and sit on the old boat down by the wharf.

Swan River Seafood Restaurant
5 Lower Country Rd., Dennisport; (508) 394-4466. Daily, 4–10.
Good, fresh seafood and breathtaking views of Nantucket Sound make this casual restaurant hard to beat. Try the steamers, the seafood pasta salad, or

just plain, delicious boiled lobster. The menu includes a wide variety of seafood and beef dishes.

Four Seas Ice Cream
360 S. Main St., Centerville; (508) 775-1394. Mon.–Thurs., 10–10; Fri.–Sun., 9–10:30.
Can't beat the homemade ice cream here. Some of the best on the Cape.

Outer Cape
(Includes Brewster, Chatham, Wellfleet, Truro, Provincetown)

Sealand of Cape Cod
Rte. 6A, West Brewster; (508) 385-9252. Daily, shows at 10, 12, 1:30, 3, 4:30, and 6; Oct.–June, closed Wed. Adults, $6.90; 5–11, $4.30; 4 and under, free.
Just what you'd expect—dolphin and sea lion shows, a marine aquarium, and a park. There are snack bars and picnic areas. Small children will love the touch pool with sea creatures.

Drummer Boy Museum
Rte. 6A, West Brewster; (508) 896-3823. May 15–mid-Oct., 9:30–5. Adults, $3.50; 6–11, $1.50.
This unique museum puts you right in the middle of the American Revolution as you walk among 21 life-size pictorial exhibits with three-dimensional backgrounds. Check out the gift shop for fascinating souvenirs. There are picnic areas and an 18th-century windmill next door.

New England Fire and History Museum
Rte. 6A, Brewster; (508) 896-5711. Daily, 10–3. Adults, $4; 4–12, $2.
This museum contains a fascinating assortment of antique fire engines—one of the largest collections in the country. "They put fires out with buckets of water?" "They had to pull this by hand?" "How fast could the horses get them to the fire?" Children are full of questions as they view this interesting collection of 18th- to 20th-century fire engines and related memorabilia.

Bassett Wild Animal Farm
600 Tubman Rd., Brewster (between Rtes. 124 and 137); (508) 896-3224. Daily, 10–5. Adults, $4.50; 2–12, $2.50.

Where the wild things are . . . tigers, lions, bears, and monkeys all live at this small children's zoo. There are picnic areas, pony rides, and hay rides.

Cape Cod Museum of Natural History
Rte. 6A, Brewster; (508) 896-3867. May–Oct., daily, 9:30–4:40; mid-Oct.– Apr., closed Sun. and Mon. Adults, $2.50; 6–14, $1.50.

Play nature detective and discover mysterious species of sea life; put your hand in a secret box and try to figure out what lurks within; test your knowledge of underwater species when you take the hands-on discovery quiz . . . these are among the many interactive displays at this nature museum. Stay awhile and hike down one of the nature trails, or watch a movie. Be sure to call ahead for a list of special activities. The museum sponsors many creative, fun children's programs throughout the year. Past programs have included bird and reptile classes, Bubble-Blowing Day, Make Your Own Kite Day, field walks, and museum sleepovers.

Nickerson State Park
Off Rte. 6A, Brewster; (508) 896-3491.

This top-notch, 1,750-acre park is perfect for hiking and biking (part of the Cape Cod Rail Trail goes through here). Swimming, camping, and fishing in one of four trout-stocked ponds are available for the sports-minded.

Stony Brook Mill And Herring Run
Stony Brook Rd., Brewster.

If you're here in the spring (March through June), join the locals as they watch spawning herring run upstream. The herring swim against the current through a series of ladders that run from Cape Cod Bay to Upper Mill and Lower Mill ponds. There's also a restored 19th-century mill. The Old Grist Mill still grinds corn every Wednesday, Friday, and Saturday from 2 to 5, July 1 through August 31.

Namskaket Farm
Brewster. 8–dusk.

This is a friendly, pick-your-own-fruit farm. Load up on fresh strawberries, blueberries, and apples, according to season. They don't want you to call ahead (the phone number is not published); just stop by when you're in the area.

Chatham Fish Pier
Shore Rd. and Bar Cliff Ave., Chatham. Daily, after 2.
Bring your camera and watch salty New England fisherman unload their
daily catch. You'll stand atop a visitor's balcony and see nets full of haddock,
flounder, halibut, cod, and more being pulled in and readied for shipping to
local markets and restaurants.

Kate Gould Park
Main St., Chatham Center. July–Aug., Fri., 8.
If you're in the Chatham area on summer Friday evenings, don't miss the
concert at Kate Gould Park. Bring a blanket and refreshments, and join
other families in sing-along folk dancing. Everyone will have fun.

Wellfleet Bay Wildlife Sanctuary
West side of Rte. 6, Wellfleet; (508) 349-2615. Year-round, daylight hours.
Adults, $3; under 16, $2.
Sign up for the wildlife tour. Climb aboard a beach buggy for an hour-long
view of salt marshes, woods, and shoreline. This 600-acre facility is
maintained by the Massachusetts Audubon Society and includes self-guided
nature walks, hiking trails, and exhibits.

Clam digging
This is the home of the world-famous Wellfleet oyster. For a true New
England experience, roll up your pants, grab a bucket, and go clam digging.
The shellfish beds here are abundant. Check the local paper for times of low
tide, when you can pick steamers, quahogs, mussels, oysters, cherrystones,
and scallops from the rich shellfish beds along the shoreline. Shellfish licen-
ses are available at the town shellfish offices near Mayo Beach and at the
Town Hall. You might ask the locals for their current recommendations of
the best places to go, as these vary throughout the year.

The New England Clambake
5 Giediah Hill (off Finley Rd.), Orleans; (508) 255-3289. Oct.–May, Mon.–
Sat., 9–6; June–Sept, daily, 9–6. $25 per person.
Imagine sitting on the beach at the Cape Cod National Seashore eating
clams steamed in seaweed, boiled New England lobster, and fresh corn-on-
the-cob. The Clambake Company in Orleans will prepare your clambake to
go and pack it in seaweed for beach parties, picnics, or boat trips. A meal
you won't forget.

Highland Light
Off Lighthouse Rd., North Truro.
Sometimes called the Cape Cod Light, this is one of the most powerful beacons on the Atlantic Ocean. The lighthouse dates back to 1797 and is the first one seen by seafaring visitors travelling from Europe to Boston. It's a pretty drive to the lighthouse, which sits atop a bluff in a quiet, country setting. There's also a small collection of materials on shipwrecks and other historical information.

MacMillan Wharf
Commercial Street, Provincetown.
This busy wharf on Provincetown harbor is the perfect spot to park your car and watch the fishing boats and yachts come and go. Leave the car here and explore the rest of the town on foot. This is where you will also pick up charter fishing boats, cruises, and whale-watching tours. Call the Cape Cod Whale Watch Hot Line for information, rates, and schedule; (508) 487-2600.

Pilgrim Memorial Monument
Town Hill (on Winslow St. off Bradford), Provincetown; (508) 487-1310. July–Sept., daily, 9–5. Adults, $2; 4–12, $1 (admission includes Provincetown Museum).
This impressive monument was built to commemorate the landing of the pilgrims here in 1620. It's the tallest all-granite structure in the U.S. The hardy can climb to the top of this 252-foot tower—116 stairs and 60 ramps in all—for a commanding view. On a clear day, you'll see Boston skyscrapers as you look across the bay and, to the southeast, the Atlantic Ocean. Even if you choose not to climb the monument, you'll enjoy a nice overview of Provincetown from its base.

Provincetown Museum
Town Hill (on Winslow St. off Bradford), Provincetown; (508) 487-1310. July–Sept., daily, 9–9; rest of year, 9–5. Adults, $2; 4–12, $1 (admission includes Pilgrim Memorial Monument).
Located at the base of the Pilgrim Monument, this museum houses some unique items of interest to adults and children. You'll see model ships (the Mayflower exhibit is especially good), marine artifacts, and a collection of toys and children's books from the 17th and 18th centuries. Small children will be attracted by the stuffed (real) animals brought to Provincetown by Arctic explorer Donald MacMillan, including a musk ox, a walrus, a polar bear, and a white wolf.

Horse and Carriage Company

Provincetown; (508) 487-1112.

If you're tired of walking, look for the Provincetown Horse and Carriage Company signs. You can hop on a buggy for an exhilarating tour of the dunes, or take a leisurely carriage ride around town. The company also offers guided horseback rides along National Seashore riding trails. They each take about two hours. Pick up dune tours on Standish Street. Horse-and-buggy rides leave regularly from the Town Hall. Call the company for information and schedules on guided riding trails.

Cape Cod National Seashore

The Cape Cod National Seashore was established in 1961 and is managed by the National Park Service. This unique, first-of-its-kind national park encompasses much private residential and commercial land. Private businesses and residents are subject to strict building regulations and restrictions as part of an effort to protect the 40-mile coastline of the Cape's outer arm. Today the government owns about 27,000 of the total 44,000 acres within the boundaries of the National Seashore. Six of the Cape's towns have boundaries within the Seashore: Chatham, Orleans, Eastham, Wellfleet, Truro, and Provincetown. The Seashore includes a wonderful variety of self-guided tours, bike trails, and ranger-guided activities, plus six spectacular beaches.

Coast Guard Beach

Doane Rd. (off Rte. 6), Eastham.

Nauset Light Beach

Cable Rd. (off Rte. 6), Eastham.

The Surfer's Beach: this is the oldest and roughest of the National Seashore beaches.

Marconi Beach

Just past Cape Cod National Seashore headquarters (off Rte. 6), Wellfleet.

Head of the Meadow Beach

Head of the Meadow Road (off Rte. 5), Truro.

Race Point Beach
Race Point Rd. (off Rte. 6), Provincetown.
If you have time, stop in at the Old Harbor Lifesaving Museum here.

Herring Cove Beach
Province Lands Rd., (off Rte. 6), Provincetown.

Province Lands and Salt Pond Visitor Centers
Salt Pond Road Visitor Center (off Rte. 6), Eastham; (508) 255-3421. The Province Lands Visitor Center (on Race Point Rd., off Rte. 6), Provincetown; (508) 487-1256.
Visit either of these two National Seashore Visitor Centers and pick up information, maps, and a schedule of activities and programs. The centers have exhibits and introductory audio-visual programs on the area. Nature films and programs are shown on summer evenings in the amphitheaters.

☐ Head of the Meadow Bicycle Trail
High Head Rd., Truro.
This two-mile marshland trail begins on High Head Road in Truro and heads toward Head of the Meadow Beach (you can also pick it up at the beach parking lot). Venture a ways from this trail to the spring where the Pilgrims took their first drink of fresh water in America (follow signs to Pilgrim Lake and Pilgrim Spring Trail).

☐ Hiking
There are many self-guided nature walks and ranger-guided tours and activities offered year-round. You don't have to be an expert trailblazer—many are short but interesting nature walks suitable for beginners and children. Particularly enjoyable are the Seashore Surprise (at which parents and children learn about the sea through scavenger hunts, stories, and games along the way), the Sunset Beach Walk (featuring stories around a campfire at sunset), and Cape Cod Whales and Historic Beach Apparatus Drill (during which divers demonstrate the methods once used to rescue shipwrecked mariners). Call the Province Lands Visitor Center for times and starting places; (508) 487-1256.

Restaurants

Bayside Lobster Hutt
Commercial St., Wellfleet. Memorial Day–Columbus Day, daily, 4:30–9.
Inside this old oyster shack you'll find some of the best seafood on the
Cape. Eat in the rough—great for families—and enjoy lobster, steamers,
fried oysters, broiled flounder, and/or whatever else is fresh that day. Yes,
there are cheeseburgers and hot dogs—sort of an unofficial kids' menu—
but why not split up the generous Fisherman's Platter instead? Veggie-lovers
can opt for corn-on-the-cob and a trip to the salad bar.

Thompson's Clam Bar
*Snow Inn Wharf, Harwich; (508) 432-3595. Mid-June–the weekend after
Labor Day, daily, noon–9:30.*
What's a trip to the Cape without fried clams? Feast on them here, along
with other local seafood specialties. The children's menu includes fried fish,
chicken, and cheeseburgers—but you can always split an order of clams.
Located right on Wychmere Harbor, with an outside patio and dining room.

Mayflower Cafe
Commercial St., Provincetown. Apr.–Oct., daily, 11:30–10.
Need a break from seafood? Try the reasonably-priced Italian and
Portuguese entrées here. Kale soup and pork chops vino Dahlos are house
specialties and, for the kids, you can't go wrong with spaghetti and
meatballs. Children's portions available. The atmosphere is low-key and
friendly.

The Lobster Pot
*Commercial St., Provincetown; (508) 487-0842. Daily, noon–10. Closed,
Jan. and Feb.*
A perennial favorite in P-Town, this restaurant is always crowded. And why
not? It's on the water and the food is great. You can bring kids along, but be
aware that there's a $7.95 minimum charge after 5 (all kids' menu items—
even hotdogs—are $7.95). Our advice: opt for an early evening meal (lunch
is served until 5), when you'll save money and also avoid waiting in line.

The Islands

Martha's Vineyard and Nantucket, accessible only by air or sea, are vacation playgrounds for thousands of travelers each year. Both islands offer miles of splendid beaches, tall, white sand dunes, nature trails, picturesque harbors, sleepy fishing villages, and bustling main streets with trendy boutiques and fine restaurants. And yet, each island has a unique personality and charm of its own.

Martha's Vineyard, located just seven miles off Cape Cod, is the largest island in New England—20 miles long and 10 miles wide. The Vineyard, as it's commonly known, is full of surprises; its textures, rhythms, and amenities are as diverse as the people who visit it. Of course, the sea is everywhere, and sunning, surfing, sailing, and exploring are favorite pastimes. Surrounding the sea are forests and salt marshes, meadows and cliffs, hills and plains.

You'll find as much, or as little, as you want on this island—from the busy, sophisticated town of Edgartown, where you're likely to rub elbows with some of your favorite celebrities, to the rustic harbor village of Menemsha, where generations of fishermen still haul in their daily catch.

Nantucket, meaning "far-away land," is 30 miles off the coast and offers a 100-year flashback in time. You'll step off the boat to enter a perfectly-preserved 19th-century village of cobblestone streets and red-brick mansions. Elegant sea captain's homes, reminiscent of a time when Nantucket was one of the great whaling centers of the world, now house fine restaurants, boutiques, and country inns. Pack up a boxed picnic lunch and venture beyond the village to where cedar-shingled homes hug the shoreline. Swim in the surrounding Island waters—the calm Nantucket Sound to the north, the mighty Atlantic to the south.

Travelers who plan ahead (book your accommodations in advance) and avoid summer traffic congestion (leave your car behind) can find the vacation they want in the Islands. Most return revitalized, refreshed by the clear, salt air which wields its therapeutic power to wash away 20th-century stress.

The Hy Line ((508) 775-7185) and the Steamship Authority ((508) 777-4000) provide regular ferry service to the Islands out of Hyannis and Woods Hole. Nantucket is 2.5 hours from Hyannis, three hours from Woods Hole. Martha's Vineyard is 45 minutes from Woods Hole and an hour-and-45-minutes from Hyannis. Call for schedules.

Martha's Vineyard

The Flying Horses
Oak Bluffs; (508) 693-9481.
Grab the brass ring as you go around on this antique carousel and you win a free ride. The challenge is as exciting as the ride for most children. A short walk from where the ferry docks in Oak Bluffs, Flying Horses is said to be the oldest operating merry-go-round in America.

Windfarm Museum
Beach Rd., Vineyard Haven; (508) 693-3658. Memorial Day–Sept., two programs daily, 10 and 2:30; Sunday, one program, 2:30. Adults, $4; under 12, $3.
A nice family spot—there's a fish pond with an "underwater windows" picnic area and farm animals to meet. You'll learn about solarpower and windpower in an interesting house exhibit. The museum offers special children's programs.

The Lobster Hatchery
Oak Bluffs; (508) 693-0060. June–Sept., hours and days vary—call ahead. Free.
A trip to New England wouldn't be complete without a real close look at one of these crustaceans. The whole family can learn all about lobsters here.

Gay Head Cliffs
These national landmark cliffs rise 150 feet above the shore, affording spectacular views. There's a small parking lot at the top of the cliffs and a trail to Gay Head Clay Cliffs Beach. Watch the children near the cliffs.

Gay Head Beaches
There are some great sandy beaches on the Vineyard, including Bend-in-the Road Beach on Nantucket Sound, Edgartown; Joseph A. Sylvia State Beach, off Beach Road between Oak Bluffs and Edgartown; and Owen Park Beach in Vineyard Haven—this calm, public beach is right next to a park. Great for kids.

Restaurants

Black Dog Tavern
On the beach in Vineyard Haven; (508) 693-9223. Mid-June–Oct., daily, 11:30–10:30.
Sit on the open porch overlooking Vineyard Haven Harbor and feast on fresh seafood.

The Seafood Shanty
Dock St., Edgartown; (508) 627-8622. Mid-June–Oct., daily, 11:30–10:30.
A moderately-priced seafood restaurant overlooking Edgartown Harbor. They offer the standard children's menu.

The Aquinnah
Gay Head Cliffs; (508) 645-3326. Mid-June–Oct., daily, 6:00–10:30.
You'll get a great view of the Atlantic at this casual Gay Head Cliffs restaurant. Sit outside for breakfast, lunch, or dinner.

Nantucket

Whaling Museum
Broad St., head of Steamboat Wharf; (508) 228-1736. Admission $2.50.
Learn what it was like during Nantucket's great whaling era as you study the museum's collections of maritime artifacts. You'll learn all about whales—how they were caught and the operations involved in processing them.

Aquarium
28 Washington St.; (508) 228-5387.
Dip your hands in the "touch me" tank to discover—and feel—a variety of marine life. Aquariums and fish displays are throughout.

Nantucket's Lifesaving Museum
Polpis Rd. in Nantucket Center; (508) 228-1885. Open mid-June–mid-Oct., 10–5.
Step into this authentic recreation of Nantucket's Surfside Station, built in 1874, and see lifesaving boats and displays of rescue equipment.

The beauty of Nantucket Harbor has enchanted visiting families for generations.

Old Windmill

Mill Hill Rd., Nantucket; (508) 228-1894. May–mid-June, daily, 11–3. Mid-June–Sept., 10–5. Adults, $1; 15 and under, 50¢.

Built in 1746, this is one of the only operating mills remaining in the country. It's preserved by the Nantucket Historical Association and is the sole survivor of four mills on the island. Visitors will delight in watching the impressive wooden gears crushing corn. After viewing the mill, stop by the old windmill store to buy a freshly-ground bag of cornmeal.

Children's Beach

North Shore/Nantucket Sound (close to town).

Aptly named because of its Nantucket Sound location (where the water is calmer) and facilities which include a playground, park, concessions, and rest rooms.

Restaurants

Claudette's Box Lunch
On the Square at Siasconset; (508) 257-6622.
Get a box lunch—or clambake—to go for the beach or a picnic.

The Downey Flake
Corner of Southwater and Cambridge Sts.; (508) 228-4533. Apr.–Oct., 6–2:30.
For melt-in-your-mouth pastries or a great breakfast, walk to this simple island eatery. The children will love the stack of pancakes served with fresh, locally-made cranberry or blueberry syrup, or homemade vanilla yogurt topped with granola and served with a bowl of fresh fruit. You can also just drop in at the counter for ready-to-go sandwiches and pastries on your way to the beach.

Maine

Southern Coastal Maine

If the word "Maine" conjures up visions of rocky shores, picturesque villages, and freshly-caught lobsters, you won't be disappointed. Maine's southern coast is a favorite with vacationing families for those reasons and more. First, it's not difficult to get there. Many visitors to Boston are surprised to learn that Maine is only 55 miles away. Then there are the sandy beaches. That's right—sandy. Although there are 3,500 miles of shoreline in Maine, fewer than 100 miles are sandy beach. Southern Maine's got them—long, silvery strands that stretch for miles. When it comes to swimming, some adults find the ice-cold North Atlantic waters a tad too brisk to be pleasurable. If you prefer being *on* the water to being *in* it, you'll find plenty of options here, including a quintessentially-Maine lobstering cruise, on which you'll help pull up the traps.

Most families try to visit a museum or two while they're here, and rainy weather usually means a pilgrimage to the family amusement centers and arcades along Route 1. A better remedy for less-than-sunny weather? Dress for it, then head outdoors so you won't miss the dramatic, foggy beauty that is Maine at its best.

Marginal Way

This mile-long shoreline footpath is not to be missed. You'll see spectacular ocean views, tidal pools, wildflowers, rock formations, and, at high tide, waves crashing against the rocky shore. Benches have been placed along the way—perfect when little feet need a rest. The footpath begins on Shore Road, near the center of Ogunquit, and continues to Perkins Cove.

Lobstering Cruise

Barnacle Bill's dock, Perkins Cove, Ogunquit; (207) 646-5227. Every half hour from 9–3:30, except Sun.; seasonal, schedule is limited in May–June and Sept.–Oct.

If you've ever wondered what it's like to trap lobsters for a living, this is your chance to find out. Take a 50-minute trip with Finestkind Cruises and learn how to bait lobster traps, read lobster buoy markings, and determine whether a lobster's a "chicken." Children are warmly welcomed.

Ogunquit Playhouse
Rte. 1, Ogunquit; (207) 646-5511.
This classic, 700-seat summer theater offers a great way for parents to spend a special evening out with older children. Helen Hayes and Bette Davis are among the famous performers who have played here. Call ahead for curtain times and reservations.

Wells Auto Museum
Rte. 1, Wells; (207) 646-9064. Mid-June–mid-Sept., daily, 10–5; open weekends only in May and Oct. (through Columbus Day), 10–5. Adults, $3; 6–12, $2.
More than 70 antique cars are on display here, some dating from the turn of the century. Kids will love taking a ride in a Model T Ford. Arcade games and nickelodeons add to the fun.

Wells National Estuarine Sanctuary
Rte. 9, Wells; (207) 646-9226. Daily, sunrise–sunset.
Budding birdwatchers will especially appreciate a visit here. The Sanctuary is also a good place to commune with nature while enjoying a picnic. This 1,600-acre site—mostly marshland—includes the Rachel Carson Wildlife Refuge and Laudholm Farm. The Sanctuary includes fields, woodlands, tidal rivers, salt marshes, dunes, and beaches, offering a protected environment for wildlife. Marked nature trails lead through the woods and along the marsh.

Seashore Trolley Museum
Log Cabin Rd. (off Rte. 1), Kennebunkport. Late Apr.–late Oct., daily, times vary. Adults, $5.50; 6–16, $3.50.
More than 100 antique trolley cars are housed here—the world's largest collection. You'll see a slide show and tour the cars on exhibit, but the real fun here is an old-fashioned trolley ride.

Dock Square
Bustling Kennebunkport is a great place for people-watching, especially at picturesque Dock Square. There are lots of shops and galleries here—our favorite is Kennebunk Book Port. Located in the loft of a warehouse built in

1775, the shop posts a sign that reads: "Ice cream, candy, children, bare feet
. . . small dragons . . . are welcome here anytime." Stop for some lunch or a
snack at one of the many outdoor restaurants and watch the world go by.

Cape-Able Bike Shop

Since Kennebunkport is so traffic-clogged in season, you may wish to park
your car and see the town by bicycle. Rentals available at Cape-Able Bike
Shop, Townhouse Corners, Kennebunkport; (207) 967-4382.

Boat Cruises

Kennebunkport offers a number of options for families who want to get out
on the water. Whale-watching, deep-sea fishing, and cruising trips are available; the following companies operate from Arundel Wharf on Ocean Avenue: Cape Arundel Cruises, (207) 967-5912, deep-sea fishing; Indian
Fishing and Whale Watch, (207) 967-5912; and Discovery Sailing Cruises,
(207) 967-2921.

Scenic Drive—Kennebunkport

A ride along Ocean Drive to Cape Porpoise and Goose Rock Beach is a
pleasant way to view Kennebunkport's coastline. Along the way, you'll see
two unmarred natural wonders, too—Spouting Rock, a spectacular ocean
fountain, and Blowing Cave, a rock formation where the waves roar in
dramatically. Look closely so you don't miss them. When you reach Cape
Porpoise, park the car and stroll around this quaint fishing village.

Old York Historic Tour

*Lindsay Rd. (off Rte. 1A), York; (207) 363-4974. Mid-June–Sept., daily, 10–
5. Admission for all buildings: adults, $6; 6–16, $2.50.*
The Old York Historical Society offers guided tours of seven historic
buildings, dating back to the days when York was a colonial village and
seaport. You'll start at Jefferd's Tavern (1750), where you'll find period
furnishings and a tap room. You're also likely to see a demonstration of
hearth cooking, basket weaving, or candlemaking during your visit.

Children also enjoy touring the Old Gaol Museum, built in 1719 as the
King's Prison for the Province of Maine and used as a prison until 1860.
You can wander through the dungeons and cells that once held criminals
and debtors, and see the "gaoler's" living quarters. An exhibit room features
the Museum of Colonial Relics, a recreated, turn-of-the-century museum
display, with old dolls, toys, and unusual objects. Other sites on the tour
include the Elizabeth Perkins House; the Emerson-Wilcox House; the

Marshall Store, a 19th-century general store; the John Hancock ___, and the Old Schoolhouse, a one-room school built in 1745.

Wiggly Bridge Footpath
Rte. 103, York Harbor.
For a lovely view of the York River that few tourists see, stroll the footpath that starts at Wiggly Bridge. Walk over the bridge, passing over an inlet to the York River, and follow the path along the river to Stedman Wood.

York's Wild Kingdom
Rtes. 1 and 1A (entrances on both roads), York Beach; (207) 363-4911. Zoo open daily, June–Labor Day, 10–7; May–June, Sat.–Sun. only. Rides open daily, June–Labor Day, noon–10, weather permitting. Zoo only: adults, $6; 10 and under, $5; under 2, free. Combination ticket: adults, $10.50; 10 and under, $9.50.

Kids have a terrific time at this combination zoo and amusement park, where they meet lions, tigers, monkeys, llamas, a zebra, and an elephant. There's also a petting area where children can feed the goats and deer. On the amusement side, rides include a ferris wheel, a merry-go-round, bumper cars, the "Octopus," and the "Jaguar"—the park's most popular ride.

Old Orchard Beach
Rte. 1, Old Orchard Beach.
Kids love the lively, carnival-like atmosphere of this seaside resort. One of the longest beaches on the Atlantic, Old Orchard Beach is lined with boardwalks full of fast food and fun. In fact, it's been called the Coney Island of Maine. The Atlantic waters here are shallow and warm, and the surrounding amusements are a hit with youngsters.

Beaches
There are several public beaches along Maine's southern coast. Most are well marked; look for signs leading to beaches on the side roads off Route 1. Arrive early to snare a parking space. The best beaches for families with small children—offering gentler surf—are Ferry Beach in Saco and Crescent Beach in Cape Elizabeth. The surf can be lively at Ogunquit beaches, but toddlers can wade safely at a protected area near the mouth of the Ogunquit River.

Restaurants

Mabel's Lobster Claw
Ocean Ave., Kennebunkport; (207) 967-2562. Daily, 11:30–9:30.
Known locally as Mabel's, this restaurant was featured in *Time* magazine for serving the best lobster rolls in the country. Adults can enjoy a glass of wine with their seafood dinner, possibly the stuffed sole (a house specialty) or lobster, prepared five different ways. The service is extremely friendly and the prices are reasonable. Children can choose from the many sandwiches and fried fish dishes on the menu. Be sure to try the onion rings: "Fresh, not frozen," says Mabel. After dinner, the family can stroll next door to Mabel's ice cream shop for dessert.

Bill Foster's Down East Lobster and Clambake
Rte. 1A, York Harbor; (207) 363-3255. Memorial Day–Labor Day, daily, noon–8. Reservations required.
Just what you'd expect: lobster, steamed clams, and all the trimmings. Steak and chicken are offered if you're not a crustacean fan (or if you've finally had your fill of 'em). Eat in the rough, then join in the old-fashioned sing-along. Little kids will love this; older children will, of course, be mortified, especially if you sing along.

1790 Candy House/Ben & Jerry's Ice Cream Shop
Ocean Ave., Kennebunk; (207) 967-5838. May–Sept., 11–10.
For a special treat, children will love a visit to this candy/ice cream shop. A large assortment of penny candy and chocolate treats awaits those with a sweet tooth. The ice cream shop offers a variety of delicious flavors made by New England favorite, Ben & Jerry's. There is a lovely seating area outside where your group can enjoy the goodies.

Portland

Maine's largest city is an intriguing blend of old and new. Wander around the waterfront and you'll see fish-processing plants and warehouses, just around the corner from specialty shops and fancy restaurants. Many stores and eateries are housed in renovated old warehouses, giving a quaint appeal to even the newest. A great way to see it all is to take a tour of historic Portland on a double-decker bus. The three-hour ride is free—catch the

ld Port Exchange (the Visitor's Bureau on Free Street has more

ng little city is rapidly becoming a cultural presence in New
land, with museums, concerts, and festivals aplenty. After visiting Portland, you'll see why it keeps cropping up on those lists of "most livable"
cities. Of course, it's a great place to visit—and you may just want to live
here.

Children's Museum of Maine
746 Stevens Ave.; (207) 797-KITE. Year-round, daily, 9:30–4:30.
Admission, $2.50.
"Please Touch" is the operative slogan here. This terrific museum has so
many things to do that your children will have the happy dilemma of
deciding where to head first. Perhaps to the "Bubbles" exhibit, where kids
can make a giant bubble screen? Or perhaps to the human skeleton, where
kids can learn how "dem bones" really work? Children from 1 to 10 are
certain to have a good time here, and you'll delight in watching them

"One ringy-dingy, two ringy-dingies . . . ."
If you've ever tried to explain to a child
how the telephone works, you'll be
grateful for exhibits that explain such
things, like this one at the Children's
Museum of Maine.

explore. Special activities and workshops are scheduled; contact the museum for details.

Portland Observatory
138 Congress St.; (207) 774-5561. June, Fri., 1–5; Sat.–Sun., 10–5. July–Aug., Wed. and Fri., 1–5; Thurs., 1–8; Sat.–Sun., 10–5. Sept.–Oct., Sat.–Sun., 10–5. Adults, $1.50; 12 and under, 50¢.
This 82-foot octagonal signal tower was once the spot where lookouts informed Portland residents of incoming ships. Now you can climb the stairway to the signal deck and enjoy the same panoramic view.

Fireman's Museum
157 Spring St.; (207) 874-8400. June–Aug., Mon. and Thurs., 7–9.
Junior firefighters will want to visit Portland's old No. 4 fire station to slide down the brass pole and admire the shiny red fire engine. That's about it, but children who love this stuff will be thrilled.

Kinderkonzerts
What does a conductor do? How does the percussionist know when to bang the big drum or clash the cymbals? To introduce children to a variety of musical instruments and how they work, the Portland Symphony Orchestra presents a series of children's concerts from October to May. Held at various sites in Maine and New Hampshire, the concerts are geared toward kids in preschool to Grade two. For reservations and information, call (207) 773-8191.

Scarborough Marsh Nature Center
Rte. 9, Scarborough; (207) 883-5100. Mid-June–Labor Day, daily, 9:30–5:30. Donations accepted; small fee for nature walks.
Located in Scarborough, just outside of Portland, the Nature Center has programs designed just for kids. With more than 3,000 acres of salt marsh to explore, the Center offers guided nature walks, hands-on exhibits, and canoe tours (canoe rental is also available). Special events are often scheduled, including a Full Moon Canoe Tour, a Wildflowers and Wild Edibles nature walk, and a Nature Art Class. Although the Nature Center is open only in summer, the Maine Audubon Society offers year-round programs for kids of all ages. Call (207) 781-2330 for information.

Boat Cruises
The Atlantic Ocean beckons. Why not take a harbor tour, or cruise to an island for a clambake? Or if you want a real getaway, take the ferry to Nova

Scotia. A number of cruise companies offer a variety of options; you'll find them along Commercial Street in the Old Port section of Portland. Some possibilities: House Island Clambake and Cruises, (207) 799-8188; Longfellow Cruise Lines, (207) 774-3578; and Prince of Fundy Cruises Limited, (207) 775-5616 (this 1,500-passenger ferry operates between Portland and Yarmouth, Nova Scotia, from May through October).

Funtown, U.S.A.

Rte. 1, Saco; (207) 284-5139. Weekends in May and Sept.; daily from mid-June–Labor Day; 10:30–11:00. Free admission and parking; you pay for rides and amusements inside.

Family fun is the name of the game here, at Maine's largest theme amusement park. The Thunderfalls Log Flume is most popular—very tall and very wet. There's also a high-speed roller coaster, tilt-a-whirl, bumper cars, and kiddie rides galore. And what better to go with those tummy-twisting roller coasters than Mexican food, taffy, and cotton candy? Antique car rides for mellower folk.

Maine Aquarium

Rte. 1 (Exit 5 off I-95), Portland; (207) 284-4512. Year-round, daily, 9–5. June–Sept. 9–9.

Giant octopuses, sharks, seals, and penguins all live here along with tidepool animals you can actually touch. Exhibits here are fun as well as educational. Don't miss it.

Balloon Rides

If your idea of a vacation is to get away from it all, why not go "up, up, and away?" It's not a cheap thrill, but if you've always wanted to try this, why not? (We recommend this activity for older children, since they're not as likely to change their minds about the idea when you're on your way up.) Call Balloon Rides By Balloon Sports, (207) 772-4401, or Hot Fun Balloon Rides, (207) 761-1735.

Aquaboggan Water Park

Rte. 1, Saco; (207) 282-3112. Daily, third weekend of June–Labor Day, 10–7. Adults, $14.95; 12 and under, $11.95; 4 and under, free.

If your children love water slides (and what kid doesn't?) this place is sure to please. Attractions include a wave pool, bumper boats, a swimming pool, and a go-cart race track. Gentler souls can tool around the pond on paddle boats.

Restaurants

DeMillo's Floating Restaurant
112 Commercial St., Portland; (207) 772-2216. Daily, Mon.–Sat., 11–midnight; Sun., 11–11.
Formerly a ferry boat, this restaurant is moored at an active marina, so you'll get a taste of the sea without ever leaving the wharf. Watch the boats coming and going as you dig into (what else?) a boiled lobster. Seafood, chicken, and steak are offered, with most entrées available in half-portions for children. Try the lobster stew. If your visit puts you in a nautical mood, sign up for the whale-watching cruise; it departs from just outside DeMillo's.

Cap'n Newick's Lobster House
740 Broadway, S. Portland; (207) 799-3090. Tues.–Thurs., 11:30–8; Fri.–Sun., 11:30–9.
This popular family restaurant offers delicious seafood at reasonable prices. The atmosphere is casual, so you don't have to worry if baby uses the drawn butter as a finger bowl or if junior discovers several unusual things to do with a used lobster leg.

Village Cafe
114 Newbury, Portland; (207) 772-5320. Mon.–Thurs., 11–10:30; Fri. and Sat., 11–11:30 p.m.; closed Sun.
This local favorite is tucked away in a warehouse district just off the waterfront. But it's worth looking for if you're hankering after good, family-style Italian food. Children's portions are available. The portions are huge, but try to save room for dessert—there's a good bakery, Amato's, next door.

Worth a Trip

Catchin' the Blues
No one's done a study, but it's probably true that when the "Blues" are running in Maine, absenteeism rates soar. No wonder—landing a fighting bluefish is pretty thrilling, for children and adults alike. Pack up some bait and tackle (locals recommend a stout rod, 20-pound test line, and wire leaders) and head for the mouth of the Kennebec River, just south of Fort Popham. You'll be in the company of lots of others as you surf cast from the

shores. The Blues run from late June/early July until September. Small children might need some help landing these fighters. Blues weigh from 8 to 15 pounds (some get as large as 22 to 23 pounds). When you bring your catch in, be careful—Blues have sharp teeth and will bite. Another good site for Blue fishing is at the mouth of the Saco River in the Biddeford/Saco area. Pick your spot on one of the jetties that stick out into the ocean.

Boothbay/Boothbay Harbor

Whether by land or by sea, Boothbay beckons. Possessing one of Maine's finest natural harbors, Boothbay is an extremely popular New England gateway. Lots of weekenders and daytrippers keep it hopping in summer months, as do sailors, who inevitably drop anchor in Boothbay Harbor while cruising the Maine coast.

The downside of all this, of course, is the crowds—on a summer weekend, you'd better have a waiting reservation for a bed and a meal when you roll into town. This is especially true if you want to hit the annual Windjammer Festival in mid-July, when the Windjammer schooners congregate in Boothbay Harbor.

The upside of Boothbay's popularity? There's plenty to do—from seal-watching aboard a schooner to star-gazing at Theater Museum. Recommended first stop for chocolate lovers: the Downeast Fudge Shop on the wharf. Chocolate-walnut fudge doesn't get any better than this.

Railway Village

Rte. 27, Boothbay; (207) 633-4727. Daily, mid-June–Columbus Day, 10–5. Adults, $4; 12 and under, $2.

This turn-of-the-century village is sure to delight young visitors. The main attraction is a two-gauge railway with a working steam train that kids can ride. There are old train cars to explore, antique automobiles on display, a player piano, a doll museum, and—every toddler's favorite—sheep and ducks that love to be fed by little hands. Eat in the diner or bring your own (no leg of lamb or roast duckling, please) and eat at the village's picnic area.

Boothbay Theater Museum
Nicolas-Knight House, Corey Lane, Boothbay Center; (207) 633-4536.
Daily, mid-June–Oct., 10:30–2. Suggested donation, $4.
Young Sarah Bernhardts and Laurence Oliviers-to-be will enjoy a look at
this unique collection of theater memorabilia, dating from the 18th century
to the present. The only museum of its kind in the U.S., the Theater
Museum is housed in historic Nicolas-Knight House (1784). Temporary
exhibitions are displayed in the adjacent barn. Elaborate costumes, stage
jewelry, playbills, and sculpture all capture the allure and magic of the
theater. Two tours are scheduled each day, by appointment only. Not for
young children (many fragile items).

Seaquarium
*McKown Pt., W. Boothbay Harbor; (207) 633-5572. Memorial Day–
Columbus Day, weekdays, 8–5; weekends and holidays, 9–5.*
Your child's first encounter with a Maine lobster will probably be rather
unpleasant for both parties—the lobster having been trapped and boiled,
and the child thinking, "I'm supposed to *eat* this thing?" A visit to this small
but interesting aquarium will provide a more complete picture of native sea
life. A wonderful "touch pool" is filled with sea urchins, starfish,
periwinkles, and other inhabitants of the deep. Even more thrilling is a
large, open shark tank with dogfish—some as long as two feet—that brave
children can reach in and pat. Toddlers will love pressing their noses
against the "baby tank" filled with tiny, squirming sea creatures. Be sure to
pack a picnic; the Seaquarium has a pretty picnic area right on the water.

Boat Cruises
Boothbay's busy harbor offers lots of choices for families who wish to try
out their sea legs. For example, you might tour nearby islands, go seal-
watching, cruise on a 90-foot schooner, learn about lobstering, or enjoy a
chicken bake or lobster fest at sea. Boats depart from Fisherman's Wharf,
Commercial Street, in Boothbay Harbor. Contact Appledore Windjammer,
(207) 633-6589. (2.5-hour sailing cruises aboard a 90-foot windjammer
schooner to outer islands and seal rocks); Argo, (207) 633-4925 (two-to-
four-hour scenic cruises of the harbor and islands with an evening chicken-
bake afloat); Linekin II, (207) 733-4925 (1.5-hour scenic cruises of Linekin
Bay, lobster fest); Marambo II, (207) 633-2284 (one-hour harbor tour near
lighthouses and islands); PinkLady, Goodtime, Goodtimes Too, (207) 633-
3244 (nature cruises, lobster hauling, sea watches).

Restaurants

Andrew's Harborside

8 Bridge St., Boothbay Harbor; (207) 633-4074. Daily, 7:30–11; 11:30–2; 5:30–8:30.

It's hard to judge what's better here—the food or the view of the harbor. Andrew's offers a variety of entrées for breakfast, lunch, and dinner. The house specialty is Lobster Pie. Be sure to save room for the strawberry shortcake or hot fudge brownie dessert. Take an evening stroll on the footbridge; then stop by Andrew's for dinner.

Ebbtide

67 Commercial St., Boothbay Harbor; (207) 633-5692. Daily, 6:30–8; Fri.– Sat. 'til 8:30.

For very casual, quick service, the Ebbtide can't be beat; just ask the locals who frequent this busy establishment. Open for breakfast, lunch, and dinner, the Ebbtide features daily seafood specials, most of which are available in half-portions for children. Prices are reasonable.

Bar Harbor Area

This region of Maine includes beautiful Acadia National Park and the prestigious resort community of Bar Harbor. Here you'll see striking stretches of coastline, where ragged cliffs meet pounding surf. The combination of fresh salt air, fragrant pines, towering cliffs, and sparkling ocean is a sensory feast you're not likely to forget.

But there's more to this area than spectacular scenery. Think of it as the ultimate place to play outside: you can hike, bike, camp, swim, paddle, cruise, or ski. Even the museums are of the hands-on variety. At the Natural History Museum, for example, you can help assemble a 20-foot whale skeleton. And the local zoo has the largest petting area in the State of Maine.

The village of Bar Harbor, formerly a vacation mecca for wealthy East Coast families, is full of shops, restaurants, and galleries. While many of its mansions were destroyed in the Great Fire of 1947, some still exist and are now in use as inns. It's a fun place to stroll, with its streets at their liveliest

*Peanut butter and jelly sandwiches
always taste better when eaten outdoors;
but if you've something more elaborate in
mind, many New England restaurants
offer gourmet picnics—or clambakes—
to go.*

ow and Musical Festival in late June and the Seafood
v. Enjoy.

National Park

22 square miles of wildlife, woodland, mountains, lakes, and valleys surrounded by the Atlantic Ocean. You'll call it paradise. The park is part of Mount Desert Island, a chunk of primitive beauty that owes its unique contours to the action of Ice Age glaciers. In 1919, President Woodrow Wilson set aside much of this lovely island as a national park. Acadia is eminently seeable, with more than 57 miles of car-free paths for hiking, bicycling, horseback riding, and, in winter, cross-country skiing. By car, a trip along scenic Ocean Drive follows the island's entire eastern perimeter.

Begin your visit at the Visitor Center, Route 3, Hulls Cove. Open from May through October (although the park is open year-round), the Visitor Center offers a free, 15-minute film to introduce you to Acadia. Here you'll find information about Acadia's Naturalist Program, which has activities especially for children. These might include guided nature walks and photography workshops, all free of charge. You'll also find lots of printed literature about camping, hiking trails, natural programs, and park history. When the Visitor Center is closed, information may be obtained at Park Headquarters on Highway 233, three miles west of Bar Harbor.

□ Swimming

Even the kids may find the ocean waters here a bit too frigid for fun. Better to swim and play in Echo Lake, which has a nice sandy beach and warmer freshwater. Lifeguards are posted, too. Open mid-June through Labor Day, the lake is located along Route 102, Southwest Harbor, and admission is free.

□ Hiking

Acadia's Naturalist Program offers several guided walks, ranging from easy to strenuous. You might want to join in a "Night Prowl" for glimpses of the nocturnal animals who share the Park. Or you can explore Acadia on your own. The Visitor Center can supply you with information on hiking trails and trail maps.

□ Bicycling

Acadia Bike and Canoe Rentals, 48 Cottage St.; (207) 288-5483. Bar Harbor Bicycle Shop, 141 Cottage St.; (207) 288-3886.

Riding a bike is a wonderful way to see the park, with more than 50 miles of car-free paths to traverse. Bicycle rental shops (children's bikes, too) are located in Bar Harbor; call for rates and information.

□ Canoeing
National Park Canoe Rentals, Rte. 102; (207) 244-5854. May–Oct., 8:30–5.
Spend a pleasant afternoon paddling along Long Pond, located within the park. Rent equipment at National Park Canoe Rentals at the northern end of Long Pond for a full day or half day. Instruction is provided and reservations are advised.

□ Horseback Riding
Explore Acadia National Park on horseback. Bridle paths are beautiful, numerous, and car-free. Arrangements may be made at Acadia National Park Headquarters, Rte. 3, Hulls Cove, in Bar Harbor or by calling (207) 288-3338.

□ Boat Cruises
Park naturalists conduct hourly or half-day cruises aboard privately-owned boats out of Bass Harbor, Northeast Harbor, and Bar Harbor. Naturalists will describe geological history and area wildlife. (Bring binoculars so you won't miss anything.) You'll see sea birds and—to the delight of children—you may spot seals and porpoises. A variety of other sightseeing cruises are also available, including seal-watching, whale-watching, and lobstering trips. You may also choose a 12-hour round-trip cruise to Yarmouth, Nova Scotia. Make arrangements by contacting the boating company directly.

Contact Acadia National Park Headquarters (Hulls Cove, Rte. 3, Bar Harbor; (207) 288-3338) for naturalist cruises. For sightseeing cruises/other specialty cruises, contact Acadian Whale Watch (55 West St., Bar Harbor; (207) 288-9776), Frenchman's Bay Boating Co. (West St., Bar Harbor; (207) 288-3322), or Bluenose Ferry/Nova Scotia (121 Eden St., Bar Harbor; 1-800-341-7981).

□ Abbe Museum of Maine Indian Artifacts
Mid-May–Oct., daily. May–June and Sept.–Oct., 10–4; July–Aug., 9–5. Adults, $1; 12 and under, free.
This tiny museum, located within Acadia National Park at Sieur de Monts Spring, contains decorative and practical items crafted by Maine Indians. Artifacts include unusual jewelry (fashioned from animal bones), pottery, baskets, and tools made of stone and bone. A museum shop offers Maine Indian crafts, books, and tapes.

Outside Acadia National Park

Natural History Museum
College of the Atlantic, Eden St., Rte. 3; (207) 288-5015. Mid-June–Labor Day, daily, 9–4.
Children will find lots to see and do here. This museum isn't stuffy, but several of its inhabitants are stuffed as part of taxidermic exhibits depicting birds and mammals in natural poses and settings. (You'll see an owl ready to grab a skunk and a coyote eyeing a chipmunk, for example.) You'll find a 20-foot whale skeleton to assemble, a moose skeleton to inspect, and many items to touch, including an array of animal skins. The Discovery Corner has a "please touch" area, featuring owl pellets to dissect under a microscope.

Mount Desert Oceanarium
Clark Point Rd. (off Rte. 102), Southwest Harbor; (207) 244-7330. Mid-May–mid-Oct., Mon.–Sat., 9–5; closed Sun. Adults, $3.75; 4–12, $2.50.
Why does the tide go out? Why is the sea salty? What do lobsters eat? If questions like these have come up during your trip to Maine, help is at hand. The Oceanarium's interactive displays offer a lively look at sea life, answering the kinds of questions kids might ask. And there's more. In the lobster room, a lobsterer explains how a lobster eats, reproduces, and gets caught. The "see and touch" room has sea urchins, starfish, and sea cucumbers that children can handle. In the Living Room, live specimens of local marine life are displayed in tanks.

Acadia Zoological Park
Rte. 3, Trenton; (207) 667-3244. Daily, early May–Columbus Day, 9:30–5. Adults, $4.50; 3–12, $3.50.
Heading north on Route 3, over the causeway from Mount Desert Island to the town of Trenton, you'll find this 100-acre mature preserve and petting farm. More than 150 native and exotic animals make their homes here, amid the woodlands, streams, and pastures. Children will delight in the petting area—the largest in Maine.

Scenic Drive—Ocean Drive to Cadillac Mountain
Ocean Drive follows the eastern perimeter of Mount Desert Island. Follow it from Sieur de Monts Spring—stopping along the way at scenic lookouts, including Thunder Hole—until you reach Seal Harbor. There, a park road will take you north to the summit of Cadillac Mountain (1,530 feet), the

highest point on the eastern seaboard. From this 360-degree vantage point, you'll see the surrounding ocean, distant mountains, and offshore islands. Breathtaking.

Scenic Drive—Somes Sound

From Northeast Harbor, take Sargent Drive to the fjord at Somes Sound. The fjord was formed when ice-age glaciers cut through existing mountains. Stunningly beautiful, Somes Sound is the only natural fjord on the East Coast.

Restaurants

Jordan Pond House

Park Loop Rd., Acadia National Park; (207) 276-3316. Late May–Oct., lunch, 11:30–2:30; tea, 2:30–5:30; dinner, 5:30–9.

A trip to Acadia wouldn't be complete without a visit here. Enjoy huge popovers and homemade ice cream on the lawn, with magnificent views all around. Elegant dinners are served in the evenings with classical music accompaniment.

Testa's

53 Main St., Bar Harbor; (207) 288-3327. Seasonal.

Seafood, steaks, and Italian specialties are featured here; children's portions are available. This restaurant/hotel has been around for more than 50 years and remains a favorite.

Beal's Lobster Pier

Clark Point Rd., Southwest Harbor; (207) 244-3202. Mon.–Sat., 11–4; Sun., noon–4.

For more than 50 years, families have enjoyed seafood "in the rough" here, on picnic tables along the pier. Fresh fish, lobsters, shrimp, clams, and crab meat are available at reasonable prices.

Worth a Trip

Sugarloaf U.S.A.

Rte. 27, Kingfield; (207) 237-2000. Lift tickets: adults, $31; 7–14, $15. Children's programs: day-care, $30 full day (includes lunch); night nursery, $4 per hour (each additional child, $2 per hour); Mountain Magic, full day, $35 (includes lunch); Mountain Adventure/Mountain Adventure Teen, full day, $35 (includes lunch, does not include lift ticket).

Skiing families who are tired of long waits in lift lines, crowded ski trails, and jammed parking lots should give serious thought to Sugarloaf. It's off the beaten path, and that's why it's so relaxed. The closest major cities are Portland, 2.5 hours away, and Montreal, four hours away, so you miss the big crowds that head to more southerly ski mountains. Located in Kingfield, in the Carrabassett Valley, Sugarloaf is a destination resort. Drive up, park your car, and spend the rest of your time on foot or riding the Sugarloaf Shuttle to the resort's shops and restaurants.

You'll find plenty to do. The resort has a well-equipped health club (including six indoor and outdoor Jacuzzis), an Olympic ice skating arena, and more than 80 kilometers of cross-country ski trails. Snowboarding lessons are also offered.

A picnic in the snow is great fun and a perfect opportunity to share ski stories.

Now about that mountain: it's big, with a vertical drop of 2,637 feet and 70 ski trails serviced by 15 lifts. You'll find long trails and a variety of terrain.

☐ Just for Children

Sugarloaf offers day-care and a nursery for children aged six weeks to six years. Children over three are introduced to skiing and spend the rest of the time playing outdoors and indoors. Arts and crafts, storytime, and group play are included in the day's activities. A night nursery is open to kids of any age, Monday through Saturday, from 6 to 10. For children aged four to six, Mountain Magic provides supervised skiing and play. Mountain Adventure is for children aged 7 to 12, and teens (13 to 16) can take part in Mountain Adventure Teen. A teen club, Rascals, offers video games, movies, dances, and a soda fountain. Advance registration is required for all programs. Hours are from 8:30 to 4:30.

Moosehead/Katahdin Region

If you've a love for the great outdoors and an appreciation for the beauty of unspoiled wilderness, this northern lakes region of Maine is for you.

This is considered one of the greatest hunting, fishing, and canoeing regions in the country. You'll see few commercial tourist attractions or concessions to modern-day extravagances. Rather, it's the wealth of natural resources that draws people to the shores of mighty Moosehead Lake or into the wilderness of Baxter State Park.

You'll stand in the shadows of Mount Katahdin, one of the highest peaks in the Northeast and the legendary home of the sacred spirits of the Abenaki Indians. Mount Katahdin, meaning "greatest mountain," rises nearly one mile above Baxter State Park. You'll get a good taste of Northern Maine wilderness in this 201,018-acre park, where you can swim in secluded mountain ponds, hike through forests, and picnic along babbling brooks.

You'll get your thrills, not from a water slide or roller coaster, but from a whitewater raft trip down the West Branch of the Penobscot River, or on a floatplane ride over the undeveloped shores of Moosehead Lake. It's easy here—and relatively inexpensive—to hire a seaplane for island exploring or to rent a canoe to get around the lakes and rivers. In the winter, you'll join snowmobilers, snowshoers, and ski tourers who traverse the surrounding forests on a network of trails and old logging roads. But whenever you come, be prepared to spend the time outdoors.

Moosehead Lake

Moosehead Lake is Maine's largest lake, more than 40 miles long and up to 10 miles wide. There are several large islands, bays, and inlets in the lake, surrounded by rugged mountains and miles of dense forests. Much of the 420-mile shoreline remains undeveloped and accessible only by floatplanes, boats, or canoes. But don't despair, as all are easy to rent or hire. Stop in Greenville, on the southern tip of the lake, where you'll find lots of local seaplanes for lake sightseeing tours. There's nothing formal here; just walk up to the plane of your choice and talk to the owner. In Greenville you'll also find a number of places to rent canoes and rowboats. This is a great way to see the lake and explore its many islands.

Be sure to bring a pair of binoculars for moose watching. More than 10,000 moose reportedly live in the Moosehead Lake region. The best time to see them is early morning or twilight, when they come out to feed in the lake's swampy areas. If you feel adventurous, explore some of the old logging roads around the lake; they will take you to secluded bogs.

Mount Kineo

While you're exploring the lake, you'll notice Mount Kineo rising dramatically more than 700 feet out of the lake itself. Located about a mile across from the lakefront town of Rockwood, Mount Kineo is made entirely of green flint. Many years ago, the Abenaki Indians sought its flint to make arrowheads and tools. Look for Indian artifacts along the trails. From here, you'll also get great views of the lake and surrounding mountains and forests.

Lily Bay State Park

East side of Moosehead Lake (8 miles north of Greenville); (207) 695-2700. Early May 'til mid-Oct.

This park, located on the shores of Moosehead Lake, just north of Greenville, is a fine recreation center. Its 942 acres include a small beach for swimming, canoe rentals, and boat launching facilities. The kids will enjoy taking the short path to the playground or picnicking in the pines.

S S Katahdin/Moosehead Marine Museum

Main St., Greenville; (207) 695-2716. Museum open year-round, daily, 9–5.

Boat excursions, Memorial Day–June, weekends; July–Oct., daily; 2.5-hour cruises, adults, $12; 5–15, $6.
Known locally as "Kate," this restored 1914 steam vessel has been converted into the floating Moosehead Marine Museum. Besides taking a ride around Moosehead Lake, you'll be able to see displays and photographs of the logging industry and steamboat operations.

Baxter State Park

North of Millinocket; (207) 723-5140. Camping, mid-May through mid-Oct. Day use, mid-Oct. through Nov. and Apr.–May.
This premier, 201,018-acre park was given to the state by Maine Governor Percival P. Baxter in 1941, with one condition: "That it forever shall be held in its natural, wild state . . ." The park is an unspoiled wilderness area, dominated by Mount Katahdin, the highest mountain in the state. It includes 46 mountain peaks and ridges (18 of which exceed an elevation of 3,000 feet) and a network of about 150 miles of trails, all surrounded by natural wildlife, mountain streams, ponds, lakes, and dense forests. Visitors can wind their way through the park on a narrow road. The auto trip through the park takes about 2.5 to 3 hours, but this includes the stops you'll want to make for picnics, swimming, and hiking.

There are trails for everyone in the park, and even families with small children can enjoy a number of hikes. Daicey Pond Nature Trail is perfect for small children. The trail is level and an easy trip around Daicey Pond. Be sure to pick up the free pamphlet on the trail that points out the wildlife as you go. It's available from the ranger station at Daicey Pond Campground. Little Niagara and Big Niagara Falls Trail is part of the Appalachian Trail, and it's great on a hot summer's day. (The Appalachian Trail, the only trail in Baxter blazed in white, terminates in the park at Mount Katahdin.) You'll pick up the trail at the Daicey Pond Campground and hike along the Nesowadnehunk Stream. You'll find lots of places to take a refreshing dip along the way. You'll pass a logger's dam before reaching Little Niagara Falls. Go a little further down the side trail to Big Niagara Falls, a picturesque spot for a picnic. From the campground to Big Niagara Falls is 1.2 miles. Families with older children will enjoy a 3.2-mile hike up Sentinel Mountain on the Kidney Pond Sentinel Mountain Trail. It's not too steep, but the summit view, overlooking a range of mountains, is beautiful. The trail leaves from the southwest corner of Kidney Pond.

There are lots of mountain pools and streams to swim in throughout Baxter State Park. Families will also enjoy South Branch Pond; this is a busy camping/picnic area also open for day use. You'll find a nice swimming area and canoes for rent. Abol Pond is a popular spot for swimming and picnicking at the southern end of the park. Take Abol Pond Road, three miles in from the park's southern gatehouse entrance. Togue Pond is open for general use. It's located just outside the entrance of the park.

Baxter State Park is a great place for animal watching. There are more than 170 bird species, and you're likely to see deer and moose in the ponds feeding on aquatic vegetation. (Look for them at Daicey and Elbow ponds.) There's also a large bear population in the park. People are warned not to feed the bears or leave waste around.

Parents should be warned that there is a serious bug population from May into August, and everyone will need the protection of insect repellent and/or nets. Finally, there is no running water, electricity, lights, food, or supplies in the park.

Lumberman's Museum
Rte. 159, Patten (at the northern entrance to Baxter State Park); (207) 528-2650. Memorial Day–Sept., daily; Oct.–Columbus Day, weekends.
You'll learn all about the lumbering industry at this museum. A complex of nine buildings contains a working model of a sawmill, a blacksmith shop, old tractors, and 3,000 artifacts of the lumbering industry.

Canoeing/Whitewater Rafting
In this area are some of the most spectacular whitewater rivers in the East, including the West Branch of the Penobscot River, the Kennebec, and the Allagash Wilderness Waterway. Canoe trips can last for a few days, a week, or longer, and are designed for beginners as well as experts. A number of licensed outfitters can arrange trips. The truly adventurous can try a thrilling ride down rushing waters in a rubber raft. Licensed outfitters arrange and guide these trips. Minimum age is usually 12 years. For a list of canoe trips, whitewater raft expeditions, and licensed outfitters, write the Maine Department of Inland Fisheries and Wildlife, 284 State Street, Augusta, Maine 04333; (207) 289-2043.

Snowmobiling
This region, full of logging roads into the northern Maine wilderness, is great for snowmobiling. There's also an extensive network of groomed trails. Rentals are available in most towns.

Cross-Country Skiing
Rte. 6, Greenville.

Miles of groomed trails and old logging roads stretch throughout the region—the possibilities are endless. Squaw Mountain Resort also offers 25 miles of groomed trails.

Restaurants

Auntie Em's

Main St., Greenville (right across from Moosehead Lake); (207) 695-2238. Year-round: summers, 5–11; fall, 4–9; spring and winter, 6–8.
You won't get served instant potatoes here—this is the place to go for no-nonsense homemade meals. This restaurant is as down-home as you can get, owned and operated by a mother/daughter team, who welcome families to their bright, child-proof dining room. There's even a safe side yard the kids can play in while you finish your dessert. Hot dogs to steak dinners and breakfast all day.

The Birches

Birches Rd., Rockwood (on Moosehead Lake); (207) 534-7305. Breakfast, 6:30–10:30; dinner, 5:30–9.
You'll share the dining room—and the view of Moosehead Lake—with hikers, canoeists, whitewater rafters, and other vacationing families. This is a favorite spot among locals and visitors, who come not only to feast in the dining room, but to stay in the adjacent log cabins, rent canoes and boats, or head out for a hunting or whitewater rafting trip. Try the shrimp or scallops. A children's menu offers the usual favorites, including a child's plate of manicotti and pork chops with applesauce.

Bethel Area

Picturebook-pretty, the Bethel area is blessed with natural beauty: mountains, river valleys, lakes, and forests. It's also blessed with snowy winters, making Bethel a desirable destination for skiing families.

Most families discover Bethel when they make plans to ski at Sunday River, one of New England's fastest-growing ski areas. Since Bethel is a fair distance from major population centers (Portland is 75 miles away, Boston, 180) crowds aren't a big problem here.

Cross-country ski trails are also plentiful. Or take it slow and enjoy winter's beauty from a seat in a horse-drawn sleigh.

The Bethel area is pretty spectacular in fall and summer, too. Hiking, camping, and rock-hounding are popular pursuits. Scenic country walks and more strenuous hikes abound. One of the best of Bethel's warm-weather attractions: a picnic near a splashing waterfall. Don't forget the swimsuits!

Grafton Notch State Park
Rte. 16, North of Newry.
Located 14 miles north of Bethel, Grafton Notch is a great place to commune with nature and is one of Maine's best spots for picnicking, hiking, and swimming. Be sure to visit Screw Anger Falls; its rocky ledges are fun to climb, and the falls make a perfect backdrop for a picnic. Other points of interest: the Moose Cave nature walk and Mother Walker Falls.

White Mountain National Forest
Rte. 2, Bethel; (207) 824-2134.
The Evans Notch Ranger District of the White Mountain National Forest is located here. Evans Notch is one of five districts in the forest, which has lands in both Maine and New Hampshire. The U.S. Forest Service maintains a number of hiking trails here that connect with the Appalachian Trail. Pick up trail maps at the Visitor Center. Take a short loop-hike or make a day of it enjoying magnificent mountain scenery.

Rockhounding
The Bethel area is noted for its wide variety of mineral and gem deposits, including tourmaline, mica, feldspar, and various types of quartz. See locally-collected specimens and get how-to information at the Evans Notch District Ranger's office on Route 2 and at the Gem Shop nearby.

Artist's Covered Bridge
Rte. 5 (two miles beyond Sunday River Ski Resort Access Rd.), Newry.
This frequently-photographed 1872 bridge is a great family swimming hole. Have a picnic on the rocky ledges beneath the bridge, downstream. (Note: this is private property, so please use discretion.)

Downhill Skiing

Sunday River Ski Resort

North of Bethel on Rte. 2 East. Ski reports, information, and reservations (including day-care and nursery reservations), (207) 824-3000. Lift tickets: adults, $30; 5–12, $15; 5 and under ski free. Ticket prices listed are for weekends and holidays; check for special weekday and package rates.

A popular family ski resort, Sunday River is composed of five mountain peaks with 56 interconnecting trails served by 11 lifts. While the skiing at Sunday River is geared toward the intermediate skier, beginners and experts will find plenty of action. Certain areas are designated as slow-skiing zones, so novices need not feel blown away by hotdoggers. Expert skiers will find "Agony" aptly named. Beginner's action is centered in the South Ridge Slope area, but novices can also ski from the top of the mountain back to the South Ridge Base via Three Mile Trail. Potential skiers in your group? Sunday River has a guaranteed Learn-to-Ski-in-One-Day program. If you don't learn to make turns and ski independently in one day, you'll get your money back.

□ Just for Children

Junior skiers can learn the sport or improve their skills in classes for every level of skier. Kids from age four to six can join the day-long Sunday Rills program. Included are morning and afternoon lessons, indoor activities, rentals, a lift ticket, and lunch. Older children, from age 7 to 12, can join Sunday Rapids. If your child has never worn a pair of skis or is a real pro, not to worry—classes are grouped accordingly. Offered daily, the fee includes morning the afternoon lessons, rentals, and a lift ticket. Sunday River has a nursery for youngsters from six weeks through two years. Day-care is offered at the same site for children from two to six. Lunch is included; be sure to reserve in advance, as space is limited.

Cross-Country Skiing

The Bethel Inn Ski-Touring Center

Rte. 2, Bethel; (207) 824-2175.

Offers 42 kilometers of marked and groomed trails, as well as rentals. Trails are rated according to difficulty; terrain is varied.

The Sunday River Inn and Cross-Country Center

Rte. 2, Bethel; (207) 824-2410.

Offers a 25-mile, groomed ski trail network. A full cross-country ski shop is on the premises; rentals are available.

Sleigh Rides/Hay Rides
Rte. 2, Bethel; (207) 824-2175. Fri.–Sun., 4–6:30. Adults, $8; under 12, $5; lap children free. (Rides free to Bethel Inn guests.) Sleigh rides are also available at Sunday River Ski Resort. Inquire at the South Ridge Lodge.
The Bethel Inn offers horse-drawn sleigh rides and hay rides (in season) around the Inn's grounds. Children will love the bumpity ride; you'll enjoy the lovely scenery. Reservations recommended.

Restaurants

Mothers
Main St., Bethel; (207) 824-2589. Mid-June–Labor Day, daily, 11–10; rest of year, 11:30–2 and 5–10, closed Wed.
This cozy, casual spot is especially welcome after a day of skiing. There are wood-burning stoves in every room. Lots of dark wood paneling gives Mothers a pleasant, rustic feel. Salads, sandwiches, good soups . . . perhaps a mellow corn chowder or a spicy lamb stew, depending on the chef's mood. Cheese fondue for two is a great winter warmer. No children's menu, but lots of items kids like at reasonable prices.

Bethel Inn
Rte. 2, Bethel; (207) 824-2175. Daily, 6–9.
This classic 1713 New England inn is a delightful choice for a special evening out. The waiters are very friendly (a big plus when you're dining with children) and the menu offers something for everyone—from native crab casserole to New York strip steak. Be sure to save room for dessert: the apple pie has been named the "best in Maine" by a national magazine and the chocolate-walnut pie is a slice of heaven on a plate.

New Hampshire

Portsmouth

There aren't many better places for a family to spend a day or two than in Portsmouth, New Hampshire. This gem of a city, New Hampshire's only seaport, is tucked away between the Maine and Massachusetts borders and often gets bypassed by hurried tourists.

In Portsmouth, being a visitor is just plain easier than in most other popular New England towns. While the city offers a list of activities to keep even the busiest of families happy, it also manages to maintain an unpretentious, relaxed atmosphere.

Don't rush through this town on your way to Maine. Plan to spend at least a day visiting its unique museums (including a great hands-on museum just for children), strolling lovely Prescott Park, cruising to the Isle of Shoals, or zipping down Geronimo at nearby Water Country. Be sure to stop by the Connecticut Fish Pier, where, if your timing is right, you'll see the fish boats hauling in the daily catches.

Strawbery Banke
Marcy St. (opposite Prescott Park and the Portsmouth Waterfront); (603) 433-1100. May–Oct. 31, daily, 10–5. Adults, $6; 6–17, $3; families, $15.
When the first settlers landed in Portsmouth they found wild strawberries growing along the banks of the Piscataqua River and so named this seaport Strawbery Banke. During the next 150 years, the site became a thriving waterfront town and later an immigrant neighborhood known as Puddle Dock.

Today, salvaged from demolition and restored, this area is a unique museum. You'll see 30 of the 35 original historic buildings, all in various stages of restoration. A number of archaeological and restoration exhibits show how we piece together facts about the past. Part of the fun is seeing restoration projects still going on, in various states of readiness.

Older children can learn how to make a barrel, spin yarn, or patch a piece of quilt by participating in daily workshops at Strawbery Banke.

Some of the houses are furnished to reflect time periods ranging from the 17th to the 20th centuries; others contain exhibits and craft shops. You're likely to see gardeners at work on the historic grounds, boat builders, barrel makers, archaeologists, carpenters, quiltmakers, weavers, and more. Older children (six and over) can get first-hand knowledge of what it might have been like to live in an earlier time by signing up for the daily workshops. During the 45-minute sessions, they will make a basket, patch a piece of quilt, spin yarn, or perform other 19th-century tasks. The museum also hosts a number of special programs and activities throughout the year, ranging from New England Gardening Day in June to Fall Festival in October.

Port of Portsmouth Maritime Museum and Albacore Park
Market Street Extension; (603) 436-1331. Dec.–Memorial Day, 9:30–3; Memorial Day–Columbus Day, 9:30–4. Adults, $4; 7–12, $2; families (two parents, three children), $10.
Sit at the controls of a real submarine and pretend you're in charge! At the Portsmouth Maritime Museum you get the chance to climb aboard the

U.S.S. Albacore and go below to its tiny engine room, captain's quarters, radio room, and dining area. A short film describes the history of the 1,200-ton submarine, and a tour guide leads you through it.

Children's Museum of Portsmouth
280 Marcy St.; (603) 436-3853. Mid-June–Sept.; Tues.–Sat., 10–5; Sun., 1–5. $3; under 1 year, free.
Where else can your children don rain slickers and fishing hats, jump aboard a lobster boat, and pull up a trap full of plastic flounders, lobsters, haddock, bass, and shrimp? And where else can they take their "catch" over to the fish market, where their playmates become make-believe customers? This cozy, three-story historic home-turned-museum is a children's paradise. When they're done fishing, children can head up to the rocket ship. They'll take turns at the controls, while a video screen before them helps them imagine their journey through space. There's lots to do and see here—dozens of hands-on exhibits and many daily-scheduled art activities. There are probably many children who never get past the yellow submarine on the first floor. This three-story play structure contains tunnels, platforms, peek-holes, slides, and poles. Relax in the convenient adjacent sitting area—they're bound to come out sooner or later.

It's okay to make a mess—as long as you're learning something—at the Children's Museum of Portsmouth.

Park

on Portsmouth Waterfront; (603) 436-2848.

time to relax (or the kids need to let off a little steam), walk over to Prescott Park. This lovely waterfront park is full of flower gardens, fountains, and room to roam. Snack pushcarts are here if you need quick replenishing, and often you'll see a variety of arts and crafts exhibits throughout the park. If you can, stay for the evening family art and music festivals held during the summer. Sit on the lawn and listen to outdoor concerts or watch dance programs. It's great family entertainment in a hard-to-beat setting.

Water Country

Rte. 1 (three miles south of downtown Portsmouth); (603) 436-3556. June–Sept., 11–6; July–Aug., 9:30–8. Adults, $15.95; children under four feet tall, $9.95. Admission does not include tube rental or boat rides. Reduced evening rates after 4:30.

On a hot summer day this place is a real treat. Tube down a quarter-mile "river" through waterfalls and caves, speed down the dips on double dive-boggan, bank around curves on the triple giant slides, or swallow your stomach down Geronimo. If that sounds a bit too active, there are just plain pools to soak in and lots of lawn chairs. For younger kids (under four feet tall) there's a special play area with mini-water slides, wading pool, and playground equipment. It's the older kids and their daredevil parents who get the most for the money here.

Boat Cruises

There's no better place to view the coastline, harbors, and islands than from a boat. Portsmouth Harbor Cruises (63 Ceres Street; (603) 436-8084) offers a 1.5-hour cruise aboard the small (49 passengers), wooden Heritage. With the Thomas Laighton Steamship Company you can cruise to the Isles of Shoals (eight miles out of Portsmouth Harbor) and listen to tales of captains, pirates, and hidden treasures (Market Street Dock; (603) 431-5500).

Isles of Shoals

Discovered in 1614 by Captain John Smith, these nine islands are natural havens for birds, wildflowers, and animals. You'll see several species of gulls on the islands, the most common being the herring gull. The largest is the black-backed gull, with a wing span of five feet. Harbor seals raise their young on one of the islands, and whales have been observed a few hundred yards off shore. Four of the islands are in New Hampshire and five are in Maine.

Restaurants

Yokens
Rte. 1 (2 miles south of the Portsmouth Traffic Circle); (603) 436-8224.
July–Aug., daily,; rest of year, Tues.–Sun., 11–8.
Most people on the East Coast know about this large, noisy, family-style
restaurant that's been around for almost five decades. The menu has
something for everyone—fish, chicken, beef, veal, spaghetti, and more.
There's a children's menu with kid favorites and smaller versions of the
turkey dinner, roast beef, haddock, and fried clam dishes. Good place to go
when you're hungry.

Fish Shanty
64 Bridge St.; (603) 436-3522. Mon.–Fri., 11–9; Sat.–Sun., 12–10.
This casual, family-style restaurant offers two levels—the first floor is self-
serve and take-out, the second floor contains a full-service dining room and
lounge. Both offer the same menu of fried and baked fish, sandwiches, and
pizza. Everything is available in two portion sizes.

New Hampshire Seacoast

This small, condensed region of New Hampshire encompasses only 18
miles of shoreline and centers around the busy resort area of Hampton
Beach. Nearly 150,000 sunbathers crowd this long stretch of beach on
sunny summer days. The hardy swim in the cold waters of the Atlantic
(averaging about 55 degrees in July); the rest soak up the sun's rays and the
area's frolicking, carnival-like atmosphere. This is the Daytona Beach of the
Northeast, full of noisy fun and enough activities to fill your days and
nights.

If you're in need of a bit more solitude, don't despair. Visit the seaside
town of Rye, where you can picnic at Odiorne Point State Park and take a
quiet oceanside nature walk. Stroll the cobblestone streets of quaint downtown Exeter, or pick fruit at a nearby orchard. If you venture just a few
miles from Hampton Beach in either direction, you're back in storybook
New England.

Hampton Beach

Ocean Blvd.; (603) 926-8717. Year-round. Free.

Your teenagers—and near teens—will love this place. There are three miles of white, sandy beach surrounded by restaurants, boutiques, game rooms, arcades, souvenir shops, water slides, hot dogs, pizza, candy, fried dough, and ice cream stands. Don't bother driving around town; you'll spend too much time stuck in traffic. Hop the town trolley car (on which you'll hear about the day's list of area activities), or walk the boardwalk on Ocean Boulevard. On Monday nights there are talent shows; Wednesday nights, fireworks; Friday nights, sing-alongs; and free band concerts nightly. At last count there were five arcades, including the granddaddy of them all—the 40-year-old Hampton Beach Casino's Funarama Arcade. Of course, the beach settles down after Labor Day, which is when the locals are to be found enjoying its special beauty on sunny fall days.

Odiorne Point State Park

Rte. 1A, Rye; (603) 436-1118 or 436-8043. Park open year-round; Visitor Center, late June–Aug.

Located just a few minutes south of Hampton Beach in Rye is this lovely oceanside park, the largest undeveloped stretch of shore on New Hampshire's coast. Stop by the Visitor Center for a look at the nature exhibits and saltwater aquarium. The little ones will enjoy the "touch table" of sea life. There are swimming areas, picnic tables, grills, and a playground in this 230-acre preserve. There are also a number of nature trails that take you along the rocky coastline or inland through water marshes.

Wallis Sands

Rte. 1A, Rye. Memorial Day–Labor Day.

This white, sandy beach is 800 feet long, 150 feet wide, and a popular summertime swimming spot. There are refreshments, rest rooms, and changing facilities. From the rocky bluff at the north end of Wallis Sands you can see Seal Rocks, frequently covered with seals sunning themselves during the colder months. On the horizon, you'll be able to see the Isles of Shoals, nine tiny islands off the coast.

Fort Constitution and Fort Stark

Fort Stark, Rte. 1B (take Wild Rose Lane to the fort), Newcastle. Memorial Day–Labor Day. Free. Fort Constitution, Rte. 1B (follow signs to Coast Guard Station), Newcastle. Weekend days only. Free.

These two sites in Newcastle provide a peek at early military installations and offer great views of the Atlantic coastline.

Fort Stark is a 10-acre former U.S. coastal harbor defense facility, where you'll get a historical look at the state's fortification system and a spectacular view of the Atlantic Ocean, Little Harbor, Odiorne Point State Park, and the Isles of Shoals. Be careful as you walk through the site: there's rough ground and slippery rocks.

On December 13, 1744, Paul Revere rode from Boston with a message that the fort at Rhode Island had been dismantled and troops were coming to take over Fort Constitution (then named Fort William and Mary). The fort was damaged in the raid, which was an important link in the chain of events leading to the Revolution. Today you can walk the site and enjoy the coastal views.

Kingston State Park
Off Rte. 125, Kingston; (603) 452-9621.
Swim in the fresh waters of Great Pond and have a picnic in this 44-acre state park; just outside Exeter.

Applecrest Farm Orchards
Rte. 88, Hampton Falls; (603) 926-3721. Year-round. Rates vary.
A visit to Applecrest is more than just a stop at an apple farm; it's also a nice family outing. One of the oldest and largest apple orchards in the Seacoast area, Applecrest also offers pick-your-own strawberries, raspberries, and blueberries. There are special activities and festivals throughout the year and cross-country skiing in winter.

Emery Farm
Rte. 4, Durham; (603) 742-8495. May–Dec., daily, 9–6; June–Sept., 8–7.
There are more than 12 acres of pick-your-own fruit on this family farm, established in 1655 in nearby Durham. A small animal petting farm and old-fashioned country store are also on the grounds.

Exeter Park Concerts
Swasey Parkway, Exeter; (603) 778-0595.
Bring a blanket and lawn chairs to sit under the stars and listen to music for all interests. Summer concerts are held early evenings (about 6:30 to 7) during the week. You're likely to hear anything from brass bands to comedy quartets. Call for a schedule of performers. During inclement weather, concerts are moved indoors to the Exeter Town Hall.

Restaurants

Little Jack's
Across from Great Boar's Head, north end of Hampton Beach, Ocean Blvd.; (603) 926-8053.
Nothing fancy—you'll be served fast, fresh seafood on paper plates with plastic dinnerware. It's reasonably priced and tasty.

Newick's Lobster House
431 Dover Point Rd. (Exit 6W off Spaulding Turnpike), Durham; (603) 742-3205. Mon.–Thurs., 11–8; Fri.–Sat., 11–9 (closed Sun.).
The quintessential down-home seafood house, complete with paper plates, picnic tables, and a water view. You'll get boiled lobster, shrimp, scallops, swordfish, sole, and more. All come with hefty orders of french fries and cole slaw. You won't go home hungry or broke.

Pirate's Cove
1200 Ocean Blvd. (Rte. 1A), Rye; (603) 436-8733. Tues.–Sun., 11:30–9.
This is a large, busy restaurant with great views of the Atlantic. Open for lunch and dinner; the menu is extensive, offering a variety of fish, meat, pork, and chicken dishes. Children's menu includes baby shrimp, fried clams, fish sticks, and hamburgers ($4.95).

Worth a Trip

New Hampshire Farm Museum
Rte. 16, Milton; (603) 652-7840. Year-round, daily, 9–5. Adults, $3; 12 and under, 50¢.
Ever wonder what it was like in the old days, growing crops for your food, weaving your clothes on a loom, churning your butter, pumping your water from a well? Children get a chance to see and touch a large collection of old farm tools and equipment as they tour the New Hampshire Farm Museum in nearby Milton. You'll see a blacksmith shop, cobbler shop, an old house and tavern, herb garden, country store, and two large barns full of all sorts of antique harvesting, planting, and woodworking tools. Often children are invited to work the special equipment—making ice cream in an old butter churn, working an antique loom, or cleaning clothes in the old wash basin. Special family events are held each weekend throughout the summer,

including Children's Day in July. More than 60 farm activities, barbecue, music, animal rides, and more take place during this special celebration.

Lakes Region

This region in central New Hampshire is dominated by Lake Winnipesaukee, the state's largest lake, encompassing 72 square miles and more than 280 miles of shoreline. This picturesque lake is encircled by three mountain ranges and speckled with 274 islands. Claiming to be home to the country's oldest summer resort (Wolfeboro), it also lays claim to being New Hampshire's "most popular vacation spot" (Weirs Beach). A look at the level of activity and number of visitors on any summer weekend makes this hard to dispute. In fact, the Lake Winnipesaukee area has developed rapidly in recent years as New England residents have increasingly sought vacation homes in this area.

On the western side of the lake you'll find busy Weirs Beach, often crowded but full of amusements. For a slower pace, visit the nearby lakes Waukewan and Winnisquam, or Lake Squam, the setting for the movie *On Golden Pond.*

Especially popular in the summer, this area by no means closes down the rest of the year. With the crowds gone, this is a nice spot to spend a warm September or October day admiring fall foliage, and winter brings cross-country and downhill skiing at the Gunstock ski area.

Lake Winnipesaukee Flagship Company
Weirs Beach Dock, Weirs Beach; (603) 366-4837. May–Oct., daily. Cruises leave at 9, noon, and 3:30. Adults, $11; 5–12, $5.
For a good view of the lake and its islands, take a cruise ship from the Weirs Beach pier. You can choose from a three-hour tour aboard the 1,200-passenger M/S Mount Washington or 1.5-hour tours aboard the smaller Doris E. and Sophie C.

Surf Coaster
Rte. 11B; (603) 366-4991. Memorial Day–Labor Day, daily; until mid-June,

weekends only; 10–7. Adults or children above four feet tall, $15; children, four feet or under, $12; under 3, free.

If you're tired of sand in your shoes, but still want to cool off in freshwater surf, a visit to Surf Coaster is in order. This attraction boasts a giant wave pool (nearly .5-acres in size), four water slides, two miniature golf courses, and a kiddie Play Park. There are lounge chairs and picnic tables with a great view of mountains and lakes.

Weirs Beach Water Slide

Rte. 3; (603) 366-5161. Memorial Day–Labor Day, daily; until mid-June, weekends only. Rates vary with height and season.

There are water slides here for all levels of bravery, from the 70-foot-long Tunnel Twister to the high-acceleration sling shot (reserved for "the slider seeking the ultimate sliding experience"). This attraction is best enjoyed by older children.

Endicott Rock Beach

Rte. 3; (603) 524-5046. Year-round. Lifeguards on duty July–Labor Day, 8:30–5.

This small, sandy beach, located next to the Weirs Beach Water Slide, is one of the few public beaches in the area. (Most of the lodging places on Lake Winnipesaukee have their own private beaches for guests' use.) There are lifeguards on duty here, with a roped-off swimming area, picnic tables, and swings.

Funspot Amusement Center

Rte. 3 (one mile north of Weirs Beach); (603) 366-4377. Year-round, 10–10; July 1–Labor Day, 24 hours a day. Free.

A rainy day is the perfect excuse to visit Funspot, home of more than 500 electronic games. You'll find all the hottest machines, along with 20 lanes of bowling (ten pin and candlepin.) The preschoolers in your group will love the "Aqua Blasta" splash guns and Kiddie Bumper cars. You'll go through a lot of quarters here.

Winnipesaukee Railroad

Weirs Beach Dock, Weirs Beach; (603) 528-2330. June–Labor Day, daily; Memorial Day–Columbus Day, weekends only. Short ride: adults, $6; 5–12, $3. Long ride: adults, $7; 5–12, $4.

Travel along the shores of Lake Winnipesaukee in this locomotive that leaves from Weirs Beach or Meredith. The one-hour round trip to Meredith is perfect for younger ones with short attention spans. There are lots of other trips to choose from, including fall foliage tours and Santa Claus specials.

Castle in the Clouds

Rte. 171, Moultonborough; (603) 476-2352. May–mid-June, weekends; mid-June to mid-Oct., daily, 9–5. Adults, $4.50; 5–11, $1.50.

Thomas Plant, an eccentric millionaire, wanted to own "from the mountains to the water." This several-acre site in the middle of the Ossipee Mountain Range is testimonial to his desires. Small children will probably not be too enthused by the guided tour of Plant's retirement home. But there's lots more to do and see here. Take a short path (off the driveway entrance) to either the Fall of Song or Bridal Veil waterfalls. Hitch a ride on a tractor-train up to the house, which sits on the estate's highest point. Here you truly are "in the clouds," with a fabulous view of mountains, woods, and lakes. Guided trail rides on horseback are offered, covering some of the more than 85 miles of bridle paths on the property. The short, half-hour or hour tours are perfect for younger children. If you have more time, have a picnic at Shannan Pond. There are tables, grills, and paddle boats to rent. Castle in the Clouds is especially beautiful in the fall, when the mountainside is ablaze with color.

Science Center of New Hampshire

Rte. 113, Holderness; (603) 968-7194. May–June, Sept.–Oct., weekdays, 9:30-4:30; Sat.–Sun., 1-4. July and Aug., daily, 9:30–4:30. Adults, $4; 16 and under, $2.

Live, native bears, deer, raccoons, reptiles, bobcats, and other animals roam this 200-acre center contained by natural barriers. You'll learn about plant and animal life through a number of unique indoor and outdoor displays and interactive exhibits. Children will push buttons, solve puzzles, skip along the nature trail lined with exhibits, and have fun learning all about nature. In the summer, attend "Up Close Animals," a live animal demonstration held twice each day.

Kids get up close to animals during twice-daily demonstrations at the Science Center of New Hampshire.

Downhill Skiing

Gunstock Ski Area

Rte. 11A, Gilford; (603) 293-4341. Adult lift tickets, $30; SKIwee, $40; nursery and day-care, $5/hour, $15/half day, $25/day.

You'll find downhill and cross-country skiing at this recreation area. The cross-country area is a quiet network of more than 30 kilometers of trails through snowy woodlands. There are trails for all levels of expertise, with rentals and lessons available. The downhill center is a good intermediate area, with 25 trails serviced by six lifts. A special section is used by beginners and children, and the staff shows a commitment to children's services.

□ Just for Children

The Buckaroos Children's Center is located at the heart of Gunstock's base complex so parents can drop in frequently throughout the day, if they wish. The nursery and day-care programs include arts and crafts, outdoor play, and social activities. They're available daily for children two months and older on a first come, first serve basis. Be sure to arrive early on weekends and holidays. Children 3 to 12 can join the SKIwee course. The full-day

program includes ski lessons, lunch, supervised playtime, and snacks.
Rental equipment is $5 extra. Children 6 and under ski free, anytime.

Scenic Drive—Eastern side of Lake Winnipesaukee

Follow Route 109 from Sandwich or Moultonborough to Wolfeboro, and
you'll see the tranquil side of the lakes region. Look past the pine trees that
line this two-lane road, and you'll see homes, farms, and cottages. (See if
you can spot the rock painted like a frog on the left.) Take the jog to Route
171 to visit Castle in the Clouds. Drive through tiny Melvin Village to
quaint Wolfeboro, America's oldest resort. Park your car and explore Wolfeboro; try the Yum Yum Shoppe for delicious pastries.

Restaurants

Hart's Turkey Farm Restaurant

*Rtes. 3 and 104, Meredith; (603) 279-6212. Mon.–Thurs., 11–8; Fri.–Sun.,
11–9.*
Every day is Thanksgiving at this turkey farm-turned-restaurant. On a busy
day, Hart's serves more than a ton of turkey. All the trimmings, too, like
mashed potatoes, cranberries, and squash pie. The children's menu
includes the "Tiny Tot Turkey Plate"—a real feast.

Weirs Beach Lobster Pound

Rte. 3, Weirs Beach; (603) 366-5713. Memorial Day–Labor Day, 12–9.
Eat in the rough at this casual spot, right across the street from the Weirs
Beach Water Slide. Enjoy barbecued ribs, chicken, steamers, burgers, and
lobster.

Franken Sundae

*Rte. 3, Meredith; (603) 279-5531. Memorial Day–June, weekends only;
July–Sept., daily, 11:30–10:30.*
Build a "monster" ice cream sundae, take it to one of the lakeside tables
here, and dig in. What a great way to enjoy a lazy afternoon!

Merrimack Valley

More than half the population of New Hampshire lives in the Merrimack Valley region, and most visitors see it only in passing, on their way north to the more popular tourist destinations. Nashua, Salem, Manchester, Concord . . . these are probably not at the top of your "places to go" list. Yet venture just a few miles from their centers, and you'll find rolling, peaceful countryside, clear rivers and lakes, and some kid-pleasing attractions. Next time you're driving by, get off the highway for more than a stop at a fast-food chain. Spend the afternoon at Canobie Lake Amusement Park, take a refreshing swim at Silver Lake, or ride a rowboat in Bear Brook State Park. You'll return to the car refreshed, and the kids will be tuckered out for the rest of the journey. Or you might just decide to stick around the area awhile to discover its other hidden gems.

Canobie Lake Park
Exit 2 off I-93, Salem; (603) 893-3506. Memorial Day–Labor Day, daily; mid-April–Memorial Day, weekends only. Adults, $12 includes all rides/ shows ($7 without rides); 7 and under, $7.
A kid's delight—all the favorite amusement rides, boats, games, an arcade, a haunted house, live puppet shows, a Sensaround theatre, and music revues. There's a large kiddie area with lots of rides and a great roller coaster for the teens. Bring your bathing suit; there's a swimming pool and a wild log flume ride. You can also take a boat cruise around the lake or a train ride around the park. On your way home, head north a few miles and take a look at America's Stonehenge.

America's Stonehenge
Mystery Hill (off Rte. 111), North Salem; (603) 893-8300. May–Oct., daily, 10–4; Nov., weekends only, 10–4. Adults, $5; 13–18, $3; 6–12, $1.50.
Some claim this series of unusual rock formations is the 4,000-year-old astronomical complex built by Celts who came here from the Iberian peninsula. There are a few trails for the kids to run on while you ponder this controversial site and take in the view.

Busch Clydesdale Hamlet
Anheuser-Busch Brewery, Rte. 3, Merrimack; (203) 883-6131. May–Nov., daily, 9:30–3:30; Dec.–Apr., closed Mon. and Tues. Free.

You can get a close-up look at the famous Clydesdale horses on this free tour through the stables. Also on display are wagons, harnesses, and other riding equipment.

Silver Lake State Park
Rte. 122, Hollis.
This is a popular family picnic area and beach in the Merrimack Valley. The sandy, 1,000-foot beach is great for toddlers. Older swimmers will enjoy diving off the raft. There's a bathhouse, rest room and concession stand. Picnic tables and barbecue grills are nestled in the pine groves surrounding the beach.

Old Sandown Depot Railroad Museum
Rte. 121A, Sandown; (603) 887-4631. Memorial Day–Oct., Sun., 2–4.
If you or your children really like trains, this is an interesting small museum filled with railroad memorabilia. You'll see a couple of flanger cars, a motorized handcar, and a collection of old telegraph equipment. Keep it in mind as a good place to spend an hour or so on a rainy day.

Scouting Museum and Library
Camp Carpenter, Bodwell Rd., Manchester; (603) 627-1492. July–Aug., daily, 10–4; Sept.–June, Sat. only, 10–4. Free.
If you have avid little Brownies or Cub Scouts in your troop, they might enjoy a visit to this museum. There are lots of scouting artifacts and memorabilia that trace scouting through the years. There's also a small picnic area.

Bear Brook State Park
Rte. 28, Allentown; (603) 485-9874. Mid-May–Columbus Day.
This 9,600-acre park offers a playground, picnic area, a nice swimming beach, and rental boats. A good place to spend the day outdoors.

Pawtuckaway State Park
Off Rte. 156, Nottingham; (603) 895-3031. Mid-May–Columbus Day. Free.
This large park is mostly forest, but you'll find a small swimming beach, picnic area, and hiking trails.

Sleigh Rides at Charming Fare Farms
774 High st., Candia; (603) 483-2307. Oct.–Mar., daily, 1–midnight. Adults, $6; children under 12, $4; be aware, however, that the ride won't begin until the sleigh is full ($72 worth of riders).

A lovely place to take a horse-drawn sleigh ride through snow-covered fields and woods.

Restaurants

Thursdays Restaurant
6–8 Pleasant St., Concord; (603) 224-2626, Mon.–Thurs., lunch, 11:30–3; dinner, 5–9; Fri.–Sat., 11:30–10.
You'll find delicious, health-conscious lunch and dinner entrées at this family restaurant. There are lots of fish and chicken dishes, plus 10 vegetarian delights. Children pay 50 percent less for smaller portions.

Clam King Restaurant
Exit 4 off I-293, Manchester; (603) 669-2868. Sun.–Thurs., 11–8.
Seafood is king here, including fried clams, haddock, scallops, shrimp, and chowders. A small selection of sandwiches and a large salad bar round out the menu. Take-out is available.

Green Ridge Turkey Farm
235 Daniel Webster Highway, Nashua; (603) 888-7020. Daily, lunch and dinner, 11:30–10.
This is like going to Grandma's house for Sunday dinner. This popular family restaurant is located off the major highway in Nashua. Smaller portions of turkey, mashed potatoes, and gravy, and all the traditional trimmings are available for children. Menu also offers roast beef and seafood dishes.

Sunapee Area

"I don't like to talk too much about Sunapee. It's the best-kept secret in New England, and I'd like to keep it that way." "You won't find boardwalks lined with t-shirt shops and fast-food stands here. It's still a relaxing, beautiful place to vacation, void of the typical tourists traps." These are some of the comments you're apt to hear from Sunapee locals and visitors.

Indeed, nestled high in the mountains of western New Hampshire, the Lake Sunapee area extends a quiet, slow welcome to its visitors. You'll find nothing pretentious or fancy here. Despite its natural beauty and bountiful opportunities for sports and activities, the Lake Sunapee area is fairly non-commercial, retaining much of its rural charm. Aware of its increasing appeal, its citizens have adopted the motto, "Preserve the Best of the Past." They're doing a good job.

That's not to say you'll spend your entire time here sitting under a white pine, skipping stones on Lake Sunapee (unless, of course, you want to). There are plenty of activities: aerial rides, band concerts, boat cruises, hiking, water- and snow-skiing, apple picking, horseback riding, science and art museums, forts, and playhouses are all nearby. Look for the Craftsmen's Fair in the schedule of events—this is the oldest craft fair in the nation, with lots of hands-on activities and crafts for children.

Mount Sunapee State Park

Rte. 103; (603) 763-2356. Beach open Memorial Day–mid-June, weekends, 9:30–8; mid-June–Labor Day, daily, 9:30–8. Aerial chairlift ride, late June–Labor Day, daily, 9:30–4:15. Chairlift, adults, $5; 6–12, $2.

If it's a nice, warm day, start with a visit to this state park located on the southern shores of Lake Sunapee. The kids will enjoy the sandy State Park Beach (so will you!). The swimmers in your family will have fun racing to the raft; toddlers are safe along the calm, shallow banks. There are picnic areas in the park, a playground, and a small concession stand at the beach.

Hiking trails are abundant. Athletic types can hike to the 2,700-foot summit of Mount Sunapee or take the easier way up—via a triple chairlift. You'll get beautiful, panoramic views of the mountains and surrounding lakes.

Sunapee Harbor

Off Rte. 11.

Sit at the edge of the lake and watch boats come and go, or picnic on the lawn that stretches from the lake to the road. Nobody hurries here. During the day you can rent boats and water-skiing equipment from Osborne's Marina—on a weekly basis only. (Sailboat, canoe, and motor rentals are also available from Sargent's Marina in Georges Mills, a few miles north of the Harbor.) Don't miss the free outdoor band concerts held here every Wednesday evening during the summer. Bring a blanket—the kids can dance and play on the lawn while you listen to the music float across the lake.

MV Mount Sunapee II

Sunapee Harbor (off Rte. 11); (603) 763-4030. Mid-June–Labor Day, daily, 10–2:30. Adults, $7; 5–12, $4.

"Who wants to take the wheel?" Captain Hargbol yells, and by the end of the boat ride, nearly every child has taken the helm and played out the fantasy of "sea captain." This 1.5-hour cruise, departing from Sunapee Harbor, takes you around Lake Sunapee past beaches, lighthouses, and summer homes. Captain Hargbol gives a lively narration on the history, points of interest, and lore of the lake. It's a pretty ride and a nice way to see Lake Sunapee.

Winslow State Park
Exit 10 off I-89, head toward Wilmot; (603) 526-6168.
Take the auto road from the park entrance up to Mount Kearsage (2,937 feet), and you'll find a peaceful picnic area with a great mountain view. From here you can take a short hiking trail to the summit. This is an extra special spot at twilight, when you'll be privy to a wonderful sunset.

Wadleigh State Park
Sutton; (603) 927-4727.
A 52-acre beach and picnic area on the south shore of Kezar Lake makes this a special spot for families. It's rarely crowded.

Pillsbury State Park
Rte. 31, Washington; (603) 863-2860.
This 5,000-acre park is a great place for fishing, hiking, and camping. There are nine picturesque woodland ponds and several hiking trails in the park. Walk to Balance Rock, a large glacial erratic in such a teetering position that it's said one can actually move it by hand.

Shaker Village
Shaker Rd., Canterbury; (603) 783-9977, May–Oct., Mon.–Sat., 10–5. Adults, $6.75; 6–12, $3.50.
As you walk through this historic communal village, you'll get a glimpse of what life was like for the Canterbury Shakers. Watch artisans make a broom, spin yarn, or weave a rug in the self-sufficient tradition of Shaker life. Skilled craftspeople use other Shaker skills to make baskets, tinware, herbal sachets, and ladderback chairs. There are six buildings on the spacious grounds, and walking tours are given by knowledgeable guides who interpret 200 years of Shaker history.

Ruggles Mine
On Isinglass Mountain (off Rte. 4), Grafton; (603) 448-6911. Late-June–

mid-Oct., daily, 9–5; mid-May–mid-June, weekends only, 9–5. Adults, $5.75; 6–11, $2.50.

Hammer and pound and chisel away as you look for precious metals and stones. Prospecting in Ruggles Mine is a real adventure, no matter what your age. The mine is big—full of caves and tunnels, high ledges, and water pools. You're allowed to pick away at the walls and take whatever you extract. The kids are sure to leave with a heavy load of "precious" souvenirs. In fact, more than 150 types of minerals have been found in the cave. You can rent hammers, chisels, picks, flashlights, and carrying sacks if you've forgotten to bring your own. Consider packing a lunch—the panoramic view of mountains and valleys makes this a nice setting for a picnic.

Fort at No. 4

Rte. 11, Charlestown; (603) 826-5700. Late May–Columbus Day, daily except Tues., 10–4. Adults, $4.75; 6–11, $3.25.

This living-history museum is a reproduction of the original fortified settlement at No. 4, Charlestown, New Hampshire, during the French-Indian War era. The 20-acre site on the Connecticut River includes a

Fort at No. 4, a living history museum, features costumed guides demonstrating crafts like musketball molding and candle-dipping.

stockade surrounding 14 buildings: a watch tower you can climb into, a blacksmith shop, cabins, and barns. As you walk through the village, you'll see costumed guides demonstrating a variety of early crafts, such as musketball molding and candle dipping.

Barn Playhouse
Main St., New London; (603) 526-4631. July–Aug.
This summer stock theater is a great way to introduce your family to the stage. The Playhouse does a nice job welcoming children. Catch the magical Mondays series throughout July and August. All programs are held in a refurbished barn. Call ahead for program information and schedules.

Gould Hill Orchards
Gould Hill Rd. (off Rte. 103), Hopkinton Village; (603) 746-3811. Aug.–May. Free (apples charged by the pound, bags furnished).
If you're in the Sunapee area in the fall, take a side trip to the Gould Hill Orchards for apple picking and fresh cider. The scenic mountain setting is a good place to view fall foliage.

Hang-gliding
Rte. 12, Claremont; (603) 542-4416.
If you're in the Claremont area, you might want to swing by the Morningside Recreation area to see if the local airborne athletes are practicing their hang-gliding stunts. On weekends there are specially scheduled events. Or parents can get a group together and try the sport themselves.

Norsk Cross-Country Skiing
Rte. 11, New London; (603) 526-4685.
Young or old, big or little, novice or expert, if you're thinking of cross-country skiing, head for the Norsk Touring Center. Rent your equipment, take a lesson, and then head for one of the 17 trails, marked according to ability level. It's a pretty location, with all the amenities right on site: lodging, restaurant, and ski-rental shop. Don't worry if you've never tried touring before—they're great at teaching the most inexperienced, and smallest, beginners.

Downhill Skiing

Mount Sunapee Ski Area

Sunapee National Park; (603) 763-5626 or 1-800-322-3300 (outside of New Hampshire). Adult lift tickets, $24/day; Little Indians, $12/session; SKIwee, $35/half day, $45/full day; children's equipment rentals, $10/day. Prices listed are for weekends and holidays; check for special weekday and package rates.

A good place to learn to ski—or to perfect your skills. This small, friendly area has 30 trails serviced by seven lifts. The majority of trails are for intermediate skiers, with a special area for beginning skiers. It's billed as the "Learn to Ski" mountain, offering a variety of ski schools and programs and claiming the staff will have you up and skiing in one day, whether you're 6 or 60. In fact, Mount Sunapee boasts a guarantee: they will help you ski linked turns on the first day or the second day is free.

□ Just for Children

The Duckling Nursery, located at the ski area, will take care of your youngsters while you ski. The nursery is free midweek on a first come, first serve basis. Reservations are suggested for weekends and holidays, when you pay by the hour. The Little Indians program will give your three- and four-year-olds a nice welcome to the sport of skiing. Class size is small, with a three-to-one child/teacher ratio, and the emphasis is on fun. Children 5 to 12 can join the nationally recognized SKIwee program.

King Ridge Ski Area

King Ridge Rd. (Exit 11 off I-91), New London; (603) 526-6066. Adult lift ticket, $15; nursery, $1.50/hour, three-hour minimum; SKIwee, $35/day. Prices listed are for weekends and holidays; check for special weekday and package rates.

You might meet the Mad Hatter or the White Rabbit as you traverse down the gently-sloping trails at King Ridge. This is a friendly, small resort that caters to families. Most of the 20 trails are for beginners—12 in all, including the Cheshire Cat, the Big Tea Party, and Alice's Return. If you haven't guessed by now, the trails are named after Lewis Carroll's most memorable characters, and the atmosphere throughout the area is casual and fun.

□ Just for Children

Besides Alice and her friends, King Ridge features two nurseries for children aged four months through six years. The nursery is open from 8 to 4:30, weekends; 8:30 to 4:30, non-vacation weekdays. Free nursery day-care is offered on non-vacation weekdays to the children of all-day, all-lift ticket purchasers. Children four years and under ski free when accompanied by a full-paying parent. The full-day SKIwee program is offered to children ages 5 to 12, and includes two lessons and lunch. Rental equipment is $13 more.

Restaurants

The Dock and Boathouse Tavern
Sunapee Harbor (off Rte. 11). Seasonal.
Nothing fancy here—except the setting, right on Sunapee Harbor. Sit on the back deck at one of the picnic tables for a great view of the boats bobbing in the lake. Barbecued ribs and pizza are favorite dinnertime choices, or order from a complete menu of soups, salads, and sandwiches.

Pizzas and Cream of New London
Colonial Plaza, New London; (603) 526-2875. Daily, 11–11.
A family-style restaurant that's popular with summer visitors. Top-selling item is the deep-dish pizza. You can also get children's portions of spaghetti, lasagna, and other Italian specialties. And homemade ice cream for dessert.

Mount Washington Area

Majestic Mount Washington, the highest peak in the Northeast, looks down upon an area rich in beauty and abundant with activities. The Presidential Range, a string of mountain peaks named after U.S. Presidents, and the surrounding national forest offer miles of fine hiking trails, cascades, waterfalls, and mountain lakes. Chug along in a steam-powered railroad car, or take the slow, climbing auto road to the top of Mount Washington. The view, of mountain peaks and valleys below, is spectacular; the air is chilly, so dress warmly.

Families that ski will enjoy the relaxed Bretton Woods ski area for cross-country and downhill skiing. Young children will enjoy a visit with Santa, and the entire family can get a taste of the Old West at Six Gun City in nearby Jefferson.

Santa's Village
Rte. 2, Jefferson; (603) 586-4445. Mid-June–Labor Day, daily, 9:30–7; Labor Day–Columbus Day, weekends only, 9:30–5. $8.95; under 4, free.
Santa is never out of season with young children. If you can tolerate the "When is Christmas?" questions that will inevitably follow, stop in to see Santa and his elves. Besides a visit with the host of honor, children will enjoy splashing down the log flume, riding in the enchanted train, and circling around on the old-fashioned carousel. There are music and bird shows, snack bars, and picnic areas.

Six Gun City
Rte. 2, Jefferson; (603) 586-4592. Mid-June–Labor Day, daily, 9–6; Labor Day–Columbus Day, weekends only, 9–5. $7; under 4, free.
This is a kid's fantasy come true—a visit to the Old West when cowboys ruled the land, sheriffs caught outlaws, and horses were the mode of transportation. Children will love to become deputies, helping the sheriff go after law-breaking outlaws or taking their own ride on a pony or burro. The live cowboy skits and Frontier Show are fun family entertainment. Throughout Six Gun City, you'll see more than 100 horse-drawn vehicles and many Old West antiques. And there are plenty of rides and bumper boats. Be sure to bring your bathing suit for a trip down the Tomahawk Run Waterslide.

Mount Washington Auto Road
Rte. 16, Gorham; (603) 466-3988. Mid-May–Columbus Day, daily, 8–4:30. $11 for car and driver; additional adults, $4; 5–12, $3.
This winding, steep, eight-mile toll road offers some of the most scenic views in the Northeast. The 45-minute trip to the summit—at 6,288 feet it's the highest mountain in New England—takes you through mountain forests 'til you reach the top. Here you'll see views stretching, on clear days, across six states. At the summit, there's an observatory and a small museum with displays of the rare, arctic flowers often found in this cold environment. Be sure to dress warmly—it's chilly up here. If you prefer not to drive yourself,

*Pint-sized cowboys and cowgirls thrill to
the Wild West-style action at Six Gun
City, especially if they make deputy.*

there are guided tour vans that will take you up, or you can ride the Cog Railway.

Mount Washington Cog Railway
Rte. 302, Bretton Woods; (603) 846-5404 or 1-800-922-8825, Ext. 5. Round trip, $32; 7–15, $16.
This ride up the mountain railway to the summit of Mount Washington is not unlike being on a slow roller coaster. The steam-powered train, dating back to 1869, hits inclines that reach a 35 percent grade, making this the second steepest railway track in the world. The round trip takes about three hours. Get a window seat, if you can, to enjoy the lovely mountain panoramas. Consider taking the early morning (8:30) or afternoon (4:30) train when fares are reduced . . . and dress warmly.

Crawford Notch
Rte. 302, Bartlett; (603) 374-2272.
One of the most scenic places in the area is this mountain park on the Saco River, surrounded by the White Mountain National Forest. Dip your toes in the clear waters of the Saco River and listen to the nearby Silver and Flume Cascades. There are lots of hiking trails nearby.

Hiking
Don't miss the chance to hike one of the many trails in the Mount Washing-ton area—the best way to enjoy its natural beauty. Stop by one of the Appalachian Mountain Club camps or huts scattered throughout the area for trail maps, recommendations, and up-to-date trail conditions. (Closest one in this area is just south of the Bretton Woods area at the Crawford Notch Camp on Route 302.) Trails listed below are short, easy hikes appro-priate for families. (Put infants in a backpack—trails are not stroller-accessible.)

□ Alpine Garden Trail
Tie in a short hike with your trip up or down the Mount Washington Auto Road. This trail leaves the road at the Alpine Gardens Junction at about the six-mile mark. This pretty hike is best from late June to early July, when the dainty alpine flowers are in bloom. It'll take about an hour to cover its 1.5 miles.

□ Jackson-Webster Trail
There are a few steep spots along the way, which make this trail best for families with older children (seven years and older). The trail, marked in

blue, leaves the east side of U.S. 302 just south of the Crawford Depot. You'll see a side trail, Elephant Head, veering to the right. Take this short side trip to the top of the ledge overlooking Crawford Notch for fine views. The main trail runs above Elephant Head Brook, crosses Little Mossy Brook, and rises, rather steeply, to Flume Cascade Brook. It's about 45 minutes and .9 miles to this point. Head back now or continue on the Webster branch (to the right) to a beautiful cascade and pool. That'll be enough for most families.

□ Sylvan Way

This is a great trail for families, particularly in the fall when foliage is spectacular. Pick it up at the Link at Memorial Bridge on Route 2, .7 miles from the Appalachian parking area in Randolph. You'll pass falls and cross brooks on this easy 2.5-mile trip. It should take about an hour-and-a-half.

Scenic Drive—Jefferson Notch

Not recommended for the meek, but worth the effort, is a ride through Jefferson Notch. This narrow, steep road is the highest in New Hampshire, reaching almost 3,000 feet. From U.S. 2, about three miles east of Jefferson Highlands, you'll turn south on the road heading from Labyan to the Mount Washington Cog Railway Station. You'll get great mountain and valley panoramas and a fine view of Jefferson Notch.

Cross-Country Skiing

Rte. 302, Bretton Woods Touring Center, Bretton Woods; (603) 278-5000. Besides the many trails within the Appalachian Mountain Club network, Nordic skiers will enjoy the well-maintained course at Bretton Woods Ski Area. The trails are generally old logging roads or rail beds that head through forests, over bridges, and down lanes. There are lots of nice views of Crawford Notch or Ammonoosuc Ravine along the way. You can warm up and replenish at the Ski Touring Center.

Downhill Skiing

Bretton Woods

Rte. 302, Bretton Woods; (603) 278-5000. Adult lift ticket, $25; Hobbit Ski School, $35; nursery, $3.75/hour (three hour minimum) or $20/day. Prices listed are for weekends and holidays; special packages are available. Bretton Woods Ski Area also offers Alpine skiing. There are 22 trails of varying degrees of difficulty, offering something for everyone. You'll be

*That first run from the top of the
mountain is a singularly thrilling
experience.*

skiing Mount Rosebrook, which has a 1,500-foot vertical drop—mostly felt in long, relaxed runs. More experienced skiers will enjoy the six difficult runs, including a short, challenging trip down the head wall on Short & Sweet or Upper Express. Just about everything the skiing family needs is here: lessons, rentals, restaurants, and nursery. And the area gets twice as much snow as other ski resorts in the vicinity, a phenomenon the locals call the "Bretton Wood flurries."

□ Just For Children
The Hobbit Ski School is open for children ages 4 to 12. The all-day program, 8:30 to 3:30, includes rental equipment, lunch, lift ticket and two two-hour ski lessons. Children are awarded badges as they progress through the program. A nursery is open daily, 7:30 to 5, for children two months to four years. Kids five and under ski free at the t-bar at all times.

Restaurants

Fabyans Station
Rte. 302 (next to Cog Railway Road), Bretton Woods; (603) 846-2222.
Lunch, 11–2:30; dinner, Sun.–Thurs., 5–9:30; Fri.–Sat., 5–10.
Housed in a restored railroad depot, this restaurant offers a selection of appetizers, salads, burgers, and sandwiches. Dinner entrées feature swordfish, pork pie, chicken, ribs, and beef dishes. Ask for half-portions for children or split the order; it will be plenty.

Darby's Restaurant
Rte. 302, Lodge at Bretton Woods; (603) 278-1500. Breakfast, 7:30–10;
dinner, 6–9:30, except Fri.–Sat., 6–10; Sun. brunch, 8–11.
This family-oriented restaurant in the Lodge at Bretton Woods offers great views of the Presidential Mountain Range. In winter you'll be warmed by two open fireplaces. The menu offers veal, chicken, steaks, and seafood. A special, $4.50 children's menu is available. Make reservations for weekend dinners; it gets crowded.

Lincoln/Franconia Area

This picturesque mountain area on the western flanks of the White Mountain National Forest is a pine-scented, four-season playground. Summer is the most popular season, when the valleys are full of flowers and the streams run with cool, clear mountain water. Each summer, thousands come to see the natural beauty of the White Mountain National Forest, to visit Franconia Notch State Park's gorges, flumes, and waterfalls, and to drive the scenic Kancamagus Highway, lined with mountain and valley vistas. Outdoor activities abound—take a hike to tumbling falls, swim in pristine mountain lakes and pools, canoe or kayak the Swift River, or take an aerial ride to the 4,200-foot summit of Cannon Mountain. The children can explore caves, zip down water slides and roller coasters, visit haunted houses and petting zoos, and learn about nature, music, and history at a variety of local museums. In the winter months, there's ice skating, sleigh rides, cross-country and downhill skiing.

Polar Caves
Rte. 25, Plymouth; (603) 536-1888. Mid-May–Oct., daily, 9–5. Adults, $6.50; 6–12, $3.
Get your first taste of spelunking as you slink through narrow passageways and climb rocky inclines. You'll explore the area where giant boulders were deposited many years ago by glaciers, forming a maze of caves. Kids who love a challenging climb—and don't mind getting their knees dirty—will enjoy finding hidden Smuggler's Cave, squirming through Lemon Squeeze, and screaming in dark Fat Man's Misery. You can back out along the way—there are detours to get you by the most challenging caves. A picnic area, museum shop, cafeteria, and ice cream bar are also on the grounds.

Lost River Reservation
Rte. 112, North Woodstock; (603) 745-8031. Mid-May–Oct., weather permitting: May, Sept., and Oct., 9–5:30; June, July, and Aug., 9–6. Last ticket sold one hour before closing. Adults, $5.50; 6–12, $2.75.
Your children will be dirty, tired, and happy when they leave this place. You'll become explorers and navigators as you climb your way up and down ladders, belly-slide under rock ledges, and slither through caves. You can take the easy way around—on the boardwalk—and simply enjoy the fine scenery. The .75-mile, hour-or-so trip follows the river as it appears and

disappears through giant, glacial boulders. You'll learn about the geological and ecological history of the river along the way. Be sure to wear comfortable shoes and outdoor clothing. A snack bar and picnic area are on the grounds.

Clark's Trading Post

Rte. 3, Lincoln; (603) 745-8913. Memorial Day–mid-June, weekends only, 10–6; late June–Labor Day, daily, 10–6. Adults $6; 6–11, $4.

From an adult's point of view, Clark's Trading Post is a hodge-podge of amusements, its best being the performance of a family of trained black bears. But the kids will skip along in amused bliss, laughing at the slanted floors in Tuttle's Haunted House and the flying pianos in Merlin's Mystical Mansion. They will even enjoy the antics of "Wolfman," who jeers at them as they ride aboard the White Mountain Central Railroad. There's a snack bar, an ice cream parlor, and picnic grounds.

The Whale's Tale and Amusement Park

Rte. 3, Lincoln; (603) 745-8810. Late May–mid-June, weekends, 10–5; late June–Labor Day, daily, 10–5. Water and amusement park: adults, $15.50; 6–12, $13. Amusement park only: $6 per person, adults and children.

Combine carnival rides and water slides and you come up with a sure kid-pleaser. At the amusement park, you'll find rides for your teenage thrill-seekers, as well as slower, tamer ones for the younger set. The kids will love bouncing in the sea of balls and getting wet on the water boats. When you're ready to cool off, walk over to the adjoining water park. Brave souls can streak down the Blue Lightning and Serpentine slides. For a more relaxing pace, you'll want to soak in the wave pool or tube down Lazy River. Younger children will love Whale Harbor, a special pool just for them. There are snack bars, changing facilities, and locker rentals.

The Flume

Rte. 3, Franconia Notch; (603) 823-5563. Memorial Day–Oct., daily, 9–4:30. Adults, $5; 6–12, $2.50.

One of the most popular attractions in the area, this natural, 800-foot chasm is a must stop along the way. The rushing waters of the Pemigewasset River carved this wonder thousands of years ago, leaving walls that rise as high as 70 feet. If you don't mind sharing space with the inevitable summer crowds, you'll enjoy the cool, misty mountain air and marvel at the surrounding natural beauty. You'll walk boardwalks and hiking trails across covered bridges to waterfalls, cascades, and river basins and pools.

Crossroads of America Museum

Main St., Bethlehem; (603) 869-3919. June–foliage season, daily, 9–6. Adults, $2.50; 6–15, $1.75.

This quiet, small museum has a good collection of model trains and railroads, old toys, planes, trucks, and ships. Children will especially like the five working railroads and villages that are set up here.

New England Ski Museum

Base of Cannon Mountain, Franconia Notch; (603) 823-7177. Memorial Day–Columbus Day and Dec. 15–Mar., daily, 10–4. Adults, $2; under 12, free.

Older children who've been bitten by the ski bug might enjoy a visit here. The exhibit that traces the evolution of ski equipment is particularly interesting—we've come a long way. The museum also features changing, ski-related exhibits and displays and a short slide show outlining the history of New England skiing.

Hobo Railroad

Rte. 3, Lincoln; (603) 745-2135. Memorial Day–late June, weekends; late June–Labor Day, daily. Trains leave at 9, 11, 1, 3, 5 and 7. Adults, $6; 6–12, $4.

For some outstanding mountain views (and a fun way to have lunch), consider taking the 14-mile trip along the Pemigewasset River aboard the Hobo Picnic Train. Your picnic lunch comes packed hobo style—wrapped in a bandana and tied to the end of a stick. (If you can't make lunch, there are other rides throughout the day and evening.) Your children will probably not let you get away without a ride on Diamond Eddie's ferris wheel. This giant wheel takes you for a gentle 10-minute ride as you sit on benches in enclosed compartments. A fun way to get an aerial view of the mountain range.

Loon Mountain Gondola

Kancamagus Hwy., Lincoln; (603) 745-8111. Memorial Day–mid-June, weekends only; mid-June–Oct., daily. Adults, $5; 6–12, $3.

The beauty of the New Hampshire mountain ranges, forests, and lakes is spectacular from the mountain summits. In the Lincoln area, ride the Loon Mountain Gondola to the top of Loon Mountain, where you'll see a panoramic view of many White Mountain peaks. The enclosed gondola ride takes about 10 minutes. Atop, there's a four-story observation tower and cafeteria.

Cannon Aerial Tramway

Rte. 3, Franconia Notch; (603) 823-5563. Memorial Day–mid-Oct., daily, 9–4:30. Adults, $5; 6–12,, $2.75; under 6, free.

In Franconia Notch, the Cannon Aerial Tramway whisks you to the summit of 4,200-foot Cannon Mountain; on a clear day, you'll be able to see into Maine, Vermont, and Canada. The ride takes six minutes. Plan to spend some time at the top. Consider packing snacks or lunch (or buy something at the Summit Cafeteria) to enjoy along one of the summit trails. The Rim Trail is perfect for families. You'll be treated to some great mountain views, and you'll find plenty of picnic spots along the way. At the end is an observation deck for more viewing. It'll take only about 20 minutes to walk (not counting time out for picnics).

Children's Festival

Mill at Loon Mountain (Kancamagus Hwy.), Lincoln; (603) 745-6032. July– Aug., Wed., 11 and 1. Adults $2.75; 12 and under, $3.

Music, mimes, puppets, storytelling, and theatre for children are all part of the Children's Festival activities held at the mill at Loon Mountain. Sponsored by the North Country Center for the Arts, festivals take place each Wednesday through July and August.

Swimming

Rte. 3, Franconia Notch.

On hot days, head for Echo Lake, a pristine, spring-fed lake at the base of Cannon Mountain. The white, sandy beach, cool mountain waters, and picturesque background are a hard-to-beat combination. There are changing and bathhouse facilities.

Fishing

For some of the best in fly fishing, head for Profile Lake in Franconia Notch State Park. This small, clear body of water is the headwater of the Pemige-wasset River. The lake, well known for its brook trout, is open for fly fishing only. In Franconia, grab a rock or wade the Gale River for freshwater fish. You'll also want to try your luck at Coffin Pond on Route 18. This is a favorite local fishing hole. Stop by Pro-Bait & Tackle on Harvard Street in Franconia for equipment, bait, and good advice on fishing spots; (603) 823-8419.

Horseback Riding

Franconia Inn, Rte. 116, Franconia; (603) 823-5542. $18/hour; Beginner's Special, $13/half hour.

A great place to match wits with brook trout: Profile Lake in Franconia Notch State Park, open for fly fishing only.

Horseback rides through meadows and forests, offering beautiful views of Mount Lafayette, Mount Mooslauke, and the Franconia Range, are available at the Franconia Inn. You'll travel with a guide on trails through the 117-acre estate on the Easton Valley. Children must be at least 54 inches tall to reach the stirrups properly.

Scenic Drive—Franconia Notch Parkway

Travel I-93 for eight miles through a spectacular mountain pass. The highway is located between the high peaks of the Kinsman and Franconia mountain ranges. As you travel through the Notch, from the Flume at the south to Echo Lake at the north, you'll see wonderful vistas, waterfalls, mountain lakes, and natural attractions. Visit the Flume, then stop for a peek at the basin. This beautiful waterfall has a granite pothole 20 feet in diameter at its base. Below the Basin look for the Old Man's Foot rock formation. Show the kids Boise Rock, where Thomas Boise, a teamster from Woodstock, New Hampshire, sought shelter during a blizzard in the early 1800's. Killing his horse, Boise skinned it and wrapped himself in its hide. Searchers cut away the frozen hide and found him alive the next day.

Just north of Boise Rock you'll see Profile Lake, headquarters of the Old Man's Washbowl. Hovering above Profile Lake is the Old Man of the Mountains. This natural rock formation was formed nearly 200 million years ago. The Old Man is made of five separate granite hedges arranged to form a man's profile. At the northern side of the Notch Parkway you'll find beautiful Echo Lake, the perfect spot to stop for a swim or picnic.

Cross-Country Skiing

Loon Mountain
Kancamagus Highway, Lincoln; (603) 745-8111. Trail fee, $4/day.
The Loon Mountain Cross-Country Center maintains more than 30 kilometers of groomed trails that run along the Pemigewasset River and traverse the mountains. There are lots of gentle trails for beginners and children. Information on trails, lessons, and rentals is available at the headquarters in the base lodge at Loon. There's also a skating rink with skate rentals available.

Echo Lake
Cross-country skiing around Echo Lake is a visual treat. You'll see Cannon Mountain in the background and glimpse the Old Man of the Mountains. Bring your own gear.

Downhill Skiing

Waterville Valley Ski Area
Rte. 49 (Waterville Valley Access Rd.); (603) 236-8311. Adult lift ticket, $33; 6–12, free during non-holiday mid-weeks when one parent buys a 3- (or more) day ticket; 5 and under, free; SKIwee $50/day. Ski equipment rentals extra.
Waterville knows how to treat families. Come for the day and ski the 53 trails serviced by 13 lifts. But it won't be enough—and you will wish you'd stayed to browse the Town Square, ice skate in the indoor arena, soak in the Jacuzzi, or enjoy the twilight sleigh ride. Despite its amenities, this family resort manages to maintain a cozy, New England village atmosphere. Recent mountain renovations have included a 7,556-foot, high-speed quad chairlift

that takes you to the top of the mountain in about seven minutes. From there you can ski any level of trail.

□ Just for Children

Waterville Valley offers a professionally-run nursery for infants six weeks and up, located at the ski area. This friendly facility includes an infant's game room equipped with cribs, playpens, high chairs, and plenty of toys. Depending on your child's age and your preferences, a typical day may include reading, arts and crafts, lunch, and indoor and outdoor play. It's available by the hour in half-day, full-day or multiple-day packages.

But if your children are old enough—that's three years and up at Waterville—enroll them in one of the children's learn-to-ski programs. "We believe in the all smiles, no tears approach to learning here," says Joseph Jung, Director of the Waterville Valley Ski School. Waterville Valley has a special children's ski area, complete with its own kinderlift. Petite SKIwee (ages three to five), SKIwee (ages six to eight), and Grand SKIwee (9 to 12) half-day or full-day programs are offered. A teenage group ski lesson is also available. There's lots of flexibility in choosing programs. It's best to talk over the options with one of the staff ahead of time (advance reservations are recommended) so you can choose the best package for you and your children—and get the most for your money.

Loon Mountain Ski Area

Kancamagus Hwy., Lincoln; (603) 745-8111. Adult lift ticket, $30; nursery, $30/day; Nitey Nite Day Camp, $44.
Loon is a popular Northeast ski resort, offering 41 trails for skiers of every level. Loon's trails ski long. Even a beginner can ride to the top of the mountain and take a gradual, easy run down to the base. It's a big place to get around, but it still manages to maintain a friendly, helpful atmosphere. The children's ski programs are first-rate, and experienced skiers will not be bored.

□ Just for Children

The Gingerbread Nursery at the Mountain Club provides care for children six weeks to six years from 8 to 4:30. Space is limited, so call ahead. The ski school offers an all-day Nitey Nite Day Camp program for children ages 5 to 12. Lessons and lunch are included. Junior (6 to 12) can ski free on five-day, non-holiday ski weeks when accompanied by a participating adult. Children five and under ski free anytime.

Cannon
Franconia Notch State Park, Franconia; (603) 823-8521. Adult lift ticket, $25. Nursery, ages 6–17 months, $8/session or $5/hour; mid-week, non-holidays only; ski workshops, $17/half-day, $45/day.

This state-owned ski area is located in lovely Franconia Notch State Park. A predominantly intermediate area, Cannon Mountain offers 25 trails, seven lifts, and a 2,146-foot vertical drop. This is a small, manageable ski area with spectacular views from its 4,200-foot summit.

□ Just for Children
The Cannon nursery offers day-care for children 18 months and older. Infants from 6 to 17 months are accepted only during mid-week and non-holidays. Care includes a morning snack, story time, games, dancing, and arts and crafts projects. The nursery offers two sessions per day, 9 to noon and 1 to 4. It's open during lunch on weekends and holidays only. Special ski workshops are offered on weekends from December 31 through March 12 and on school vacation weeks for children 6 to 12. You can choose between half- or all-day instruction. Lifts and equipment are optional.

Restaurants

Govani's
Rte. 112 (Lost River Rd.), North Woodstock; (603) 745-8042. Seasonal, daily, 4:30–9.

This cozy restaurant has been in operation since 1914, when Granny Govani first started feeding the lumberjacks. On the edge of a beautiful waterfall, you'll feast on northern Italian dishes like garden lasagna, manicotti, pesto linguine, and shrimp scampi. Entrées range from $6.95 to $15.95. They're happy to serve half-portions or provide extra plates for children. Go early to avoid the crowds and to enjoy a walk along the river.

The Chalet
Main St., North Woodstock; (603) 745-2256. Sun.–Thurs., 11:30–8; Fri.–Sat., 11:30–9.

This very popular family restaurant in the heart of North Woodstock serves large portions of good food at reasonable prices. There's a wide variety of entrées to choose from—beef, chicken, seafood—along with the popular prime rib and lobster dishes. Children's menu offers the usual (hot dog, hamburger, chicken fingers), plus fried scallops, shrimp, and spaghetti. Save room for a make-your-own-sundae dessert.

Polly's Pancake Parlor
Rte. 116, Sugar Hill; (603) 823-5575. Seasonal, Mon.–Thurs., 7–3; Fri.– Sun., 7–7.
Sometimes there's nothing better than a stack of homemade pancakes and syrup. For more than 50 years, Polly's has been serving country breakfasts all day long. Pancakes, waffles, and french toast, all made from home-ground flours, are offered with a variety of toppings (try yogurt, ice cream, or the coconut or walnut syrup). There are also eggs and bacon, homemade country sausage, soups, sandwiches, and salads for lunch or early dinner.

Dutch Treat
Main St., Franconia Village; (603) 823-5542. Daily, 7 a.m.–9 p.m.
The real treats here are the scenic views of Cannon Mountain and the homemade Italian dishes. This is an area favorite, and you're likely to be sitting next to a group of locals recounting their day's catch. It's friendly and casual. The homemade pizza is popular—comes child-size, too.

Conway/Jackson Area

If your family has a love of the great outdoors, you'll revel in the natural beauty and abundance of activities available at the rugged mountain village of Jackson. This is the home of the Appalachian Mountain Club and center for hiking, mountain climbing, and cross-country skiing. The beauty of this area is best seen on a hike into the White Mountain National Forest, a picnic on the shores of a mountain lake, or a horse-drawn sleigh ride through a covered bridge and past the white-steepled church in the village center. There's fishing, swimming, hiking, canoeing, rafting, kayaking, golfing, tennis . . . and more. And, in the winter, there's some of the best cross-country and downhill skiing. Drive a few miles south to North Conway and you're in a different world of factory outlets and discount shopping.

Amid the natural beauty of the mountains, you'll find an abundance of commercial attractions to delight children. Your family can visit Cinderella

New Hampshire's White Mountain region offers a variety of options for outdoors-loving families, including hiking, fishing, and swimming in freshwater lakes and streams.

at her castle, ride a gondola to the top of a mountain, and zip down it on a water slide. It's a wonderfully diverse and popular area for family vacationing.

Heritage, New Hampshire

Rte. 16, Glen; (603) 383-9776. Mid-May–late Oct., daily, 9–5; mid-June–Labor Day, daily, 9–6. Adults, $6.50; 4–12, $4.50.

This museum puts you in the middle of history-in-the-making as you journey through time, from 1634 to the 20th century. You'll be carried across the ocean aboard the ship *Reliance*. From there you'll walk through history, as special effects and audio-visual techniques do a good job of putting you right in the middle of the action. The kids' imaginations will run wild, and you'll learn about early American history along the way.

Story Land

Rte. 16, Glen; (603) 383-4293. Father's Day–Labor Day, daily, 9–6; Labor Day–Columbus Day, weekends, 10–5. $11; under 4, free.

Look, it's Cinderella and Little Bo Peep . . . with her sheep! Youngsters will squeal with delight as they meet their favorite story-book characters. Take a ride on a pirate's ship, a swan boat, or around the track in a miniature Model T. There are amusement rides, a castle, live animals, and daily shows.

Attitash Alpine Slide, Cannonball Express, and Aquaboggan
Rte. 302, Bartlett; (603) 374-2368. Memorial Day–mid-June, weekends only, 10–6; mid-June–Labor Day, daily, 10–6. Adults, $5, single ride; 5–12, $4, single ride; under 4, free.
Combine a scenic ski-lift ride with an exhilarating trip down Alpine Slide. The .75-mile slide takes you through woods and meadows—at your own pace. You control your own sled, going as fast or as slow as you like. Little ones can hop on with you. On hot days, you can cool off with a trip down the water slides—the Cannonball Express or Aquaboggan.

Conway Scenic Railroad
Rte. 16, North Conway; (603) 356-5251. Mid-June–late Oct., daily; May, weekends only. Trains depart at 11, 1, 2:30, and 4. Adults, $6; 4–12, $4.
Several trips depart daily from the old Victorian railroad station in North Conway. The hour-long ride is a peaceful trip through scenic New Hampshire countryside.

Community Center Playground
Main St., North Conway.
This is where all the kids hang out. The outdoor playground is full of monkey bars, tunnels, slides, swings, and jungle gyms. Right next to the Conway Railroad Station in the center of North Conway Village.

Eastern Slope Playhouse
Main St., North Conway; (603) 356-5776. Tues.–Sat., 8.
For a special evening, consider attending a performance of the Mount Washington Valley Theater Company, held throughout the summer at the Eastern Slope Playhouse. The renowned summer theater performs first-rate productions of Broadway musicals. A nice, upbeat, toe-tapping night out with older children. Call starting mid-June for schedule, reservations, and ticket prices.

Arts Jubilee
Box 647, North Conway, NH 03860; (603) 356-9393. Performances held at Settler's Green, intersection of Rtes. 16 and 302, North Conway.
Magicians, dragons, and acrobats; folk dancing and ballet; barbershop quartets, jazz reviews, and classical orchestras; knee-slapping country music

and bagpipes—you're liable to see anything under the Arts Jubilee tent in North Conway. This ongoing arts festival is well known for its weekly summer family-entertainment series (monthly events are held the rest of the year). Call or write for a schedule of events.

Grand Manor Antique Car Museum
Junction Rtes. 16 and 302, Glen; (603) 356-9366. 9:30–5; Mid-June–Labor Day, daily, 9:30–5; year-round, weekends, 9:30–5. Adults, $5; 6–12, $3.
Auto buffs will like this museum, filled with 40 mint antique and classic models from 1908 to 1963. Take a close-up look at the car Bonnie and Clyde drove in the infamous movie. There are lots of cars of the "rich and famous" and old movie cars. There's a vintage movie theater and radio shows to enhance the setting. Enjoy a ride in the paddleboats or a picnic on the grounds.

Wildcat Mountain Gondola
Rte. 16, Pinkham Notch; (603) 466-3326. Mid-May–July 4, weekends, 10–4; July 4–mid-Oct., daily, 10–4. Adults, $6; 12 and under, $3.
Enjoy the views atop the 4,100-foot summit at Wildcat Mountain without having to ski down it. Take a 25-minute (round-trip) sky ride to enjoy the fabulous views of the White Mountain National Forest and beyond. A great place for a picnic, if you have the time. Picnic areas, snacks, and nature trails are at the summit.

Mount Cranmore Tramway
Skimobile Rd., North Conway; (603) 356-5543. July–mid-Oct. Adults, $6; 6–12, $4.50.
Ride the open-air skimobile to the top of Mount Cranmore and enjoy aerial views of Mount Washington and the valley below. It's a fun place for a summer picnic; you can grab hamburgers and chicken for lunch at the outdoor barbecue. During the fall, when views of the foliage are spectacular, lunch is served in the Summit Pub. Sometimes you can catch a local hang-gliding demonstration.

Echo Lake State Park
Rte. 302 (just off Rte. 16), North Conway; (603) 356-2672. June–Labor Day.
This small park is the perfect spot to stop for a refreshing swim or a relaxing day outing. The clear, spring-fed lake has a good swimming area for children. There are trails to take around the lake and to ledges above,

depending on your time and inclination. There are picnic tables, grills, and boats for rent. This is a very popular hot summer day spot.

Swimming

There are plenty of places to pull off the road here and take a refreshing dip in the pristine mountain rivers and falls. On hot summer days, you'll see lots of people sunning on rocks and swimming in the clear waters of the Saco and Swift Rivers, accessed from the Kancamagus Highway (Route 112) and Route 302. If you want to avoid crowds, prowl around a bit. You'll find lots of good swimming holes a bit off the highway that are easily accessible.

Canoeing

Rte. 302, Center Conway; (603) 447-2177. Also, Main St., North Conway; (603) 447-3801. Or write for brochure: Saco Bound, Box 119, Center Conway, NH 03813.
The Saco River is well known for its excellent canoeing. You need not be experienced. Stop by the Saco Bound offices in North Conway, where you'll get all the equipment and instruction you need. You can go for a few hours or make a day of it. The scenery is wonderful, the waters are calm and shallow in summer, and there are lots of great places along the way to stop for a picnic and swim. In the spring, when the waters are swifter, you might consider an exhilarating kayaking or whitewater rafting trip. Be sure to plan several weeks ahead for weekend rentals to avoid disappointment.

Fishing

You'll need nothing fancy to sink your hooks into a freshwater brook trout: give the kids a pole, some #8 hooks, and a can of worms and head for the Swift River. Pick your rock and cast. Adults will need a license if they join in the fun.

Gold-Panning

The locals swear there's gold in them thar rivers (Swift and Saco), but the rangers are quick to add that while many have found gold, no one's struck it rich yet. Pack a couple of shallow pans and try your luck. It's a fun way to spend a few hours on the river. Who knows?

Horse Logic Hay and Sleigh Rides

Rte. 116, Jackson; (603) 383-9876.
There's something special—for kids and grown-ups alike—about a sleigh ride through freshly fallen snow around a picturesque New England village. Relax in a wagon or sleigh pulled by horses as they prance around Jackson

Village. Take the kids (of course, they'll love it), or get a baby-sitter and reserve it for a romantic night out!

Hiking

Your first stop should be a visit to the Pinkham Notch Camp at the base of Mount Washington. This serves as the Northern New England Headquarters for the Appalachian Mountain Club, and everyone is welcome to use its facilities and services. The AMC is a non-profit organization offering a wide variety of recreation and conservation activities. Besides expeditions, these include research, back country management, trail and shelter construction and maintenance, conservation, mountain search and rescue, book publishing, and outdoor education.

Pinkham Notch is the hub of White Mountain hiking activity. You'll see mountain climbers and backpackers, downhill and cross-country skiers (in the winter), novices and experts, all gathering about, planning the day's activities. You'll want to talk to the people on staff here for updated information on trail conditions, recommendations for families, and to pick up trail maps. You might even want to stop for a hearty meal at the center's dining room. The Saco Ranger Station at the junction of Route 112 (Kancamagus Highway) and Route 16 is another good spot to stop in for hiking information. The folks here are always friendly and helpful.

There are thousands of miles of trails for hiking in the White Mountain area and many are appropriate for the inexperienced hiking family. (Most, however, do not accommodate strollers or wheelchairs, so put baby in a backpack.)

□ Glen Ellis Falls

Off Route 16, .8 miles south of the Pinkham Notch Camp, is a very easy walk to Glen Ellis Falls. The trail passes under the highway through a tunnel and reaches the falls in .3 miles. The main fall is 70 feet high, with many pools and smaller falls below.

□ Winneweta Falls Trail

This trail leaves Route 16 three miles north of Jackson. You'll cross the Ellis River (watch out in the spring when the water is high) and follow the Miles Brook until you get to Winneweta Falls. A refreshing, wet, hot-day hike— it's a mile long and takes about 40 minutes.

□ Mountain Pond Trail

This trail begins .6 miles up the road that leaves Maine 113 at a spot .2 miles north of the Congregational Church in Chatham. You'll walk through a birch and fir forest to the pristine Mountain Pond. From here, take the northerly route around the pond and head back (you'll want to stop first for a dip in the pond or a picnic along its shores). If you continue south, passing the AMC cabin, you'll be in for a much longer (three-hour) hike. Otherwise, it's a short, easy hike to the pond and back.

□ Sawyer Pond Trail

This trail leaves the Kancamagus Highway two miles east of the Sabbaday Falls Picnic Area. You'll head north and cross the Swift River, pass through between Coreens Cliff and Owls Cliff, and cross Sawyer Brook. Here, Sawyer Pond will come into view. The pond is clear and inviting—a great place for a swim after your hike. There's a nice, sandy area for sunning and picnicking. You can continue on the trail (you'll pass across a couple of streams) and end up on Sawyer River Road, from which you'll need transportation back to your starting point. (AMC runs a shuttle service; arrange for it before you start out.) It will take about 3.5 hours to go the entire six miles. A better option for families with young children might be just to head back the way you came. This will take you about 2.5 hours on an easy four-to-five-mile trail (not counting your time-out on the pond).

□ Sabbaday Falls Trail

This is a pleasant, easy walk to a picturesque series of cascades. The trail begins off the Kancamagus Highway (about 15 miles west of Route 16) and has a number of descriptive signs along the way pointing out wildlife and rock formations. It'll take about a half hour to go its .4 miles.

□ Black Cap Mountain

Drive to the top of Hurricane Mountain Road. There's an easy trail from here to Black Cap Mountain, at which you'll be rewarded with great views of the National Forest, mountain peaks, and Maine, to your east. Watch for the migrating hawks that are often seen here. The trail will take about an hour to go its 1.2 miles.

□ Black Mountain Trail

This trail begins as a toll road leaving Carter Notch Road, one mile north of the junction of Routes 16A and 16B. You'll walk along woody slopes and rocky outcrops to the summit of Black Mountain. The small spur trail heading east a short walk up from here leads to fabulous mountain vistas with fine views of Mount Washington, Wildcat Mountain, and Carter Notch. The trail is less than two miles long and will take about 1.5 hours.

Scenic Drive—Cathedral Ledge

For several years, this area has been honored with the presence of a pair of nesting Peregrine falcons, seen on Cathedral Ledge. When the falcons are in town, cars are not allowed to drive to the ledge (hikers only!). But if you're here when they're not, take the short, winding road off Route 16, just north of North Conway (it's just past the Echo Lake State Park). The view from Cathedral Ledge is fantastic—the entire valley stretches below you, with the Saco River running through the middle.

Ice Skating

There are three rinks open to the public in this area. Watch for signs in Conway Village, Jackson Village, and North Conway Village. You can rent skates at Joe Jones' Ski and Sports Shop in North Conway.

Cross-Country Skiing

Jackson Ski Touring Foundation, Jackson; (603) 383-9355. Appalachian Mountain Club, Rte. 16, Pinkham Notch; (603) 466-2727. Intervale Nordic Center, Intervale (off Rte. 16A), North Conway; (603) 356-5541.

The Jackson, New Hampshire, area had been rated as one of the four best places in the world for cross-country skiing. The Jackson Ski Touring Foundation maintains more than 90 miles of trails throughout the area—beginning in the village of Jackson and running into the White Mountain National Forest. The trails are well-maintained and marked for all abilities. In addition, many of the Appalachian Mountain Club trails are perfect for cross-country skiers. (Some of the trails described in the preceding hiking section are also good for beginner ski tourers.) The Intervale Nordic Center offers lessons and ski rentals plus 40 kilometers of scenic trails. There's a pleasant dining area on the grounds. You'll also notice a number of cross-country skiers and snowshoers right in the middle of Jackson as they traverse across the town golf course.

Downhill Skiing

Many of the ski resorts in this area offer interchangeable tickets, allowing you to ski at a variety of places throughout a week. Lift ticket rates listed below are for full days and weekends. Reduced rates are available for mid-weeks, limited areas, and junior skiers. Many money-saving packages are offered, as well. Contact ski resorts for more information.

Mount Cranmore Ski Resort
Off Rte. 16, North Conway; (613) 356-5544. Adult lift tickets, $29; nursery, $15/day; Rattlesnake Program, $45/day.
Conveniently located in North Conway, Mount Cranmore has old-time appeal, nothing too flashy or fancy. Skiing is easygoing and gentle on 28 trails. Take one of five lifts or, for something different, ride the unique skimobile to the 1,665-foot summit.

□ Just for Children
The nursery, open to children of walking age to six years, offers a structured program of activities that includes arts and crafts, games, and outdoor play. As soon as youngsters are willing and able (about 2.5 to 3 years old), the staff takes them out for ski lessons. Kids 4 to 12 can join the Rattlesnake Ski Program. The daily program runs from 10 to 3, and includes a morning ski lesson and an afternoon mileage program (they take to the trails with the instructor for some real skiing!). The Rattlesnake program includes a supervised "bring-your-own" lunch. It does not include equipment. Rentals are $15 more. Each year at the end of February Cranmore sponsors Kid's Week, when cartoon characters don skis and take to the rails. There are also games, contests, races, and cartoon nights during this special week.

Attitash
Rte. 302, Bartlett; (603) 374-2368. Adult lift tickets, $30; 6–12, $16. Children's ski program, $40; Nursery, 6 month–1 year, $4/hour, $24/day; 2–5, $3/hour, $20/day; Beginner's Special (age 6–adult): lesson, novice lift, and full rentals, $27.
A nice, intermediate ski area, offering 20 trails: 5 expert, 10 intermediate and 5 novice. There's snowmaking from top to bottom on 95 percent of the terrain. Trailside lodging, ski rentals and lessons, a nursery, restaurant, and lounge are available.

□ Just for Children
The on-site nursery is available for children from one to six years old. It's

open seven days a week and provides lunch, ski lessons if you choose, and fun and games. It's well-run, friendly, and well-equipped with high chairs, cribs, and toys. The children's ski programs are available during weekends and holiday weeks only for 6- to 12-year-olds. The day-long program, 9:45 to 3:45, includes two lessons, lunch, and a novice lift ticket. Children aged five and under ski free on the novice lift.

Wildcat Mountain
Rte. 16, Jackson; (613) 466-3326. Adult lift tickets, $31; Kitten Club, $15/ day; SKIwee, $40/day.
Wildcat's 2,100-vertical-foot drop and its 4,100-foot elevation make it an exciting ski area for the more experienced skier. That's not to say there's nothing here for beginners: there are easy trails, ski lessons, a nursery, and SKIwee programs available for novices. But you'll also find a large collection of more serious skiers here. The views at the top of this mountain are fabulous.

□ Just for Children
The Kitten Club Childcare Center offers day-care for children starting at age

Young skiers perfect their wedge turns— in tandem—at Wildcat Ski Resort.

18 months. The center has a large area for toddlers to play and climb in, an arts and crafts space, and a separate room for napping. Children ages 3 to 5, who are enrolled at the Childcare Center, can take private ski lessons at a reduced rate ($15, includes rental equipment). A SKIwee Program is offered for children ages 5 to 12, and includes lunch, supervised play, and two ski lessons. Rental equipment is not included; that costs $10 more.

Black Mountain
Rte. 16B, Jackson; (603) 383-4490. Adult lift ticket, $25; Youth Program, $42/day, $26/half day; nursery, $14/day, $8/half day.
Billed as the Great American Family Ski Place, Black Mountain offers gentle, sheltered slopes and a slow, relaxed atmosphere that are welcoming for family skiers. There are 20 trails here, with snowmaking on 95 percent of the mountain. There are great savings programs, including the family pass offered during non-holiday mid-weeks: Mom, Dad, and all the kids, 12 and under, ski for $44.

□ Just for Children
The nursery is open seven days a week (reserve ahead) for children six months to five years. The Youth Proficiency Program is a structured program for children 5 to 12. Offered weekends and holidays only from 9:30 to 3, participants get a lift ticket, two lessons, and lunch. A half-day program is also available.

Restaurants

Snug Harbor
Rte. 16, North Conway; (603) 356-3000. Daily except Tues., 4–10.
This is a relaxing place for family dinners with no compromise on quality. Fresh seafood dishes are the specialty here (try the shrimp scallopini or sole wrapped around artichoke hearts). There are a number of chicken, veal, and beef dishes on the menu, too. Kids love the nautical setting and have their choice of burgers, chicken, haddock, pasta, or shrimp from the Little Pirates menu.

Merlino's
Rte. 16 (at junction with Rte. 302), North Conway; (603) 356-6006. Daily, 11–9.

This family restaurant specializes in steaks and chops, but you can get just about anything you want. The Italian dishes, made with Merlino's homemade sauce, are especially popular. A unique Juniors & Seniors Menu is offered—"A special menu for the young set . . . over 65, and the younger set . . . under 12." Kids can choose from a wide variety of dishes, including pasta, chicken, steak, and seafood dishes. Homemade bread pudding or Indian pudding are favorite dessert choices.

Elvio's
Main St., North Conway Village; (603) 356-3307. Sun.–Thurs., 11–10; Fri.–Sat., 11–11.
If you're in the mood for pizza, there's no better place than Elvio's in North Conway Village. Locals argue that it's the best pizza in the world. Three different types are offered: the regular, round, thin-crust pizza baked in a stone deck oven; a rectangular, thick-crust, Sicilian pan-cooked pizza; and white pizza, a round pie made without tomato sauce but with mozzarella and ricotta cheeses, olive oil, garlic, and spices. All can be purchased whole or by the slice. Dine in or take out.

Monadnock Region

White-steepled churches set in village centers, old-fashioned country stores, covered bridges, and rolling hills all set in quiet, meandering valleys and farmlands—welcome to rural New Hampshire. The area surrounding Keene is New Hampshire countryside at its best. You won't find neon lights, flashy hotels, or amusement parks here. This is the place to come for lazy Sunday drives (be sure to drive Route 10 from Keene to West Swanzey—you'll see six covered bridges along the way), hikes in the woods, swimming in rivers, casting in lakes, and sleigh rides in the snow.

Mount Monadnock State Park
Rte. 124, Jaffrey; (603) 532-8623. Year-round.
Getting to the top of Mount Monadnock is a popular pursuit. If you've the energy for the two-mile trek up to the 3,165-foot summit, you'll be rewarded with lovely views of Boston to the east and Mount Washington to

the north. It will take about three hours to complete the round-trip hike. If that sounds too ambitious for your group, there are more than 30 miles of trails to choose from at the park. Stop in the Ecocenter, where you'll find exhibits and programs on nature and ecology as well as information on the various hikes.

Friendly Farm
Rte. 101, Dublin (.5 miles west of Dublin Lake); (603) 563-8444. May–Columbus Day, daily, 10–5; weekends only after Labor Day; 10–5. Adults, $3.50; 1–12, $2.50.
Children will enjoy a visit to this farm where they can pet and feed their favorite animals. At the hen house, you're likely to see eggs hatching (and you can hold and cuddle baby chicks). Brilliantly-plumed peacocks strut their stuff alongside a pen housing baby bunnies; take a look at the observation beehive. The natural setting is pleasant; bring a packed lunch to enjoy in the picnic area.

Sure to be on every toddler's list of favorite things to do: a visit to a petting farm.

Miller State Park
Rte. 101, Peterborough; (603) 924-9963.
While you're in the Peterborough area, consider taking the scenic drive to the summit of Pack Monadnock Mountain. You'll find walking trails, picnic sites, and a great view at the 2,280-foot summit.

Greenfield State Park
Rte. 136, Greenfield; (603) 547-3497. Mid-May–Columbus Day.
This is a nice family park of more than 350 acres along Otter Lake. The sandy beach is great for sunning and swimming, and children will enjoy the small playground. If you'd like to do some rowing or fishing, you can rent small boats. The picnic area includes tables, grills, and a refreshment stand. There are hiking trails in the park. Pack your trout-fishing gear and head for Hogback and Mud ponds; locals say the fishing is good.

Clough State Park
Off Rte. 114, Weare.
This is a great place on a hot summer day. Take a dip in a cool river pool, rent a boat, or explore the park's 150 acres. The beach and picnic area are large enough to accommodate the summer crowds.

Sleigh Rides at James Anthony Farm
Dudley Brook Rd., Weare; (603) 529-1123.
This charming, 175-year-old farm is a nice setting for a winter sleigh ride through snowy fields and country lanes. Call ahead to confirm availability.

Fox State Forest
Center Rd., Hillsborough.
This area in Hillsborough offers more than 20 miles of trails through more than 1,400 acres of woodlands and forest. Stop by the Visitor Center on Center Road just outside of Hillsborough Center for detailed information on the trails most suitable for your family.

Cross-Country Skiing
Many of the trails in the Greenfield State Park and at Pisgah State Park (off Routes 63 or 119 in Chesterfield or Hinsdale) are good for cross-country skiing. There are also a number of ski touring centers, including B.U. Sargent Camp and Temple Mountain Touring in Peterborough, (603) 525-3311; and Tory Pines Resort in Francestown, (603) 588-2000.

Little Nature Museum
59 Boyce St., Weare; (603) 529-7180. Year-round. Adults, $2; 12 and under, $1.

This 34-year-old private museum is open to the public and boasts an extensive collection of Indian artifacts, shells, fossils, and insects. Children will glow with wonder at the mounted birds and fluorescent minerals and will enjoy the many hands-on activities. A lovely nature hike is also available (weather permitting). Call ahead to let them know you're coming and to get directions (the museum is tough to find).

Monadnock Children's Museum
147 Washington St., Keene; (603) 357-5161. Tues.–Sun., 10–4. Admission, $2.50; 1 and under, free.

This hands-on museum for children of all ages is housed in a renovated 1850s colonial home that's chock full of learning fun. There's a little bit of everything here to please all interests and to help fill the insatiable curiosity of small children. In the Crystal Room, budding scientists will perform tests to identify crystals. Children will learn about other cultures in the World Room and about sea life from the variety of fresh and saltwater fish tanks. On Wednesdays in the summer, there are Clubhouse Mornings, when children are admitted to the museum simply by bringing something to add to the museum's tree house area. The tree house is filled with collections of unusual objects that children have donated.

Restaurants

Colony Mill Marketplace
222 West St., Keene; (603) 357-4011. Mon.–Sat., 10–9; Sun., 11–6.

Instead of opting for a fast-food lunch, consider stopping here, where your group can select anything from corn dogs to gourmet salads. Order from one of the take-out eateries, then find a table in the adjacent courtyard. Good choices to try: a chicken burrito at Portable Feast; then a chocolate lollipop to go from Ye Goodie Shoppe.

Addison's Restaurant
Rte. 124, Jaffrey; (603) 532-7062. Daily, 11–8.

This casual family restaurant offers fried clams, scallops, burgers, and the like. It's self-serve, with a large indoor seating area. Dessert is right next door at Addison's Ice Creamery. Try a black raspberry frappe ("frappe" is the New England term for "milkshake").

Foodees
65 Roxbury St., Keene; (603) 357-8600. Wed., Thurs., and Sun., 3–9; Fri.– Sat., 3–10.
You can get pizza any way you like it here, and they've got some combinations you've probably never tried, like Mexican pizza (with beans, cheeses, and onions) and pesto-sourdough pizza.

Vermont

Manchester and the Mountains

Long before there were ski-lifts and condominiums, Manchester was an elegant summer resort—Vermont's answer to Newport, Rhode Island, and Saratoga, New York. Instead of waiting in lift lines, guests queued up for a game of croquet. Then as now, the combination of fresh mountain air and charming countryside proved too enticing to resist.

Happily, some of that gentility remains today. Visiting families can tour Manchester Village, where time seems to have stood still, on a horse-drawn carriage complete with a top-hatted driver. Guests can picnic on the manicured laws of Hildene, the Robert Todd Lincoln estate, as past Presidents once did. Or you can bundle up for a sleigh ride, stopping back at the mansion for hot mulled cider.

In Manchester Center, a more modern pastime predominates—shopping. There is a plethora of specialty stores, antique shops, crafts studios, and designer outlets. You'll also find one of the best selections of child-pleasing restaurants in New England here.

What makes this area a truly superlative place to visit is the fact that you can sample all of these pleasures and still have ample opportunity to play outside. Southern Vermont is a great place for trout fishing, canoeing, camping, swimming, hiking, skiing, horseback riding—you name it.

There's also a prominent resident your children will want to meet—Santa. Where else would the Claus family choose for their summer home?

Hildene
Rte. 7A, Manchester; (802) 362-1788. Mid-May–Oct., daily, 9:30–5:30 (last tour begins at 4). Adults, $5; 14 and under, $2.
This gracious Georgian Revival mansion was built by Robert Todd Lincoln, the only one of Abraham Lincoln's four sons to live to maturity. Lincoln's descendants lived at Hildene (the name means "hill and valley") until 1975. Your visit will begin with a brief slide show on Robert's life; then you can

walk through the rooms of the house. Children will appreciate the toy room, decorated with fairy-tale scenes, and the 1908 player pipe organ, demonstrated for visitors. From the garden terrace, you can view the Green Mountains on one side and the Taconic Mountains on the other. Nature trails and a picnic area are also on the grounds. Open-air concerts are often scheduled in summer, performed by the Vermont Symphony Orchestra. If you visit in late December, treat your family to a candlelight tour of Hildene. You'll enjoy cookies and hot mulled cider, along with a horse-drawn sleigh ride and a look at this beautiful house in its holiday finery.

Stratton Scenic Chairlift Rides
Stratton Mountain Rd., Bondville (off Rte. 30); (802) 297-2200. July–mid-Oct., daily, 9–4. Adults, $10; 12 and under, $6.
Grab your camera, pack a picnic, and don some sensible shoes for a trip to the top of Stratton Mountain. Commune with nature awhile, then take the chairlift back down.

Bromley Alpine Slide
Rte. 11, Peru (6 miles east of Manchester); (802) 824-5522. 9:30–6; mid-June–Sept., daily; mid-May–mid-June, weekends only. Adults, $4; 7–12, $3.25.
The action at Bromley Mountain doesn't stop when the snow melts. Come spring, you can board the chairlift to the mountaintop, then career down to the bottom on your own sled. Daredevils can take it fast, wimpy souls can take it slow.

Bromley Scenic Chairlift Ride
Rte. 11, Peru (6 miles east of Manchester); (802) 824-5522. 9:30–6; mid-May–July 4, weekends; July 4–foliage season, daily. Adults, $4; 7–12, $3.25.
For a family picnic with an unforgettable view, ride to the top of Bromley Mountain. You'll see five states (okay kids, name them) and spectacular scenery. Work off your lunch by hiking along the ski trails—then ride the chairlift back to the base of the mountain.

Sugarhouses
Maple Tree Vermont Products (3 miles north of Emerald Lake off Rte. 7, Danby; (802) 293-5566), James A. Twitchell (Winhall Hollow Rd., South Londonderry; (802) 824-3605), or Harlow's Sugar House (Rte. 5, Putney Village; (802) 824-5852. At Harlow's you'll also find a cider press, plus apple picking in the fall and berry picking in summer; call ahead to see what's happening).

If you're visiting the area during winter or early spring, a trip to a sugar house is a must. Watch maples being tapped, and see sugarmakers boil the sap to make syrup. Call ahead; the maple sugaring season varies, usually beginning in late February and lasting from six weeks to two months.

Scenic Drive—Equinox Skyline Drive

Take Rte. 7A south from Manchester to Sunderland; (802) 362-1114. May–Nov., 8 a.m.–10 p.m. Toll is $6 per car.

For beautiful vistas and a view of five states, drive to the summit of Mount Equinox. At 3,835 feet above sea level, Mount Equinox is the highest peak in the Taconic Mountains. Below in the valley, you'll see triangle-shaped Lake Madeleine and the granite walls of the Monastery of the Transfiguration. At the top is a picnic area and a hotel, the Skyline Inn. Get out of the car and take a deep breath—the air is full of the wonderful fragrance of balsam pines. This 10.5-mile round trip is especially breathtaking during foliage season.

Windhill Farm

North Rd., Manchester Center; (802) 362-2604. Open daily, year-round, weather permitting. Reservations are required. Sleigh rides: a fee of $35 is charged for the first five people; $5 per person thereafter. Trail rides: $10 per person; $2 per child for pony rides.

This is a special place for families, no matter what the season. In winter, a team of Belgian and Percheron horses will take you on an old-fashioned bobsled ride. Traversing fields and woodlands, the rides are about an hour long. The rest of the year, Windhill Farm is the perfect place to go horseback riding. Trail rides through the countryside are offered, as well as pony rides for the little ones.

Santa's Land

Rte. 5 (between Exits 4 and 5 off I-91), Putney; (802) 447-1571. Mid-June–Christmas, daily, 9:30–5; May–mid-June, weekends only. Adults, $7; 3–15, $5.50.

Ho! Ho! Ho! This very merry theme park has lots of child-pleasing features, including a petting zoo, a child's train ride, a carousel, and a playground. The highlight of your child's visit will likely be a chat with the Jolly Old Elf himself, who'll ask, "Do you take care of your toys?" not, "What do you want for Christmas?" To avoid the obvious North Pole questions, tell the kids that Santa's Land is Mr. and Mrs. Claus' summer home. Have lunch at the Igloo Pancake House on the grounds.

Taking a ride on the Santa's Land Express is one of several child-pleasing options at Santa's Land in Putney.

Green Mountain Flyer Scenic Train Ride

Green Mountain Railroad Corp., 1 Depot Square, Bellows Falls; (802) 463-3069. Trains depart Bellows Falls at 11 and 2, Chester at 12:25, and Chester South (Chester Marble Mart) at 12:30. July 1–Labor Day and mid-Sept.–mid Oct., daily; weekends only through Oct. Special foliage excursions scheduled; call for details. Adults, $7; 5–12, $4.

View the splendor of central Vermont's countryside by train. You'll see Quechee Gorge, covered bridges, river valleys, and rolling hillsides—all the more spectacular during foliage season.

Bennington Museum/Grandma Moses Gallery

Rte. 9 (West Main St.), Old Bennington; (802) 447-1571. March–Dec., weekends; Jan.–Feb., 9–5. Adults, $4.50; 12–17, $3.50.

You'll take a trip back to the 19th century when you view this collection of paintings, furniture, military artifacts, and toys. Even better is the gallery devoted to Anna Mary Robertson, better known as Grandma Moses. This legendary woman began painting seriously at age 78 and continued to do so until her death at age 101. The story will inspire you and her work will delight you—and any aspiring artists in your group.

Hiking

In southern Vermont, two legendary trails merge together: the Appalachian Trail and the Long Trail. These trails provide opportunities for a number of day hikes with spectacular views, including one to the top of Bromley Mountain. For details, call the U.S. Forest Service, Route 11, Manchester; (802) 362-2307. Supervised nature hikes originate from the Stratton Sports Center at Stratton Mountain; call (802) 297-2525.

Emerald Lake State Park

Rte. 7, North Dorset; (802) 362-1655.
This 430-acre state park offers swimming, boating, and fishing in Emerald Lake along with a playground and a marked nature trail. Picnic tables, a snack bar, and canoe and boat rental are available.

Hapgood Pond Recreation Area

Rte. 11, Weston (2 miles north of Peru); (802) 362-2307.
Part of the Green Mountain National Forest, this popular spot offers swimming, fishing, and picnicking.

Jamaica State Park

Rte. 30, Jamaica; (802) 874-4600.
Have a picnic on the banks of the West River or go hiking, fishing, canoeing, kayaking, or swimming. Follow the nature trail to Hamilton Falls. Boat rentals are available.

Lake Saint Catherine State Park

Rte. 30, Poultney; (802) 287-9158.
Lake Saint Catherine offers swimming, fishing, and boating. A marina on the west shore of the lake rents canoes and motor boats. You'll also find a nature trail, a nature museum, and a playground. Also offered: picnic tables, fireplaces, and wood.

Townsend Lake Recreation Area

Rte. 30, Townsend; (802) 874-4881.
Here you'll find swimming, boating, picnicking, hiking trails, and, most notably, a dam. Boat rentals available.

Battenkill River

Originating in Dorset and East Dorset, the Battenkill flows into New York State and the Hudson River. Its water is lively, clear, and perfect for canoeing and trout fishing. Canoe rentals are available at Battenkill Canoe, Route

313, West Arlington; (802) 375-9559. Fishing gear and fly-fishing lessons—if you want to get serious—can be found at the Orvis Company, Route 7A, Manchester; (802) 362-3622. Orvis also stocks detailed maps of the river.

Bromley Summer Music Series

Bromley Mountain, Rte. 11, Peru (6 miles east of Manchester); (802) 824-5522. The series begins the first weekend in July and continues every Sat. and Sun. 'til Labor Day, 1–5. Free.

What a way to unwind after a busy weekend . . . live music and a country barbecue! On the deck/cafe at Bromley Mountain, you'll hear jazz, country music, and bluegrass. This informal atmosphere is just fine for families with kids, and the festivities are free. (There's a charge if you partake of the barbecue.)

Village Carriage Company

Rte. 7A, Manchester. Departs daily, weather permitting, from in front of the Equinox Hotel or at the Equinox Golf Course. 20-minute ride, $20; 30-minute ride, $30.

A visit to historic Manchester Village is special; a tour by horse-drawn carriage is unbeatable. A top-hatted driver will take your family to town in style.

Bicycling

You'll find bicycle-rental shops throughout southern Vermont. Some shops rent mountain bikes as well as touring bicycles. A couple of possibilities: Battenkill Sports Cycle Shop (Route 7 and 11, Manchester Center; (802) 362-2734) and Valley Cyclery (Wilmington; (802) 464-2728).

Cross-Country Skiing

Southern Vermont is a Nordic skier's paradise. There are numerous ski-touring centers nearby; great for families because you get detailed maps, advice, rental equipment if you need it, groomed trails, even lessons. Here are some possibilities: Hildene Ski-Touring Center (Route 7A, Manchester; (802) 362-1788), Nordic Inn Touring Center (Route 11, Londonderry; (802) 824-6444), Stratton Cross-Country Center (Mountain Road, Stratton Mountain; (802) 824-3933), Viking Ski-Touring Center (Pond Road, Londonderry; (802) 824-3933), Sitzmark (East Dover Road, Wilmington; (802) 464-3384).

Downhill Skiing

Mount Snow
Rte. 100, Mount Snow; (802) 464-3333. Lift tickets: adults, $34; 12 and under, $19. Pumpkin Patch day-care, $37 a day, includes lunch; PeeWee SKIwee, 3–5 years, $51, includes lift ticket, two lessons and lunch; SKIwee, 6–12 years, $51, includes lift ticket, lessons and lunch; half-day rates available. Rates listed are for weekends and holidays; special packages available.

One of Vermont's largest ski resorts, Mount Snow offers good skiing for beginners and intermediates, and the challenging North Face area for black diamond lovers. With a vertical lift of nearly 2,000 feet and more than 70 trails serviced by 16 lifts, you'll have a grand time trying to cover it all. Although Mount Snow is perhaps less fashionable than Stowe, it nonetheless draws big crowds from Massachusetts, Connecticut, and nearby New York.

□ Just for Children
Mount Snow helped develop the nationally-known SKIwee program, designed to make it fun, not fearsome, to learn how to ski. For children aged 3 to 5, Mount Snow offers PeeWee SKIwee, combining two hours of ski instruction with indoor play. They learn how to put on their ski gear indoors too, where it's less slippery. Youngsters from 6 to 12 can participate in a half day or full day of SKIwee instruction. Beginners can try out their ski legs on a gentle slope; more advanced skiers can spend the day skiing the main mountain. The Pumpkin Patch provides day-care for non-skiing children aged six weeks and up. Infants, toddlers, and older children (in separate rooms) take part in arts and crafts, cooking, story hours, and sing-alongs. Visit Mount Snow during a Teddy Bear Ski Week, scheduled throughout the season, and children 12 and under ski free when accompanied by their teddy bears. A magic show, a teddy bear parade, and a ride on a snow grooming machine add to the fun. Reservations are required for Pumpkin Patch and PeeWee SKIwee programs.

Bromley Mountain
Rte. 111, Peru (6 miles east of Manchester); (802) 824-5522. Lift tickets: adults, $32; 7–14, $20. Day-care, 1 month–6 years, $27/day, $16/half day. Beginner Discoverski, $15 (one hour); Discoverski Lift, $18 (two hours); Discoverski School (includes lunch), $40–$50. Rates listed are for weekends

and holidays; half-price weekday rates, half-day rates, and packages are available.

The best thing about skiing at Bromley? Its southern exposure makes the Alpine experience a tad warmer here than at other New England ski resorts. Amen to that. You'll find a cozy, family atmosphere here, along with 35 trails served by seven lifts.

□ Just for Children

Bromley offers a day-care center for non-skiing tots, as well as Discoverski programs for children of all abilities. Choose from Beginner Discoverski for three- to five-year-olds, lasting one hour; Discoverski Lift for children of all ages and abilities, lasting two hours; or Discoverski School for all levels of skiers from age 6 to 14—this program lasts four hours and includes lunch.

Stratton Mountain

Rte. 11 east from Manchester to Rte. 30, Bondville (follow Stratton Mountain Road); 1-800-843-6867. Lift tickets: adults, $35; 12 and under, $20; Big and Little Cub, $40/full day (includes lessons and lunch; does not include lift ticket). Rates listed are for weekends and holidays during high season; discounted weekday rates and special packages are available.

Stratton has expanded from an Alpine ski resort to a full-fledged sports center, so even non-skiers will find plenty to do here. Swimming, racquetball, tennis, and other activities are available. (Tennis enthusiasts, take note: Stratton is the site of the Volvo International Tennis Tournament, so its facilities are superb.) Downhill skiers will find 86 trails, many of them rated "difficult," serviced by ten lifts. You'll ski alongside plenty of locals and perhaps a celebrity or two: actor Christopher Reeve and tennis player Ivan Lendl are said to be regulars here.

□ Just for Children

Stratton offers a day-care center for children six months to five years and Cub programs for kids aged 3 to 12. Little Cub participants, aged 3 to 6, can enroll all day (from 8:30 to 3:45) or for a half day, with ski lessons and supervised activities included. Big Cub skiers, aged 6 to 12, take part in ski lessons geared to ability level and a variety of activities.

Restaurants

You'll find restaurants scattered throughout this area. Your best bet for dinner? Head to Manchester Center, where a number of dining spots offer good food and fun surroundings.

Laney's

Rtes. 11 and 30; (802) 362-4456. Sun.–Thurs., 5–10; Fri.–Sat., 5–11.
This movie-themed restaurant is decked out in film posters, many of them signed, and entrées are named accordingly. "Adam's Ribs" are deservedly popular, along with Laney's squiggly french fries. While you're mulling over the possibilities, the kids will be busily coloring the tablecloth. (Not to worry—it's a big sheet of white paper. Crayons are provided.) Kids' choices include Dumbo (barbecued chicken) and Muppets (a child-sized pizza), each $4.35, as well as ribs and chicken. Children's meals include fries, a beverage, and a scoop of ice cream.

Sirloin Saloon

Rte. 7; (802) 362-2600. Sun.–Thurs., 5–10; Fri.–Sat. 5–11.
This restaurant, part of a local chain, features steak, seafood, and chicken cooked over mesquite wood. The salad bar, available on its own, is wonderful, as is the home-baked whole-grain bread. Tiffany lamps, paintings and American Indian artifacts provide lots to look at and a cozy atmosphere. The kid's menu (a place mat illustrated with games and puzzles) includes steak, chicken, and burgers priced from $3.75 to $5.95. Children's meals include the salad bar, baked potato, rice or chips, a beverage, and ice cream. Adult entrées range from $7.95 to $15.95.

Mother Myrick's

Rte. 7A; (802) 362-1560. Daily, 10:30–5:30; Sat., 10:30–6.
This is goody heaven: an ice cream parlor, bakery, and chocolate shop all in one. Children will enjoy watching the candymakers prepare fudge and dip chocolates in the candy room. (Tell yourself this is an educational trip.) Can't decided what you want? Indulge in a scrumptious ice cream sundae now, and take some fudge home for later.

Woodstock Area

If your family loves the outdoors and can appreciate a healthy dose of gorgeous scenery at the same time, start packing. This is your place.

Many visitors are attracted to this region for downhill skiing; most, to mammoth Killington with its six mountains, highly-regarded ski school, and extensive children's programs. And certainly, you can spend days here on skis—of either the Alpine or Nordic variety—while your kids are merrily making snowmen, joining in sing-alongs, and perfecting their wedge turns. Not a bad way to beat the winter doldrums.

Come summer, you'll discover a whole new side of central Vermont . . . actually, an old side. This is the time to visit the towns that existed before the ski resorts arrived, especially picturesque Woodstock, and to see a natural wonder that dates back to the Ice Age—Quechee Gorge.

And, since this is Vermont, there's no need to simply play tourist. Hike, bike, swim, ride, horseback, and enjoy a side of central Vermont that less-savvy families usually miss.

Petting zoos offer children the chance to meet animals native to New England, from goats and sheep to black bears, red foxes, and bobcats.

Pond Hill Ranch

Rte. 4A, Castleton; (802) 468-2449. First Sat. in July–Labor Day. Adults, $5; under 12, free.

Bronco busting, bull riding, calf roping—it's a rodeo! The fact that you don't expect to find a rodeo in Vermont makes it all the more fun, right, Buckaroo? Special events for kids include calf catching. (If you catch the tag on the calf's tail, you win a dollar.)

Billings Farm

Rte. 12, Woodstock; (802) 457-2355. Mid-May–Oct., daily, 10–5. Adults, $5; 6–18, $2.50.

Watch cows being milked, churn cream into butter, nuzzle a sheep, pet newborn calves—these are some of the pleasures awaiting your family at Billings Farm. This working dairy farm has prize Jersey cattle, draft horses, oxen, and a petting nursery. It's also the home of a farm museum, focusing on the rigors and traditions of farm life in the 1890s. Demonstrations will show you how to hook a rug, spin wool, and do other country chores. Visit on a weekend for a horse-drawn wagon ride. Special events are scheduled each month. If you can, visit on Children's Day, when old-fashioned games are played.

Vermont Industries, Inc.

Rte. 103, Cuttingsville Village; (802) 492-3451. Year-round, daily, except Sun., 8:30–4:30. Free.

Don't let the boring name keep you from stopping here. This is the largest blacksmith shop in Vermont, and you can watch blacksmiths at work, hand-forging wrought-iron products. There's also an Iron Worker's Museum and a retail shop. Of course, children will find it most exciting to watch the molten iron flow and see the sparks fly.

Vermont Institute of Natural Science

Church Hill Rd., Woodstock; (802) 457-2779. May–Oct., 10–4, closed Tues.; Nov.–Apr., 10–4, closed Tues. and Sun. Adults, $3.50; 5–15, $1.

Most children have never seen a real live owl, only the cartoon variety. Visit the Vermont Raptor Center, and you'll meet 26 species of owls, hawks, and eagles native to northern New England in an outdoor living museum. There's also a self-guided nature trail.

Wilson Castle

West Proctor Rd. (near Rutland, off Rte. 4), Proctor; (802) 773-3284. Daily, May–Aug., 9–6. Adults, $5; 6–12, $2.

If you've ever imagined living in a fairy tale castle, you might have envisioned a place like this. Built by a local physician and his monied British wife, Wilson Castle boasts turrets, arches, parapets, and balconies—the whole thing made of imported materials, including the bricks. On the grounds are cattle barns, stables, and—to the delight of children—an aviary with Indian peacocks. The Wilson Castle fairy tale, alas, has an unhappy ending. Soon after the castle was built, the lady of the house fled, taking all of her money with her. The town ultimately seized the castle for taxes and sold it.

New England Maple Museum
Rte. 7, Pittsford; (802) 483-9414. Oct.–Dec., daily, 10–4; May–Oct., 8:30–5:30. Adults, $1; 6–12, 50¢.
Vermonters call it "nature's gold," and you won't want to miss a sample of the state's sweetest product. While you're taste-testing, you can learn how sap becomes syrup.

Pico Alpine Slide
Rte. 4 (9 miles east of Rutland), Sherburne; (802) 775-4345. May–June, daily, 11–5; July–Sept., daily, 10–6; Sept.–Oct., daily, 12–5. Adults, $4, single ride; 6–12, $3, single ride; under 6, free. Unlimited riding: adults, $20; 6–12, $15.
Every kid loves a wild ride on a slide—and face it, don't most grown-up kids? In summer, ride the chairlift up the side of Pico Peak, enjoying beautiful mountain views . . . then *whoosh* down the slide (you control the pace). Try a single ride or opt for an all-day ticket. You'll leave wind-burned, exhausted, and happy. (The kids will have fun, too.)

Killington Playhouse
Killington Rd., Sherburne; (802) 422-9795. July–Labor Day.
Treat your children to an afternoon of musical theater at a just-for-kids Wednesday matinee. The Green Mountain Guild performs Broadway favorites at Killington Ski Resort's Snowshed Base Lodge during the summer season.

Montshire Museum of Science
Rte. 10A, Norwich; (802) 649-2200. Year-round, Mon.–Sat., 10–5; Sun., 1–5. Adults, $3; 4–17, $1.50.
Children will marvel at the wonderful collection of hands-on indoor and outdoor exhibits at this science museum. In the physics playground, your child's whisper will travel 100 feet and be clearly heard without the aid of

Learning about science is wild and wonderful at the Montshire Museum of Science.

electronic wizardry. You'll see a self-contained colony of more than 250,000 leaf-cutter ants, and you'll create bubbles larger than life. The museum has a number of changing, interactive natural history, physical science, ecology, and technology exhibits. There's also a variety of scenic nature trails at the 105-acre site.

Killington Gondola

Killington Gondola Base Lodge, Rte. 4, Sherburne; (802) 422-3333. 10–4; daily, mid-Sept.–Oct.; weekends, July–Labor Day. Adults, $12; 12 and under, $8.

Summer, winter, or fall, you can ride to the summit of Killington Mountain without ever putting on a pair of skis. The gondola (an enclosed cable car) will take you 3.5 miles up. At the peak you'll find a cocktail lounge, a cafeteria, and an observation deck. From the deck you'll see the Green Mountains, the White Mountains (see if you can spot majestic Mount Washington), the Berkshires, and the Adirondacks. This is a great way for little people and non-skiers to get to the top of the mountain. The view, especially during foliage season, is spectacular.

Quechee Gorge
Exit 1 off I-89, then west on Rte. 4, Quechee; (802) 295-7600.
Vermont's most intriguing natural wonder, Quechee Gorge is a mile-long,
165-foot deep channel that dates back to the last Ice Age. From the bridge
spanning the gorge on Route 4, you can stare down into the seemingly-
bottomless chasm. Or, if your group includes older children, try the shaded,
mile-long trail to the bottom. It's a fairly easy hike along the fenced-in edge
of the precipice. Best bet for everyone: take the short stroll to the falls at the
top of the gorge and indulge in a picnic. Plan to visit in mid-June, if you
can, to coincide with the annual Quechee Hot-Air Balloon Festival.

Bicycling
This is the best way to see Vermont—you won't miss a thing. Routes 106
and 12, running north and south from Woodstock, are good possibilities.
From Rutland, the best routes are to the south, where you'll find winding,
hilly rural roads and little traffic. Rentals are available at Cycling Plus (Route
4, west of Woodstock) and Green Mountain Schwinn (133 Strongs Avenue,
Rutland).

Hiking
You'll find plenty of hiking opportunities here, from easy strolls to rigorous
mountain hikes. Quechee Gorge, for example, offers easy hiking with great
views into the gorge. Quechee Village is a pleasant place to stroll; cross the
covered bridge by the falls and follow the river bank upstream. Mount Tom,
in Woodstock, offers a graded footpath with benches along the way. Start at
Faulkner Park and follow the switchback trail to the top of Mount Tom.
Lake Bomoseen State Park off Route 4A offers nature trails and hikes of a
mile or so.

Swimming
There are more places to take a dip—or just wade along the shore—in
land-locked Vermont than you might imagine. Here are your best bets on a
warm day: Crystal Beach (on Lake Bomoseen, off Route 4A north of Castleton—a nine-mile lake with beaches; lifeguards posted) and White River
(there are several swimming holes here; the best way to find them is to look
for parked cars along the river on hot days).

Boating
Duda's Rentals, on the west shore of Lake Bomoseen in Hydeville, rents
fishing boats, water-skiing equipment, and paddle craft.

Horseback Riding
Rte. 106, Woodstock; (802) 457-1473.
At Kedron Valley Inn & Stables, guided trail rides and hourly and daily
rentals are offered. Kids will love taking a ride on a horse-drawn wagon or,
in winter, a sleigh ride.

Downhill Skiing

Killington
*20 Killington Rd (off Route 4), Sherburne; (802) 773-1500. Lift tickets:
adults, $34; children, $18. Children's Center rates: age 6 weeks–2 years: all
day, $35 (no lunch); half day, $20; age 2–8: all day with lunch, $25; half
day, $13; Intro to Ski program: all day (lunch included), $40; half day, $21.
Rates listed are weekend rates; weekday discounts and special packages are
available.*
Killington is undeniably a popular place with skiers, and for good reason:
it's huge. With six different mountain peaks and 100 trails, there's plenty of
action for skiers of every level. Even those who are new to the sport will
find plenty of territory to cover. Killington Peak, the highest mountain of
the six, has a vertical rise of 3,000 feet. Since it gets crowded here and lift
lines get long, plan to hit the slopes early. Also, after dropping off the kids
at the Children's Center at the Snowshed Base Lodge at Killington Village,
you may want to head over to the less-populous Sunrise Mountain or Bear
Mountain areas, where you'll get more runs in.

□ **Just for Children**
The Children's Center accepts kids from six weeks to eight years old. Open
daily from 8 to 4, the program is separated into three sections: Child-care,
Intro to Ski, and the Young Skier Program. In the Child-care Program,
children take part in supervised free-play activities indoors and outdoor
exercise. Lunch, snacks, and a one-hour rest time are included. The Intro to
Ski Program, for ages three to eight, includes two one-hour lessons per day.
(Most participants are aged six or under.) Hoops, cones, and obstacles are
used to make learning fun. The program has three levels, from the first-time
skier to the independent skier, who learns to ride the chairlift. The Young
Skier Program, for ages four to six, includes a two-hour lesson in both the
morning and afternoon. To qualify, a child must be able to hold a wedge,
ski in control, and ride the chair alone. From age six, children at this level

can take lessons through Killington's ski school. Reserve well in advance, as spots fill up quickly. Courtesy phones are provided so that you check on your child periodically. A 50 percent deposit is necessary to confirm reservations. Caution: Reservations are held only for the first hour of the day (8 to 9 a.m.). Depending on weather conditions, the ski season can last from November to May. (Believe it or not, we've seen diehards ski down Superstar Trail on Mother's Day.)

Pico Peak

Rte. 4 (9 miles east of Rutland), Sherburne; (802) 775-4345. Lift tickets: adults, $32; juniors (14 and under), $19. Children's Program rates: Pico Children's Center, full day, $22; half day, $14; Explorers, $39 (all-inclusive); Mountaineers, $39 (all-inclusive).

In the shadow of massive Killington, Pico Peak is smaller, less hurried, and less crowded—in short, an appealing option for the family that prefers a more low-key ski resort. The vertical rise of the mountain is 1,967 feet. Trails are geared toward skiers of intermediate ability.

□ Just for Children

Pico divides its children's programs into three categories, geared to kids from 6 months to 12 years. The Pico Children's Center accepts children from 6 months to 6 years. Infants and toddlers meet at the lower-level nursery; upstairs, the older children engage in active play. Story time, arts and crafts, games, and other activities are offered, along with lunch and a quiet time for napping. Explorers are children from 3 to 6 years old who are ready for ski instruction. Two one-hour classes are included in a full day, grouped into four levels. Experience levels range from the first-timer to children who can confidently ski most of the mountain. The Mountaineers is made up of four levels of children aged 6 through 12. Experience levels range from the first-time skier to the child who is ready for challenging terrain, like gates and bumps. After age 12, kids are ready for Pico's regular ski school. Advance reservations recommended, especially for infants and toddlers. Special note: Mom and Dad can enjoy an evening out, sans children, while kids enjoy a Saturday night pizza party at Pico. For $17, children aged 3 to 12 are invited for pizza and supervised activities from 6:30 to 10. The program is available without the meal, from 7 to 10, for a reduced rate. Parties are held every weekend during the winter and weeknights during holiday weeks.

Cross-Country Skiing

Nordic skiers will find abundant trails, varied terrain, and plenty of extras at Woodstock Ski-Touring Center (Route 106, Woodstock; (802) 457-2114) and Mountain Meadows (Thundering Brook Road (off Route 4), Sherburne; (802) 775-7077). Most downhill ski areas also have cross-country centers.

Restaurants

Spooner's at Sunset Farm
Rte. 4 (east of the Village), Woodstock; (802) 457-4022. Sun.-Thurs., 5–10; Fri.–Sat. 5–11.
Mesquite-broiled items are the specialty here. Choices include steak, seafood, prime rib, and eggplant Parmesan. Children's dinners include salad bar, baked potato or rice, beverage, and a scoop of ice cream, with entrées ranging from grilled shrimp ($7.50) to hamburgers ($3.75).

Mountain Creamery
33 Central St., Woodstock; (802) 457-1715. Sun.–Thurs., 7–5; Fri.–Sat., 7–6.
Head to the take-out side of this little restaurant and order a homemade ice cream cone or a fruit smoothie. Then walk over to Woodstock Green in the center of the Village (just a few yards away), grab a bench, and watch the world go by.

The OTT-Dog
Rte. 4, Quechee; (802) 295-1088. Mid-May–Oct., daily, 9–6.
Located right at Quechee Gorge, this popular snack bar serves—you guessed it—hot dogs, with a variety of tasty toppings. Other sandwiches are available, as are pastry and ice cream. Try the double-dip blueberry cheesecake. Picnic tables here and (for better scenery) at the Gorge.

Lake Champlain Valley

Burlington, the largest city in Vermont, reigns over the Lake Champlain Valley region, blessed with spectacular views of mountain peaks on both sides and a large, glistening lake in the middle. The most urban of Vermont's cities sits on the eastern shore of Lake Champlain and is home to nearly a quarter of the state's population. But "urban" to most of us does not mean what it does to Vermonters. You'll find a thriving, vibrant city, but one that has not lost its small-town charm and rural influences.

The rejuvenated waterfront area, once one of the country's busiest seaports, is a nice place to stroll; at dusk you'll be rewarded with breathtaking sunsets across the lake. Nineteenth-century buildings have been restored and now house cafés, specialty shops, and pedestrian marketplaces. There are five public parks and benches from which to enjoy water views and lake activities.

Do not leave the area without visiting Champlain's Grand Islands, only a short half-hour drive away. You'll discover the small rural town of South Hero, the countryside of Grand Isle, the pretty, tiny village of North Hero, and the beautiful seashore of Isle La Motte. The islands are connected by bridges, surrounded by mountains, and laced with lovely state parks and lakeside beaches.

Everywhere there are opportunities to enjoy the sparkling, 110-mile-long Lake Champlain. Beaches are plentiful; there are power boats, sailboats, and wind-surfers to rent; ferries and schooners to carry you across; and scenic vistas everywhere you look. Waterlogged and happy, you can travel inland and visit horse and dairy farms, a 1783 log cabin, and the popular Shelburne Museum and Farm.

Champlain Ferries
Lake Champlain Transportation Co., King Street Dock, Burlington; (802) 864-9804.
An easy way for the family to see Lake Champlain is to hop on one of the ferries that go across to New York. There are three crossings on Lake Champlain. Catch the ferry in Charlotte, just south of Burlington, for the 20-minute ride to Essex, N.Y. You'll enjoy the stop-over in Essex—it's a charming lakeside village. The drive from Burlington to Charlotte is worthwhile, too, and you might want to visit a few other sites (Wildflower Farm, Mount Philo State Park) in Charlotte, before or after the ferry ride.

The ferry leaving Charlotte is open April through December. A 12-minute ferry between Grand Isle and Plattsburgh, N.Y., is open all year. This is a good side trek to remember on your visit to Grand Isle. A longer, one-hour ferry between Burlington and Port Kent is open mid-May through Columbus Day, and provides great views of Lake Champlain.

Spirit of Ethan Allen

Departs from Perkins Pier, Burlington; (802) 862-9685.
This is a lively, narrated lake excursion aboard a replica of a vintage stern-wheeler. With children, you might want to opt for the shorter day cruise or perhaps the sunset ride. On either one, you'll see fine scenery. This is especially popular during fall foliage season.

Homer W. Dixon Schooner

Most kids will find just the sight of this gaff-rigged schooner exciting—the chance to ride on it is a real treat. This graceful windjammer can be chartered for a very special cruise of Lake Champlain.

Perkins Pier

This small waterfront park in town is a good place for lake viewing and sunset watching. The children will enjoy watching the many boats that come in and out.

Burlington Waterfront

□ Farmer's Market

College St. (next to City Hall Park), Burlington. Wed. and Sat., 9–2.
You can see some local color and pick up some local fruit and vegetables at this lively market held every Wednesday and Saturday. It's also a good time to wander the side streets and browse the gourmet shops, bakeries, and specialty stores. Give the kids a few bags and a dollar or two and have them do their own bartering at the market.

□ Bike Path

This 10-mile recreation path follows the lake from the mouth of the Winooski River. You'll share the route with strollers, joggers, and bikers. Pick up the path at Perkins Pier, Leddy Park, Oakledge Park, or North Beach.

□ Burlington Public Beaches

There are five public beaches in Burlington where you can enjoy the clear, cool waters of Lake Champlain. North Beach is the largest, most popular of the town's beaches. It has a sandy area for sunbathers and swimmers. You'll also get a view of the Adirondacks in the distance. Oakledge Park is a more rugged, scenic beach. It has a picnic area and rocky ledges to toss your blanket on. Red Rocks, a small, sandy beach in South Burlington, is good for kids. Lifeguards are always on duty. Leddy Park has a playground and a small beach kids will enjoy. There's also an ice skating rink, if you've brought your skates, open mid-July through March. Ethan Allen Park is close to Leddy Park. At this small local park, you can climb up a stone turret for a view of the city and lake.

UVM Morgan Horse Farm
R.D.1 (Weybridge Rd.), Middlebury; (802) 388-2011. May–Oct., daily, 9–4. Adults, $2.50; under 12, free.
This farm, once owned by Joseph Battell, an eccentric local landowner, was one of the first centers for the development of the purebred Morgan horse. Now operated by the University of Vermont, the stables are open for guided tours to see the Morgan descendants. From the short audio-visual presentation shown on the tour, you'll learn that the Morgan was the first breed of horse developed in America.

The Discovery Museum
51 Park St., Essex Junction; (802) 878-8687. Sept.–June, Tues.–Fri. and Sun., 1–4:30; Sat., 10–4:30. July–Aug., Tues.–Sat., 10–4:30; Sun., 1–4:30. Adults, $2.50; 2–14, $2.
This wonderful hands-on museum includes a natural science area with live animals; a physical science area, where kids can make giant bubbles or work at WFUN-TV station; and an art hall, with changing art exhibits and programs. The museum is best enjoyed by children ages 2 to 12. In July and August, the outdoor animal wildlife center is open, where you can meet native Vermont critters like the great horned owl, fox, and raccoon.

Shelburne Museum and Heritage Park
Rte. 7, Shelburne; (802) 985-3344. Mid-May–Columbus Day, daily, 9–5. Adults, $12; 6–17, $4.
This is a museum for people of all ages. The children will enjoy its park-like setting, covering 45 acres and filled with an interesting collection of buildings and memorabilia. You'll be able to board the steamboat Ticonderoga, cross a covered bridge, peek in at a one-room schoolhouse, shop in an 1840s general store, circle the round barn, and climb the lighthouse. There are 37 buildings in all; most have been moved here from

Kids make friends with pure-bred Morgan
horses at the Morgan Horse Farm,
operated by the University of Vermont.

Kids of all ages enjoy a trip to the past at Shelburne Museum.

other sites. The buildings are filled with wonderful collections of treasures. You'll see old dolls and toys, a first-rate quilt collection, antique wagons and tools, and some of the best of American primitive antiques. It's a fun peek at our past and a great family outing.

In the summer and fall, stop by Shelburne Farms, located right down the road from the museum. As you walk this pretty, 1,000-acre lakeside estate, you'll see beautiful gardens, dairy barns, and the Shelburne House. This 1899 brick manor is now an inn open for summer and fall guests. Stop by the gatehouse on your way out to pick up some cheese made from the herd of Brown Swiss on the farm.

Vermont Wildflower Farm

Rte. 7, Charlotte; (802) 425-3500. May–mid-Oct., daily, 10–5. No admission fee until July. July–mid-Oct., adults, $2; under 12, free.
This farm is well known to many New England gardening aficionados. The farm's seed catalog is the bible for wildflower growers. In July and August, the farm is ablaze with color and the air filled with accompanying music. You'll walk the self-guided pathways through acres of wildflowers and trees. Not the place to spend hours with rambunctious toddlers or bored teens,

but worth a quick stop en route. Before leaving the area, stop at Mount Philo State Park.

Mount Philo State Park
Off Rte. 7, Charlotte.
Mount Philo is the only mountain available to climb in this region, and it's small at that. But don't let that stop you from driving to its 980-foot summit. There's an access road in the state park (you pay a nominal toll) that will take you to some of the best views in the area.

Kill Kare State Park
Rte. 36, Saint Albans.
A good place, if you're in the Saint Albans area, to stop for a picnic and swim. You can catch a ferry to Burton Island from here.

Burton Island State Park
For those who like a solitary look at natural beauty, this island is paradise. There are no cars allowed on the island; you reach it by boat or a launch service from Kamp Kill State Park (Town Road (off Route 36); (802) 524-6021.) Pitch a tent or come for the day to enjoy its scenery. There are hiking trails, great fishing, and a small nature center.

Champlain's Grand Islands
You'll not want to miss a drive through these peaceful lakeside gems. Traveling north from Burlington, you'll cross the lake to the islands of South Hero, Grand Isle, North Hero, and Isle La Motte. These island villages, connected by bridges, form one county, 30 miles long and eight miles wide. Surrounded by water, with views of the Adirondacks to the west and Mount Mansfield to the east, they offer some of the best in water activities, solitude, and scenery. Parks and beaches on the islands include: Grand Isle State Park (this park has great views, a small beach cove, and rowboats to rent; U.S. 2, Grand Isle; (802) 372-4300), Knight Point State Park (a good family beach with a large, sandy swimming cove, picnic area, nature trails, concession stand, and boat rentals; U.S. 2, North Hero; (802) 372-8389), and North Hero State Park (this beach is open to campers only—others can fish, hike, and rent boats; U.S. 2, North Hero; (802) 372-8389).

Saint Anne Shrine on Isle La Motte
Rte. 89, Isle La Motte; (802) 928-3362.
Even if shrines are not high on your list of attractions to see, come here for the peaceful setting. The shrine, which draws crowds of worshippers on

Sundays, is the site of Fort Saint Anne, the earliest settlement in Vermont. You'll enjoy a walk around the grounds and the surrounding lake views. There's even a picnic area, small beach, and snack bar.

The Hyde Log Cabin on Grand Isle

Rte. 89, Grand Isle. July–Labor Day, daily except Tues. and Wed., 9:30–5:30.

Built in 1783, this is probably the oldest log cabin in the country. It was certainly one of the first homes on the island. It's now maintained by the local historical society and filled with 18th-century antiques. A good place to stop and stretch your feet on your drive through the islands.

Downhill Skiing

Bolton Valley Resort

Rte. 2, Bolton Valley; 1-800-451-5025. Adult lift tickets, $30/day; nursery, $22/day; PreSki, $35/day.

Winter guests to this year-round resort enjoy skiing on 38 slopes and trails serviced by six lifts. The resort is a complete European-style slopeside village with restaurants, grocery store, sports club, and shops at the base. There's also night skiing.

□ Just for Children

The Henry Bear Nursery is open for children from three months to six years. The structured program includes games, outdoor play, and lunch. Henry Bear PreSki is offered for four- to six-year-olds and includes a two-hour ski lesson, lunch, and nursery stay. Equipment rental is not included ($14/day).

Restaurants

Stroll through Burlington's downtown pedestrian marketplace, and you'll find all kinds of things to eat—lots of delis, take-out food, candy shops, sidewalk cafes, and indoor and outdoor restaurants. Two family favorites are featured below, as is a restaurant recommendation for your tour of the Champlain's Grand Islands.

Carbur's

115 Saint Paul St., Burlington; (802) 862-4106. Mon.–Thurs., 11–10; Fri.–Sat., 11–11; Sun., noon–10.

Like no other, this zany restaurant is perfect for families. From the moment you glance at the menu (a 16-page newspaper entitled *The National Injester*) 'til the moment you wipe your face and hands with the fluffy hand towels, you'll enjoy your meal here. There are close to 200 items on the menu. (The staff recommends you glance at the table of contents, decide what you're in the mood for, and turn to the pages for descriptions!) The favorite items on the kids' menu are the peanut butter and jelly, honey, and sliced banana sandwich, or the peanut butter and fluff sandwich (fluff of marshmallow). If those offend your good taste, there's the kid's bowl of tricolored pasta and sauce, mini-pizza, fish and chips, and more.

Henry's Diner
Bank St., Burlington; (802) 862-9010. Daily, 11–10.
A real diner with real diner food. Try the pig-in-a-poke—a hot dog wrapped in bacon and cheese on a grilled roll.

Sandbar Motor Inn and Restaurant
Rte. 2, South Hero; (802) 372-6911. Wed.–Sun., dinner, 5–9; Sat., breakfast, 8–11; Sun., brunch, 8–1.
On Champlain Lake, in a pretty harbor in South Hero, this popular restaurant offers fresh seafood and meat dishes. The food is fine, the location is great. You can walk off your meal on the beach across the street.

Montpelier Area

Take a deep breath, let it out, and relax. As you gaze up at Montpelier's elegant, gold-domed Capitol, you'll get a sense that time has passed you by. The nation's smallest state capital is nestled in the valley of the Winooski River and surrounded by the green hills. There's a simple elegance and beauty about Montpelier. But it's not at all pretentious; it's a friendly place to be. Your family will feel comfortable running about the town streets or tumbling on the front lawn of the Capitol. Best of all, from here you have all Central Vermont to explore. You won't need to look hard, or far, for recreation. The area mountains, forests, lakes, and streams offer great skiing, hiking, biking, swimming, fishing, and sight-seeing.

An après-ski sleigh ride is cozy, delightful, and a real treat, even for sleepy children.

Meander the back roads for a view of rural Vermont's rolling farmlands and tiny villages. Follow the winding mountain road through dramatic Smuggler's Notch or the twisting side road that follows the Lamoille River over scenic covered bridges. If you're looking for something more lively, visit the cosmopolitan, four-season resort town of Stowe. (Stowe is one of six places in the area for families to downhill ski.)

This is also a great place to learn about how things are made. Visit the Cabot Farmers' Cooperative Creamery to see cheese being made. At the Maple Grove Museum, you'll see a maple-sugaring operation. In nearby Barre, you can visit the world's largest granite quarries. Take the tour of the Capitol and learn how laws are enacted. And everyone's favorite is a tour of the Ben & Jerry's Ice Cream Factory, which includes samples!

Vermont State House Tour
State St., Montpelier; (802) 828-2228. July–Oct., Mon.–Fri., 8–4. Free.
On this friendly, 20-minute tour of the State Capitol, you'll get an introduction to how state government works. You'll see old Civil War flags in the governor's ceremonial office and take a look at Representatives' Hall. If you're here when the Legislature is in session (January to April), you can watch the proceedings, although tours are not given at that time.

Vermont Historical Society Museum
State St., Montpelier; (802) 828-2291.
You'll get a peek at Vermont history in this small, hands-on museum, located at the Pavilion Office Building. The city band presents plays here on summer evenings. Call for details.

Hubbard Park
This 121-acre network of trails, directly behind the State Capitol, is a favorite place to go for short hikes. Pack a picnic to enjoy en route; there are scenic places along the way to stop.

Morse Farm Sugar House
Country Rd., (3 miles from the State Capitol), Montpelier; (802) 223-2740.
Year-round, daily, 9–5. Free.
The best time to visit this rustic sugar house is in March or April, when the sap is gathered and transformed into syrup. But you can tour the farm and learn about the equipment and process of maple sugaring at all times. There's a short slide show and a chance to taste samples of maple syrup.

Rock of Ages
Exit 6 off I-89, Barre; (802) 476-3121. May–Oct., daily, 8:30–5.
You can stand atop an observation platform and look over the world's largest granite quarry in the nearby town of Barre. Rock of Ages has been operating since the Civil War, producing granite for buildings and monuments across the world. On the guided walking tour, you'll see and hear (this is a noisy place) the work being done here. You can also take an open-air rail car to the work areas farther uphill. Visit the Craftsman Center on your way out to see how the granite is used in final products.

Stowe Gondola and Alpine Slide
Mountain Rd., Stowe Ski Area; (802) 253-7311. 10–5; Memorial Day–June, weekends; July–Oct., daily. Adults, $5; 12 and under, $3.50.
Take a scenic ride to the summit of 4,393-foot Mount Mansfield aboard the enclosed, four-person gondola. For a faster ride, take the Alpine Slide down Spruce Peak. You control your own speed through woods and fields and around turns and curves.

Mount Mansfield Auto Road
This 4.5-mile gravel road twists and turns its way to the top of Mount Mansfield. At the top, put on your coats—it's cold up here—and take a look at the 33,881-acre Mount Mansfield State Forest that stretches before you.

Because of the cold climate, you'll see Alpine plants found only in arctic temperatures.

Bingham Falls

This is a nice hiking trail down to a beautiful gorge. Pick up the trail on Route 108, just past the Mountain Toll Road entrance.

Stowe Aviation

Rte. 100 (7 miles north of Stowe); (802) 888-7845. May–mid-Nov., daily, 8–sunset. Rates vary.
For a bird's eye view of Mount Mansfield, stop by Stowe Aviation and inquire about their airplane, sailplane, and hot-air balloon rides. If you've always wanted to soar above mountaintops or float silently across treetops, this is your chance.

Top Notch Riding Stable

Mountain Rd. (Rte. 108); (802) 253-8585. Memorial Day weekend–Oct., daily, 9–5.
Top Notch offers great one- and two-hour guided horseback tours through the pretty Vermont countryside. You'll trot up hills, ford streams, and cross bridges on your way.

Stowe Recreation Path

Get a good tour of this mountain city as you walk or bike its recreation path. The three-mile path meanders through town. In winter, it's a popular cross-country ski tour. The path begins behind the white-steepled community church on Main Street.

Ben & Jerry's Ice Cream Factory

Rte. 100 (Exit 10 off I-89), Waterbury; (802) 244-5641. Year-round, daily, 9–4. Over 12, $1.
It's not quite Willie Wonka's Chocolate Factory—but close enough! For ice cream lovers, it's next to heaven. The fun-filled tour takes you through the factory where all the famous Ben & Jerry's ice cream is produced. You'll learn the steps it takes to produce the ice cream, and just when you think you can wait no longer . . . you've reached the Scoop Shop. (The tour includes free samplings of ice cream, but not nearly enough.) Enjoy your Chunky Monkey cone (or other favorite flavors) at a picnic table overlooking the pasture of cows and backdrop of mountains. In the summer, Ben & Jerry's offers free outdoor family movies, once a week at dusk. Call for schedule.

New Englanders eat more ice cream than residents of any other region in the country—which may explain why you'll see a homemade ice cream shop on every corner.

Cold Hollow Cider Mill

Rte. 100, Waterbury; (802) 244-8771. Year-round. Free.
Also in Waterbury, you'll find a barn full of homemade Vermont goodies—and lots of apples. In the fall and winter, you can see the cider press working.

Lamoille Valley Railroad

Rte. 100, Railroad Depot, Morrisville; (802) 888-4255. Mid-July–mid-Oct., two trips daily, 10–12 and 1–3. Adults, $15; 5–13, $7.
Take a scenic mountain trip aboard 1920s rail cars. This 60-mile excursion is very popular during fall foliage season. Call ahead for reservations.

Cabot Farmer's Cooperative Creamery

Rte. 2, Cabot; (802) 563-2231. Year-round, Mon.–Sat., 8–4:30; Sun., 12–5 from May 15–Oct. $1 donation for tours.
If your family has not tired of factory visits, go to the Cabot Creamery, where you'll see all kinds of dairy products being made. The cooperative comprises more than 500 farmers and nearly 30,000 cows. The countryside setting is pleasant, the staff friendly, and the video presentation interesting.

Fairbanks Museum and Planetarium
Main St., Saint Johnsbury; (802) 748-2372. Sept.–June, weekdays, 10–4:30, weekends, 10–5; July–Aug., Mon.–Sat., 10–6, Sun. 1–5. Adults, $2.50; 5–17, $1.25; families, $6.

This museum was founded by Colonel Franklin Fairbanks, a naturalist and born collector of wildlife. You'll find yourself nose to nose with stuffed polar bears, wild boars, alligators, penguins, bison, foxes, moose, opossums, an armadillo, and more. You'll be surrounded by an unbelievable collection of mounted birds and mammals peeking out through holes under limbs from behind glass environment displays. The eclectic collection also includes mosaic pictures made of insect parts, Indian artifacts, dolls, photomicrographs of snowflakes, dinosaur bones, Fairbanks scales, and lots of folklore. The lower level contains one of the country's oldest continuous weather stations, where you'll see regional weather broadcasts being prepared. The red sandstone Victorian building, with its 30-foot-high, barrel-vaulted oak ceiling, is an architectural treat. If you've time, attend one of the ongoing planetarium shows, offered daily in July and August and on weekends the rest of the year.

Maple Grove Maple Factory
Rte. 2, E. Saint Johnsbury; (802) 748-5141. May–Oct., daily, 8–5. Admission, 50¢; under 12, free.

Billed as the world's largest maple candy factory, you'll get a sweet-smelling, 10-minute tour of operations and see a short film showing how the sap is extracted from maple trees and brought to the sugar house.

Catamount Arts
60 Eastern Ave., Saint Johnsbury; (802) 748-2600.

Be sure to call ahead for this non-profit organization's performance schedule. It brings internationally known performers to the stage, and often hosts an impressive series of children's plays.

Groton State Forest
Rte. 232, Groton.

This is one of the best places for outdoor family recreation in the region. The 28,000-acre area is the state's largest recreational center, covering six towns. There are several lakes in the forest for swimming and boating (you can rent boats and canoes in the park) and more than 40 miles of hiking trails. The summer nature programs are fun.

Lake Elmore State Park
Rte. 12, Lake Elmore; (802) 888-2982.
A pleasant park about 25 minutes from Stowe. You can swim in Lake
Elmore, rent boats, hike, and walk up a lookout tower for a view of the
Green Mountains.

Scenic Drive—Smuggler's Notch
If you can endure the hairpin turns and narrow curves on this steep, winding scenic drive, you'll be rewarded with a dramatic view of Smuggler's
Notch. Travel Route 108, just beyond Spruce Peak, where you'll begin your
climb to the top of the Notch. It's been said that the Notch was used as a
hideout and as a passageway between Canada and the United States during
the War of 1812. At the top, there's a small rest area from which to view the
gnarled chasm created by glacial waters. You'll be at an elevation of 2,162,
where the air is cool. On the way down the back side, you'll pass a waterfall
before reaching the Smuggler's Notch ski resort. The road is closed from
late fall until May.

Downhill Skiing

Stowe
*Stowe; (802) 253-7311. Lift tickets, adults, $35; 6–12, $18. Kanga's Pocket
Nursery, $32/full day, $20/half day; Pooh's Corner, $48/full day (includes
two lessons and lunch); $24/half day (includes one lesson).*
Stowe has been called one of the best ski resorts in the country. It's big and
challenging, and its reputation as a world-class ski area draws plenty of
trendy, lively crowds. There are 44 trails, serviced by 10 lifts, covering two
mountains: the mighty Mount Mansfield and Spruce Peak. In recent years,
Stowe has actively targeted the family business, offering special family
vacation packages and top-notch day-care and children's ski programs. If
you're serious about skiing, this is the place to go.

□ Just for Children
Stowe offers two day-care centers: Kanga's Pocket, for infants to 3-year-olds,
and Pooh's Corner, for 3- to 12-year-olds. Both are located at Spruce Peak
and staffed by a registered nurse, certified teachers, and licensed day-care
professionals. Day-care includes arts and crafts, story hours, lunch, and the
option of ski lessons (three years or older at Pooh's Corner). Children in the

ski program at Pooh's Corner (3 to 6 years old) are assigned to an instructor and a Winnie the Pooh animal, according to age and ability. Children 7 to 12 are assigned to one of six different levels, identified by numbers one through six, in the Stowemasters program. When kids have progressed from Pooh's Corner they can join the Mountain Adventure Workshop for kids up to 17 years old. Children under five ski free anytime.

Smuggler's Notch

Rte. 108, Smuggler's Notch; (802) 644-8851. Adult lift ticket, $38; Ski Camps, $38/day; Parents Night Out, $15 per child; nursery rates vary with length of stay.

The folks at Smuggler's Notch bend over backwards to make families feel welcome. In fact, they offer a kid's FUN GUARANTEE—if your youngster does not enjoy the program, your money will be refunded. You'll ski three interconnected mountains—Morse, Sterling, and Madonna—with 2,610 feet of vertical that offer challenges for skiers of all levels. The village at Smuggler's Notch is a self-contained resort with restaurants, sports centers, shops, horseback riding, and sleigh rides, all within walking distance. Special family weeks are held throughout the season.

Not all the action at Smuggler's Notch Ski Resort takes place on the slopes, as this peek inside the daycare center indicates.

□ Just for Children

Kids and parents alike will enjoy Alice's Wonderland, the large, brand new nursery and day-care center. The bright nursery, for children age three months to six years, is open daily from 8:30 to 4. Activities center around toys and crafts, books, a closet of costumes, and a water/sand table. For indoor exercise, padded mats, a ski ramp, and jungle gym are used. Infants play in the Crawler Room, equipped with a soft sculptured gym, mirrors, and a wide selection of toys. The smallest children do their first skiing indoors on the carpeted ski ramp. They get the feel of sliding on skis before they go outdoors for their first 20- to 30-minute lesson on snow. Three- to six-year-olds can join Discovery Ski Camp; 7- to 12-year-olds, Adventure Ski School. Activities for both programs include two 1.75-hour ski lessons, hot chocolate breaks, lunch, games, sleigh rides, story telling, guided skiing, and on-mountain games. Smuggler's Notch also offers a Parents Night Out. This program is available on selected evenings from 6 to 10, and is limited to kids three and older.

Sugarbush

This big, popular area includes skiing at two mountains—the South Basin, with 36 trails and nine lifts, and Mount Ellen, with 26 trails and seven lifts. A free shuttle bus service runs every half hour (about a 15-minute ride) between South Basin and Mount Ellen and also to village services and restaurants. There's skiing for everyone here, with a wide variety of trails.

□ Just for Children

Warren; (802) 583-2381. Lift tickets, adults, $33; 7–12, $18. Sugarbear, 6–12, $76/full day, includes lift ticket, lunch, two lessons; Minibear, 3–5, $50/ full day, includes three one-hour lessons.

The Valley Day School, within skiing distance of the slopes at South Basin, accepts infants to 12-years-old, providing ski instruction as well as child-care. The Sugarbear Program for kids 6 to 10 provides a full day of supervised skiing, with a two-hour lesson at 10, lunch, and another two-hour lesson at 2.

Cross-County Skiing

A special place for Nordic skiers is the 1,700-acre Trapp Family Lodge. Skiers of the more than 60 kilometers of trails have some of the best views in the area. Five miles along the trail you can stop for hot soup and a cup of chocolate at the Slayton Cabin. Ski lessons and rentals are available (Luce Hill Road, Stowe; (802) 253-8511). Cross-country skiing is also available at the Top Notch Ski-Touring Center, (802) 253-8585; Jay Peak Touring Center, 1-800-451-4449; Edson Hill Ski-Touring Center, (802) 253-8954; Mount Mansfield Touring Center, (802) 253-7311; Hermansmith Farm Touring Center, (802) 754-8866; Hazen's Notch Touring, 1-800-326-4708; and at all area downhill ski resorts.

Restaurants

The Stowe area has about 35 to 40 restaurants, most located along the mountain access road. You'll find a variety of cuisines, from elegant, country-inn dining to casual, take-out delis. Those mentioned below are especially appealing to families.

The Shed
Mountain Access Rd.; (802) 253-4364. Daily: breakfast, 8–11:30; lunch, noon–4:30; dinner, 5–10.
More families eat here than at any other restaurant in Stowe. They serve breakfast, lunch, and dinner, offering a wide variety of dishes. They go through lots of barbecued baby-back ribs and mighty Shed burgers (voted "Best in Stowe"). The seafood strudel, with shrimp, scrod, and crab, is worth trying.

About Thyme Cafe
40 State St.; (802) 223-0427. Mon.–Fri., 7:30–7:30; Sat., 9–7:30.
This small, bright eatery in downtown Montpelier offers a variety of well-prepared hot and cold salads, sandwiches, soups, stews, and dinner entrées. The health-conscious menu caters to families who want to eat quickly and well—it's fast, reasonable gourmet food. You can also pick up lunch or dinner to go.

Tubbs, LaBrioche, Elm Street Cafe
The Jailhouse Common, Elm St. Tubbs: Mon.–Sat., 11:30–2 and 6–9:30. La Brioche: Mon.–Fri., 7:30–3; Sat., 7:30–1. Elm Street Cafe: Mon.–Sat., 7–10, 11:30–1:30, and 5:30–9.
These are the three restaurants operated by the students of the New England Culinary Institute, all located near each other in downtown Montpelier. If you're in the mood for something creative, stop by: you might find bluefish tuna with lemon soy butter, herbed lamb with roasted peppers and mint yogurt dressing, or a variety of other great-tasting dishes. The

atmosphere is casual, and there's always something the kids are sure to enjoy. (How about the turkey-and-apple-topped-with-cheese sandwich?)

Burlington Bagel Bakery
Rte. 2; (802) 223-0533. Mon.–Fri., 6:30–6; Sat., 7–5; Sun., 8–3.
For a quick breakfast in downtown Montpelier, you can't beat the bagel factory. Plenty of room to sit down and enjoy the wide assortment of bagels and toppings while you watch people go by.

Connecticut

Mystic Area

The community of Mystic is tremendously popular with families, and for good reason: it boasts two world-class attractions, Mystic Seaport and Mystic Marine Life Aquarium. Downtown Mystic—sliced down the middle by the Mystic River—has a seafaring charm all its own. There you can participate in the town's most popular spectator sport: watching boats go by. You may not have a choice regarding this activity: the bridge goes up in the middle of downtown approximately every hour-and-15-minutes in summer.

The nearby towns of Stonington, Norwich, Groton, and New London also offer some interesting attractions for families, including the Thames Science Center, the Nautilus Submarine Museum, and Ocean Beach Park.

Where there's lots of fun and activity, there are crowds. This is especially true of Mystic Seaport, with more than a half a million visitors annually. So arrive early, and be prepared to spend some time waiting in lines if you visit in summer. Or plan your trip to Mystic in the less hectic spring or fall. Another possibility: consider Christmastime. Mystic makes the most of it. Mystic Seaport hosts Children's Victorian Christmas Tours and Downtown Mystic recreates the spirit of a 19th-century Christmas, complete with carolers and yuletide refreshments.

Mystic Seaport
Exit 90 off I-95, Mystic; (203) 572-0711. Year-round, daily, 9–5. Adults, $12.50; 5–18, $6.25. Ice Cream Tour: $1 per child. Horse-and-carriage ride: $2 per person; under 3, free. Steamboat Sabino River Cruise: adults, $2.50; 5–18, $1.75.

Many visitors have the mistaken notion that the name "Mystic Seaport" refers to a Connecticut town. It's actually the name of America's largest maritime museum, a 17-acre waterfront site boasting tall ships and a recreated 19th-century seaport village. If you're visiting Mystic Seaport from mid-June through Labor Day, make your first stop the Children's

*Children won't be bored at Mystic
Seaport, where tall ships provide the
backdrop for lots of seafaring fun.*

Museum. Here you can make reservations for an hour-long Ice Cream Tour, for children only. Supervised by an adult guide, kids aged 5 to 10 will take part in waterfront activities, such as sail stitching and raising the arm of a ship. (Children under four can participate if accompanied by a parent.) At the end of the tour, back at the Children's Museum, there's ice cream for everyone. Small fry will adore the quaint Children's Museum (despite the long wait to enter it in high season). A treasure-trove of 19th-century toys and games awaits inside; outside, on the green, children can try rolling a hoop or walking on stilts.

Your family could spend a whole day at Mystic Seaport and not be bored. For starters, you'll want to explore the Seaport's historic homes and village, where "role-players" demonstrate 19th-century skills such as boat building and wood carving. Climb aboard the 1841 whaleship, *Charles W. Morgan*, and you'll see the magnificent result of one of the lengthiest restoration projects in the Seaport's history. The *Morgan* is the last of the wooden whaleships. You won't want to miss a river cruise on the *Sabino*, the last coal-fired steamboat in America. The *Sabino* departs hourly for 30-minute cruises, from mid-May to mid-October.

A great way to end your day at Mystic Seaport: give your legs a rest and take a ride on a horse-drawn carriage at Chubb's Wharf. Children will enjoy clip-clopping around the Seaport Village, and you'll all get one last look at this special place before heading back to the 20th century.

Mystic Marinelife Aquarium
Exit 90 off I-95, Mystic; (203) 536-9631. Daily, 9–4:30; grounds close at 6. Adults, $7; 5–17, $4.

More than 6,000 marine animals live here, and the best part about this aquarium is that you can get up close to many of them. The aquarium houses 48 exhibits, with every kind of fish and sea creature you can imagine, including a blue lobster and an octopus. Most kids are fascinated by sharks, and they'll love exchanging menacing stares with three kinds of sharks in the Open Sea exhibit. There's even a special step up, alongside the tanks, so that toddlers won't miss anything. Of course, you'll want to see as many of the marine mammal shows as possible. Dolphins, sea lions, and whales perform here; children are especially delighted when the dolphins walk on their tails and the Beluga whale kisses his trainer. Outside, Seal Island features five species of seals and sea lions in natural settings, and the Penguin Pavilion houses a colony of African black-footed penguins. Plan to spend a couple of hours here to see it all.

*Marine mammal shows are the highlight
of a visit to Mystic Marinelife Aquarium.*

Denison Pequotsepos Nature Center

Pequotsepos Rd., Mystic; (203) 536-9248. Nature Center: Apr.–Oct., Mon.–
Sat., 8–5; Sun., 1–5; Nov.–Mar., closed Mon. Adults, $1; under 16, 50¢.
Homestead open May 15–Oct. 15, Tues.–Sun., 1–5. Adults, $1.75; under 16,
30¢.

If you're worn out from fighting the crowds at Mystic Seaport and
Marinelife Aquarium, this peaceful place could provide the perfect respite.
You'll find more than 125 acres of wildlife sanctuary and four miles of
hiking trails, with ponds, fields, lowland and upland woods to explore. The
Nature Center maintains a year-round trailside museum, where you'll learn
about birds, insects, reptiles, and pond and marine life. The non-profit
Nature Center is dedicated to increasing environmental awareness. Special
programs are offered on weekends throughout the year; call ahead. Nearby,
the Denison Homestead (1717) showcases heirlooms from all generations of
the Denisons, one of Connecticut's first families.

Old Lighthouse Museum

Water St., Stonington; (203) 535-1440. May–Oct., Tues.–Sun., 11–4:30.
Adults, $2; 6–16, $1.

Drive out to the Lighthouse Museum on Stonington Point (a short trip from
Downtown Mystic on Route 1) and you can see three states at the same
time: Fisher's Island, New York, to the south, Watch Hill, Rhode Island, to
the east, and Connecticut, under your feet. Stonington Lighthouse operated
as a lighthouse until 1889; now it's a museum, housing 19th-century
portraits, a collection of whaling and fishing artifacts, swords and firearms,
and, in the children's room, toys and a doll house. To most kids, the best
part is just being inside a lighthouse.

Nautilus Memorial Museum

Exit 86 off I-95, Groton; (203) 449-3174. Wed.–Mon., 9–5, mid-April–Sept.;
9–3:30, Oct. 15–Mar.; closed the first week in Jan. and the first two weeks
in Apr. and Oct. Free.

What child hasn't fashioned a periscope out of a cardboard tube and played
submarine? At the Nautilus Memorial Museum—part of the U.S. Naval
Submarine Base—kids can peer through real periscopes and tour a real
submarine, the Nautilus. The Nautilus, the world's first nuclear-powered
vessel, was commissioned into the U.S. Navy in 1954. Once on board (you
might have to wait in line, as only 60 people are allowed aboard at one
time), you'll carry an electronic wand that activates narration about each
area of the submarine. You'll see the navigation center, the radar room, the
attack center, and more. Elsewhere in the museum, there are working

periscopes, an authentic submarine control room, and several midget submarines.

Project Oceanology
Cruises depart from Avery Point off Eastern Point Rd., Groton; (203) 445-9007. July 3–Labor Day, Sun.–Fri., 10 and 1; Sat., 9, noon, and 3. Labor Day–Columbus Day, weekends only. Adults, $11; under 12, $9. Reservations recommended.
Climb aboard a 50-foot Enviro-Lab research vessel for a cruise you won't forget. Marine scientists and instructors will teach you how to use oceanographic instruments, test seawater, identify fish, and measure lobsters. You'll also help take core samples from the bottom of the ocean and examine them. Recommended for older children, the trips last 2.5 hours.

Fort Griswold State Park
Monument St., Groton; (203) 445-1729.
This 17-acre park was the scene of a massacre in 1781. Benedict Arnold led an attack by the British forces, taking the fort and burning Groton and New London. On the hilltop near Fort Griswold, a 135-foot monument dedicated to victims of the massacre bears their names. Today you'll find the spot a considerably more pleasant place, with beautiful views of the Thames River and Fisher's Island. Bring a picnic.

Bluff Point State Park
Depot Rd., off Rte. 1, Groton; (203) 445-1729.
Located between Mystic and Groton on Long Island Sound, this unspoiled stretch of shoreline is a great place to take a hike or nature walk, have a picnic, or fish from the shore.

Lyman Allyn Museum
625 Williams St., New London; (203) 443-2545. Year-round, Tues.–Sat., 11–5, Sun., 1–5. Free.
This small museum, a memorial to whaling captain Lyman Allyn, houses period furniture, a glass collection, and displays of Oriental, Greek, Egyptian, and Roman art. You'll find a terrific collection of doll houses, toys, and dolls. The dolls are especially intriguing, with heads made of wax, paper-maché, bisque, china, and wood. Walking dolls, too.

Connecticut Arboretum/Thames Science Center
Williams St., New London; (203) 442-0391. Arboretum: daily, dawn–dusk.
Science Center: Mon.–Sat., 9–5; Sun., 1–5. Adults, $1; 5–17, 50¢.
Two sites on the Connecticut College campus are worth a visit. The 415-
acre Arboretum offers several hiking trails, including one that leads to Balles
Wood, a hemlock forest. The Thames Science Center features a marine
touch tank, where kids can make friends with local sea life. Also thrilling: a
working beehive under plexiglass, squirming with life. Kids will enjoy
hearing bird calls on tape—and you're sure to hear kiddie versions of same,
long after you've left the Science Center.

U.S. Coast Guard Academy
Mohegan Ave., and Rte. 32 (off I-95), New London; (203) 444-8270.
Visitor's Pavilion: May–Oct., daily, 9–5. Free.
There are two advantages to visiting the Academy in spring and fall: you
might see the cadet corps on dress parade (usually on Friday afternoons),
and you can board the 295-foot training barque, *Eagle* (on weekends). Call
first to avoid disappointment. The Visitor's Pavilion features a multi-media
show depicting cadet life, while the museum at Waersbe Hall displays
historical nautical items.

Ocean Beach Park
Ocean Ave., New London; (203) 447-3031. Memorial Day–Labor Day,
9–midnight. Adults, $1; 15 and under, 50¢.
This is one of the most popular beaches on Long Island Sound. In addition
to a wide white-sand beach, you'll find a boardwalk, eateries, and
concessions.

Mohegan Park
Rtes. 2 and 32, Norwich; (203) 889-6516. Year-round. Free.
The best feature of this 350-acre park overlooking the city is a children's
petting zoo. You'll also enjoy swimming in Mohegan Park Lake. A beautiful
rose garden, honoring the World War II dead, is in full bloom from late
June to early July.

Slater Memorial Museum
108 Crescent St., Norwich; (203) 8878-2506. Sept.–June, weekdays, 9–4;
Sat.–Sun., 1–4. July–Aug., Tues.–Sun., 1–4. Closed holidays. Free.
This Romanesque building, on the grounds of Norwich Free Academy,
houses sculpture; Egyptian, Greek, Roman, and Native American artifacts;

American primitives; and African and Oriental art. Young artists will find lots of inspiration in this varied collection.

Tantaquidgeon Indian Museum
Rte. 32, Uncasville; (203) 848-9145. May–Oct., Tues.–Sun., 10–4. Donation requested.
This unique museum presents a personal look at the Mohegan Indians. Begun in 1931 by direct descendants of Uncas, the chief of the Mohegan Nation, the museum houses numerous artifacts. Among the unusual and beautiful objects here are headdresses made of deer hair and tiny, intricate straw baskets. Objects made by Plains and West Coast Indians are also displayed, including a wolf kachina doll. Behind the museum are replicas of Indian dwellings.

Boat Cruises
From Mystic, sail aboard a windjammer schooner on Long Island and Block Island sounds. Or, from Groton, cruise past the U.S.S. Nautilus up to the Coast Guard Academy and back on a replica of *The African Queen.* Suggested cruise companies: Out O'Mystic Schooner Cruises, (203) 536-4218, departing from Whaler's Wharf, Mystic; Voyager Cruises, (203) 536-0416, departing from Steamboat Wharf, Mystic; and *River Queen/River Queen II,* departing from Thames Harbor Inn, 193 Thames Street, Groton, (203) 455-8111.

Ballooning
17 Carriage Dr., Stonington; (203) 535-0283. Daily, mornings only. $20.
Want a bird's eye view of Mystic? If the kids in your party are 10 or older and you want to splurge, call Mystic River Balloon Ride.

Bicycling
Explore Mystic by bicycle. Rentals are available at Bicycle World, 75 W. Main Street, Mystic; (203) 536-4819.

Restaurants

Abbott's Lobsters
117 Pearl St., Noank (10 minutes from Mystic off Rte. 215); (203) 536-7719. May–Labor Day, daily, noon–9; Labor Day–Columbus Day, weekends only, noon–7.
Enjoy lobster-in-the-rough at this casual waterfront restaurant. Choose a picnic table at the edge of Island Sound or eat inside in the dining room.

The selection of fresh seafood includes shrimp, clams, mussels, and lobster rolls. Hot dogs are also available.

Avanti's

Rte. 1, Mystic; (203) 536-2639. Sun.–Thurs., 11–10; Fri. and Sat., 11–11.
Most children love Italian food, and this small family restaurant is the place to get it. Nothing fancy, but all your favorite pasta dishes are on the menu, as well as Avanti's popular pizza.

Steak Loft

Olde Mistick Village, Mystic; (203) 536-2661. Daily, 11:30–9:30; Fri.–Sat., 11:30–10.
This popular restaurant is well located, being just off the highway and right across the street from Olde Mistick Village and Mystic Marinelife Aquarium. Its interior is interesting, with old farm implements hanging from beams and along the walls. Steaks and seafood are among the offerings here. The children's menu ranges from the salad bar alone ($1.95 at lunch) to burgers and fried chicken with a kiddie cocktail and a visit to the salad bar included.

Hartford Area

When most people think of Hartford, they think "insurance," not "vacation wonderland." However, the city of Hartford—Connecticut's second-largest—offers several attractions that will delight visiting families. Museums are a main attraction, with a wonderful hands-on science museum, the Mark Twain House, and, on a more offbeat note, an unusual collection of antique medical and dental devices. Hartford also serves as a good base for exploring other sites in central Connecticut. They're varied and loaded with kid-appeal, ranging from a state park with real dinosaur tracks to an aviation museum.

What you probably won't see are stags roaming the streets. Although an insurance company has perpetrated this image in their advertising, locals assure us it's just not true.

Mark Twain House
351 Farmington Ave. (Exit 46 off I-84), Hartford; (203) 525-9317. June–Aug., daily, 9–4; Sun., noon–4. Sept.–May, Tues.–Sat., 9:30–4; Sun., noon–4. Mark Twain House and Beecher Stowe House combined ticket: adults, $6.50; 6–16, $2.75.

Twain's bright red Victorian-Gothic house reflects the eccentricity of its owner. For example, Twain slept with his head at the foot of his bed so he could admire the ornate Venetian headboard, and he kept his telephone in the closet because it drove him crazy. You'll see the study where Twain wrote *Tom Sawyer* and *Huckleberry Finn*—and took billiards breaks at the full-sized pool table. Visitors soon realize that the author enjoyed drinking, smoking, and billiards at least as much as he liked writing. The Mark Twain House is part of Nook Farm, an intellectual community formed in the mid-19th century by Twain and cultural luminaries Isabella Beecher Hooker, women's rights activist; William Gillette, playwright and actor; author Harriet Beecher Stowe, and others.

Harriet Beecher Stowe House
73 Forest St., Hartford; (203) 525-9317. June–Aug., daily, 9:30–4; Sun., noon–4. Mark Twain House and Harriet Beecher Stowe House combined ticket: adults, $6.50; 6–16, $2.75.

Also on Nook Farm, adjacent to the Mark Twain House, is the restored home of *Uncle Tom's Cabin* author Harriet Beecher Stowe. Most of Stowe's original furniture is here, including the small desk where she wrote 33 books.

Science Museum of Connecticut
950 Trout Brook Dr., West Hartford; (203) 236-2961. Mon.–Sat., 10–5; Sun., 1–5. Adults, $4.50; 3–12, $3.00; under 2, 75¢.

This museum is filled with exhibits and hands-on activities kids will love. You can explore the mysteries of the solar system at the planetarium, shake hands with a starfish in the touch tank (part of a 25-tank aquarium), and learn by doing in the Discovery Room, where one of the most enjoyable exhibits is an echo tunnel. The museum also houses a small indoor/outdoor zoo where 50 species of animals live. Children especially love the antics of Nora, the rhesus monkey; other zoo inhabitants include a bobcat, a raccoon, an eagle, and some snakes. In 1992, an expanded Science Museum is scheduled to open in East Hartford at Commerce Center. Features will include an IMAX Theater, a planetarium, and lots of exhibit space.

Travelers Tower

700 Main St., (1 Tower Square), Hartford; (203) 277-2431. Apr.–Oct., 11–2:30; June–Aug., 10:30–3:30. Call for an appointment. Free.

At 527 feet, this building—home of Travelers Insurance Company—is one of the tallest in New England. Climb up 72 steps to the observation deck for a panoramic view of the city.

Bushnell Park

Jewel St., Hartford; (203) 728-3089. Mid-May–Labor Day, Tues.–Sun., 11–5; early Apr.–mid-May and Labor Day–Sept., Sat.–Sun., 11–5. Carousel rides, 25¢.

What child doesn't adore a carousel? And the one at Bushnell Park, built in 1914, is something special, with 48 hand-carved horses and ornate, lavish lovers' chariots. It operates daily in summer and weekends in spring and fall. Also on the grounds are two Farragut cannons. Located in the center of the city, within steps of the Capitol, the park is a great place to people-watch or just relax under a tree. You can even grab a hotdog and a soda from a pushcart vendor.

In addition to lovely gardens and beautiful grounds, some city parks offer special features, like the antique carousel at Hartford's Bushnell Park and the zoo at Roger Williams Park in Providence.

Wadsworth Atheneum

600 Main St., Hartford; (203) 247-9111. Tues.–Sun., 11–5. Adults, $3; under 13, free. Free, Thurs., 11–1.

America's first public art museum, the Atheneum has a collection that includes paintings, sculpture, furniture, costumes, bronzes, firearms, and mummies. Items date from prehistory to the present. For kids, the staff has prepared special tours on cassette tapes, designed to make art more accessible. The tapes combine fun (treasure hunt-type questions and clues about the works) and facts (design concepts and how art is made). Wearing the headphones makes kids feel involved, not merely dragged along. Adults can plug in, too. On your way out, don't miss Alexander Calder's huge stegosaurus sculpture.

Historical Museum of Medicine and Dentistry

230 Scarborough St., Hartford; (203) 236-5613. Mon.–Fri., 9–5. Free.

This offbeat attraction may not be for everyone. The museum traces the progress of medical technology from the Revolutionary War to the 20th century, featuring a 1919 dentist's office. There's also a collection of unusual medical devices, some rather gruesome. Older children, reassured by the fact that times have changed, may be intrigued. Obviously, this is not the place to bring small children—especially those who have not yet visited a dentist. According to the staff, most kids from the age of 10 or so don't find the experience scary (lots of school groups come through).

New England Air Museum

Bradley Airport, Windsor Locks (10 miles north of Hartford on Rte. 75, off I-91); (203) 623-3305. Year-round, daily, 10–5. Adults, $5; 6–11, $2.

Older children who think airplanes are neat will enjoy taking a look at the aircraft exhibited here. More than 80 examples are on display, from an 1897 replica of a piloted glider to a modern F-105 jet. All have been meticulously restored. Children (and adults) will get a kick out of playing with the flight simulator; you must be supervised by a museum attendant to do so. Aviation-related films are shown several times a day.

Connecticut Trolley Museum

58 North Rd. (Rte. 140, take Exit 215 off I-91), East Windsor; (203) 623-7417. Nov.–May, Sat. and Sun., noon–5. Adults $4; 5–15, $2.

Take a ride on an old-fashioned trolley car.

Allen's Cider Mill

Mountain and N. Granby Rds. (Rte. 189), Granby; (203) 653-6438. Mid-Sept–Nov., Sat. and Sun. Confirm they're pressing cider before you visit.
Watch cider being pressed—and, even better, sample the results—at this 1919 mill.

Massacoh Plantation

800 Hopmeadow St., Simsburg; (203) 658-2500. May–Oct., Sun.–Fri., 1–4. Phelps House open Mon.–Fri. all year. Adults $3; 5–18, $1.50. Phelps House admission (when rest of Plantation is closed), $1.
This complex represents three centuries of local history. Older children will enjoy seeing the Phelps House (1771, formerly a hotel and tavern), the one-room schoolhouse (1741), and the stocks and pillory. Also on the grounds: an herb garden, a 1683 meeting house, and a Victorian carriage house. Guided tours, from 1 to 3:30, are lively and geared toward children.

Heublein Tower

Rte. 185, Simsburg. Late April–Labor Day, weekends only.
Drive up to Heublein Tower in Talcott Mountain State Park for panoramic views of the mountains and, below, the Farmington River.

Old Newgate Prison and Copper Mine

Rte. 20 West to 115 Newgate Rd., East Granby; (203) 653-3563. Mid-May–Oct., Wed.–Sun., 10–4. Adults, $3; 6–17, $1.50.
This colonial copper mine served as a Revolutionary War prison—the nation's first state prison—housing British sympathizers. Prowl the dungeon-like chambers to see where the prisoners ate and slept, and hear of their attempted escapes. You can take a tunnel stairway down to the celebrated Simsbury copper mine and walk the narrow mine paths. The mine was worked from 1707 to 1773. Later the Newgate prisoners were kept in the mine at night. It's an unusual glimpse of American history. Today the crumbling jail walls set against a backdrop of foothills and valley forests appear picturesque. The picnic area on the grounds is a pleasant setting. If you have the time, take the Newgate Wildlife Trail from the parking lot. The six-mile self-guided nature trail winds around Newgate Pond.

Lutz Children's Museum

247 South Main St. (Exit 59 off I-89), Manchester; (203) 643-0949. Tues.–Wed., 2–5; Thurs., 2–8; Fri., 11–5; Sat.–Sun., noon–5. Adults, $1.50; 1–7, $1.

Don't look, just touch . . . what is it? Yes, deer antlers. The "feel boxes" are just one of many exhibits children get their hands on here. This small facility is chock-full of fun spaces where children can put on life jackets and steer a boat through a storm, climb aboard the Alphabet Express, or put on their own hand puppet show, among other things. The museum also has a live animal exhibit, where you might see crows, raccoons, rabbits, a boa constrictor, even a great horned owl. Many of the animals are part of the museum's rehabilitation and release program, making this an ever-changing exhibit. Save energy for the large Playscape area outside.

Old Tolland Jail Museum
Town Green (Exit 68 off I-84), Tolland; (203) 875-7552. Jail museum: May–Oct., Sun. 1–4. Hicks-Sterns House: May–Oct., Wed. and Sun., 1–4. Donations accepted at both.
This site on Tolland Green housed prisoners until the 1960s; now visitors can go into the jail's cells (c. 1856) and tour the country house connected to it where the jailer and his family lived. If you have time, pop into the Hicks-Sterns Family Museum right across the street. This colonial inn-turned-summer cottage was occupied by Hicks and Sterns, and is filled with their belongings and souvenirs of European travel.

Benton Homestead
Metcalf Rd. (Exit 68 off I-84), Tolland; (203) 875-7552. May–Oct., Sun., 1–4. Donations accepted.
The best feature of this historic house is its romantic-yet-spooky ghost story. The guide tells it beautifully, and locals swear it's true. Visit and decide for yourself whether the Benton house is haunted.

Dinosaur State Park
West St. (Exit 23 off I-91), Rocky Hill; (203) 529-8423. Year-round, Tues.–Sun., 9–4:30. Adults, $1; 6–17, 50¢.
Imagine finding real, 185-million-year-old dinosaur tracks! That's what happened here in 1966 during excavation for a new state building. The fossil tracks—three-toed impressions, ranging from 10 to 16 inches in length—are now protected in a large geodesic dome. What type of dinosaur made these tracks? Nobody knows for sure, but you'll see a full-size replica of the scientists' best guess, a dilophosaurus, on display here. Bring 10 pounds of plaster of paris and one-quarter cup of vegetable oil, and you can make your own cast of a dinosaur footprint. Nature trails and gift shop, too.

Mill Pond Falls

Garfield St., Newington; (203) 666-4661. Year-round.
Once surrounded by Indian wigwams, this area is now a lovely town park with its own natural waterfall. Enjoy a picnic here, as ducks paddle across the pond.

New Britain Youth Museum

30 High St., New Britain; (203) 225-3020. Oct.–Apr., Tues.–Fri., 1–5; Sat., 10–4; Summer hours: June–Sept., Tues.–Fri., 11–5.
Dolls, a miniature circus display, and a small petting zoo are featured here, along with changing exhibits.

Lake Compounce

Lake Ave. (Exit 31 off I-84), Bristol; (203) 582-6333. In May, Sat. and Sun. only, 11–10. June–Sept., daily, 11–10. Adults, $14.03; 4–9, $12.93.
Had your fill of museums? Ready for some action? Consider Lake Compounce, America's oldest amusement park. Recently renovated, the park is a blend of Victorian charm (old-time shops, a carousel) and wild rides, like the mountain flume and the Wildcat roller coaster. There are live performances and several eateries; the lake itself adds a touch of serenity.

Fruit-Picking

There's plenty of picking outside the city of Hartford—especially to the south of town. Here are some possibilities: Bell Town Orchards (475 Matson Hill Road, South Glastonbury; (203) 633-2789; apples and blueberries), Szoda's Farm (Woodland Street, South Glastonbury; (203) 633-4004; apples and blueberries), Rose's Berry Farm (Matson Hill Road, South Glastonbury; (203) 633-7467; strawberries, blueberries, and raspberries).

Elizabeth Park

915 Prospect Ave. (Exit 44 off I-84), Hartford; (203) 722-6543.
A perfect place to try some lawn bowling surrounded by beautiful rose gardens. More than 10,000 plants of 50 varieties are in full bloom from June 25 through July 4 at this urban oasis. Ice skating in winter.

Wickham Park

1329 W. Middle Tpke. (Exit 92 off I-384), Manchester; (203) 528-0856.
An aviary, a small zoo, and a 1927 log cabin are the featured attractions at this unusual park. The 215-acre site has beautifully manicured grounds with Oriental and lotus gardens, play areas, and picnicking facilities. Cross-country skiing in the winter.

Opportunities to pick your own raspberries, strawberries, and blueberries abound in rural areas of New England.

Stanley Quarter Park

451 Blake Rd., New Britain; (203) 224-2491.
Don your swimsuits, grab your fishing gear, and head for the lake. In addition to swimming and fishing, Stanley Quarter Park offers hiking and bicycling trails and picnicking facilities. Cross-country skiing is the attraction in winter.

Restaurants

The Pavilion

State House Square, Hartford. Daily, 7–midnight.
For variety and ease, you can't beat Café Court on the second floor of the Pavilion. The building is smack in the middle of all the action at State House Square and is an architecturally interesting bit of art deco, featuring lots of plants, glass, and lights. Ride the glass elevator to the second floor

and take your pick of fare: stuffed potatoes, deli sandwiches, tacos and enchiladas, salads, pizza, and more. Save room for dessert; on the first floor you'll find Ben & Jerry's ice cream and Jessica's Cookies.

Sweet Gatherings
219 Main St. (Exit 29 off I-91), Old Wethersfield. Tues.–Sun., 7–10:30, breakfast; 11:30–2:30, lunch.
Fresh homemade soups, quiches, and salads (create your own omelettes for breakfast) are on the menu here. But the real draw is the homemade ice cream on a freshly-made cone. This small, casual place is just minutes off the highway in quaint Old Wethersfield. It's about 10 minutes from downtown Hartford; a great place to stop when heading south or just plain tired of the city life. You'll want to spend a few minutes after your meal walking through the pretty, historic town center.

Manchester Seafood Market and Restaurant
43 Oak St., Manchester; (603) 649-9937. Daily, 11–5.
Nothing fancy; just good, fresh seafood at this local fish market and restaurant. A quick and inexpensive place to stop before or after your visit to the Lutz Children's Museum. Try the clam fritters or chowder.

Sharpy's Lobster Spa
159 Rainbow Rd. (Rte. 20 West), East Granby. Mon.–Fri., 9–6; Sat. 9–5.
This take-out eatery is north of Hartford, convenient to visitors going to the Newgate Prison or New England Air Museum. The front of this small establishment is a fish market (kids can take a peek at the lobster pool), the back is a take-out sandwich counter. Try the lobster croissant or, for hearty appetites, the lobster grinder. Other deli sandwiches and hot dogs also available. From the picnic tables outside, you'll get a runway view of the planes taking off from Bradley International.

Essex and the Connecticut River Valley

A visit to charming, picturesque Essex is like a trip to the past. Stroll down tree-lined Main Street, and you'll see gracious old colonial homes where sea captains and shipbuilders once lived with their families. Once an important shipbuilding town, Essex is where America's first warship, the *Oliver Cromwell*, was built.

Stand at the lower reaches of the Connecticut River, and you can almost picture an old side-wheeler riverboat churning up the river on its voyage from New York to Hartford. Although schooners have been replaced by pleasure craft and riverboats have given way to automobiles, it's possible for visitors to get a taste of the river's glory days. You can even take a ride on the authentic riverboat. Combine your cruise with a steam-train ride, and you'll get a delightful tour of the Connecticut River Valley, albeit the 20th-century version. For more river lore, visit the River Museum. And, for something completely different, tour the fantasy castle-turned-state park or the museum that's positively nutty.

Steam Train and Riverboat

Valley Railroad Co. (Exit 3 off Rte. 9), Essex; (203) 767-0103. Schedules change depending on season; check locally for exact departure times. Every train connects with the riverboat except the last train of the day. No boat service with Christmas train rides. Adults, $12.95 (train only, $7.95); 2–11, $5.95 (train only, $3.95). Additional fare of $1.95 per person for parlor-car rides.

"All aboar-r-d-d!" There's something magical about a train ride. Kids find it exciting—with smoke billowing and whistles blasting—while adults find it relaxing. This attraction combines a steam-train ride from Essex to Chester with a riverboat cruise; the whole trip lasts about 2.5 hours. The scenery is beautiful, and includes rolling hills, flowering meadows, and local attractions such as Gillette Castle and the Goodspeed Opera House. Bring a picnic to enjoy on the riverboat if you wish. Off-season, visit in fall for an unforgettable view of autumn foliage. Or come at Christmastime, when you'll share the train with Santa, Mrs. Claus, and their elves.

River Museum

Main St., Essex; (203) 767-8269. Apr.–Dec., Tues.–Sun., 10–5; Jan.–Mar., weekends only, 1–4. Adults, $2.50; under 12, free.

At the foot of Main Street in Essex, where the old steamboat dock has been restored, you'll find a full-size replica of America's first submarine. Constructed in 1775, *American Turtle* was clumsy and ineffective against the British. Still, it's interesting to look at. The River Museum also houses ship models, instruments, and shipbuilding displays.

Gillette Castle State Park

Rte. 82, East Haddam; (203) 526-2336. Castle: Memorial Day–Columbus Day, daily, 10–5. Park: daily, 8–dusk. Adults, $1; 6–11, 50¢.

Your kids may not know who actor William Gillette is, but it doesn't matter—they'll find his 24-room fantasy castle quite intriguing. Gillette, known for his role as Sherlock Holmes, was a rather eccentric character himself, and the house is full of creative mechanical touches. It's also full of cat artifacts; Gillette shared the castle with 15 felines during his residence from 1919 to 1937. After his death, the estate became a state park. Picnicking, hiking, and camping are available.

Goodspeed Opera House

Rte. 82, East Haddam; (203) 873-8668. Tours offered on Mon., mid-July through mid-Oct. Adults, $1; under 12, 50¢.

This wonderful Victorian "gingerbread" structure was a popular riverside theater from the late 1800s to the 1920s. Nearly demolished in the 1950s this unique landmark was rescued, restored, and now features musical theater productions. Take a behind-the-scenes tour of the opera house or take in a show. Older children who enjoy the performing arts will find a visit to the Goodspeed a real treat.

Down on the Farm

Banner Rd. and Rte. 149, Moodus; (203) 873-9905. July–mid-Jan., Tues.–Sun., 11–5; rest of year, Thurs.–Sun.

See glass blowing, candlemaking, woodworking, and other skills demonstrated at this craft center, located in a former chicken farm. Not recommended for toddlers or young children (there are lots of breakable items), but older kids will love watching the glass blowers at work. Numerous items are available for sale.

□ Special note:

While in Moodus, listen for the "Moodus Noises." These strange, subterranean rumblings have been variously explained as the threats of evil spirits (according to Indian legend), witches in the mountain (according to early white settlers), and emanations from pearls (according to a British scientist, who disappeared while researching the subject). Modern scientists believe the sounds are caused by movement along intersecting fractures in the earth's crust.

Nut Museum
303 Ferry Rd., Old Lyme; (203) 434-7636. May–Nov., Wed., Sat., Sun., 2–5. Admission, $2 plus one nut, any variety.
This museum is nuts—literally. Proprietor Elizabeth Tashjian pays homage to the noble nut with her collection of nut-themed artifacts and art objects. Laugh if you will, but Tashjian has appeared on the "Tonight Show." Only in America.

Fruit Picking
Rtes. 147 and 157, Middlefield; (203) 349-1566. Store open daily, 9–6.
At Lyman Orchards, pick your own sweet corn, raspberries, tomatoes, squash, pumpkins, apples, peaches, and strawberries in season. The farm store offers produce and baked goods, as well as special events scheduled on certain weekends in summer and fall.

Bicycling
Rentals are available at Sew 'n' So in Essex; (203) 767-8188.

Hammonasset Beach State Park
Exit 62 South off I-95, Madison; (203) 245-2785.
A two-mile stretch of white, sandy beach is the main attraction at this popular recreation area. Swim in Long Island Sound, try your luck at fishing, or hike along marked trails through salt marsh areas. Picnicking and snack bar available.

Rocky Neck State Park
Rte. 156, Niantic; (203) 739-5741.
This resort has a .75-mile long, gently sloping beach with swimming and fishing in Long Island Sound. Boardwalk; lifeguards posted.

Devil's Hopyard State Park
Rte. 82, East Haddam; (203) 873-8566.
This scenic area offers 15 miles of hiking trails—one steep side, one gentler side. Hike along the stream to Chapman Falls, a 60-foot cascade. Fishing is

permitted in the stream, stocked with trout. Legend has it that the devil lived here; perhaps he has a taste for beer?

Chatfield Hollow State Park
Exit 63 off I-95 (.5 miles west of Killingworth Center on Rte. 80), Killingworth; (203) 663-2030.
An old waterwheel, a covered bridge, a pond, a brook, and red pine groves make this a truly exceptional park. Swim in Schreeder Pond, walk the nature trail along the brook, or hike the well-marked trails. (A 4.5-mile loop passes points of interest.) The pond is stocked with trout. The park is part of Cockaponset State Forest, where you'll find additional hiking trails, cross-country skiing, and snowmobiling in winter.

Hurd State Park
Rte. 151, East Hampton; (203) 566-2304.
Located on the east bank of the Connecticut River, this park features several hiking trails—some through the woods, some along the river, and some to high points with scenic views. Features fishing in the Connecticut River, cross-country skiing in winter.

Boat Cruises
In addition to the riverboat ride previously described, other cruises are available. Choose a 1.5-hour trip to Essex Harbor or a two-hour trip around Long Island Sound, departing from the Dock Restaurant pier at Saybrook Point. One-hour sunset cruises also offered. Deep River Navigation Company, River St., Deep River; (203) 526-4954. May–Labor Day.

Cruise from Haddam to the ports of Sag Harbor and Greenport, N.Y. (across Long Island Sound). Explore for three hours, then return to Haddam. Evening music cruises also offered. New England Steamboat Lines, Marine Park, Haddam; (203) 345-4507. July–Labor Day.

Restaurants

Many of the restaurants in this area are found in fine country inns. Your best bet is to go into Old Saybrook, where you'll find fast-food chains and the family restaurants listed below.

Pat's Kountry Kitchen
Corner of Mill Rd. and Rte. 154, Old Saybrook; (203) 388-4784. Mon.–Sat., 6–9; Sun., 6–12:30.

There's a little bit of everything on the menu, including steaks, Italian dishes, seafood, soups, and sandwiches. Pat's is a good, quick place for breakfast, too. Children's lunch and dinner menu features the usual hamburgers, hotdogs, and grilled cheese ($3.50). Casual table and booth seating. For the best deal, try one of the daily lunch or dinner specials.

O'Brannigan's
Saybrook Junction Marketplace, Rte. 154, Old Saybrook; (203) 388-6611. Mon.–Thurs., 11:30–9; Fri.–Sat. 'til 10. Sun., brunch, 10:30–2:30; dinner, 3–9.
You'll find a complete menu of steaks, seafood, chicken, salads, and sandwiches in this restaurant, located at Saybrook Junction Marketplace. Children's menu runs from $1.95 to $2.95 and features the usual favorites, as well as a hefty plate of ravioli. Special kids' sundaes for dessert. Best-selling entrées are the barbecued ribs and steaks.

Dock & Dine
Old Saybrook Point; (203) 388-4665. Sun. brunch, 11–2. Adults, $10.95; under 12, $6.95.
The ocean view from the Dock & Dine dining room can't be beat. For a special treat, attend the locally-famous Sunday brunch and feast on Belgian waffles topped with fresh strawberries or omelettes to order. The brunch spread includes a host of breakfast items, lots of homemade breads and salads, crepes, and meat dishes. The restaurant welcomes families, but suggests you call for reservations.

New Haven

The next time you lick a lollipop, fish with a steel fishhook, or pop open a bottle with a corkscrew, thank the folks of New Haven. Those items were invented here, along with the first steamboat and rubber footwear. The city also takes credit for creating the sport of football (dreamed up by a Yale rugby coach) and Frisbee throwing (inspired by Yalies tossing their pie plates into the air.) Of course, New Haven residents have a couple of other reasons to boast. The most obvious is Yale University, one of the country's oldest and most respected colleges. Yale's outstanding museums are not to be missed, especially the Peabody Museum of National History.

New Haven is also a center for regional theater, the most famous being the Yale Repertory Theater where many top-flight actors have honed their skills, and the Long Wharf Theater, birthplace of several Broadway plays. Whether you're in town for museum hopping, theater going, or attending a Harvard-Yale game, you'll realize that New Haven is a college town—and more.

Don't forget your lollipop.

Peabody Museum of National History
170 Whitney Ave.; (203) 432-5050. Mon.–Sat., 9–4:45; Sun. and holidays, 11–4:45. Adults, $2; 5–15, $1. Free on Tues.
You don't have to know a pterodactyl from a triceratops to be impressed by this museum. A massive mural provides a dramatic backdrop for life-size prehistoric creatures in the Hall of Dinosaurs. Youngsters will be amazed— and delighted—by the sight of a 65-foot brontosaurus skeleton. Elsewhere the natural history of our planet is traced through mineralogy, meteorites, and zoology. The Peabody is one of the best museums of its kind in the country.

Yale Collection of Musical Instruments
15 Hullhouse Ave.; (203) 436-4935. Mon.–Wed., 1–4; Sun., 2–5 when Yale University is in session. Free.
Budding musicians will be inspired by this collection of 850 exquisite instruments, some dating back to the 16th century. Included are historical violins, harpsichords, and woodwinds, with Western and non-Western pieces on display. Concerts are presented periodically; call in advance for dates. The building is located on Hullhouse Avenue, the street described by Charles Dickens as the most beautiful in America.

New Haven Colony Historical Society
114 Whitney Ave.; (203) 562-4183. Tues.–Fri., 10–5; Sat.–Sun., 2–5. Free.
Local antiques are the focus here, including beloved playthings of New Haven children who lived 300 years ago. In addition to the antique dolls and toys, older children will enjoy seeing the photographs of old New Haven and comparing them to the city of today. Other noteworthy items: Eli Whitney's cotton gin and the sign from Benedict Arnold's drugstore on Chapel Street.

Shore Line Trolley Museum
17 River Rd. (Exit 51 East from I-95), East Haven; (203) 467-6927.
Memorial Day–Labor Day, daily, 11–5; May and Sept., weekends only; Apr.
and Nov., Sun. only; Adults, $3.50; 2–11, $1.50.
Guaranteed kid-appeal here, where the highlight is a three-mile ride on a
vintage 1911 trolley car. Adults will get a chuckle out of the old advertising
slicks posted in the cars. More than 100 trolley cars are on view—many
antique—from the U.S. and Canada. Bring a picnic.

Connecticut Children's Museum
567 State St.; (203) 562-5437. Year-round, hours vary according to school
vacations. Call in advance for hours and location; the museum may be
moving. Admission, $2.
This delightful museum is set up like a little village where kids can indulge
in imaginative role-playing. There's a hospital, a grocery store, a school, a
restaurant, and more, each equipped with plenty of props and dress-up
clothing. Parents won't feel silly joining in—in fact, the museum staff
encourages it. Young visitors will learn by doing, and have lots of fun in the
process. Recommended age range is toddler to age seven.

Grove Street Cemetery
227 Grove St. (between Prospect and Ashmun Streets). Gates close at 4.
Visit the gravesites of Eli Whitney, Charles Goodyear, Noah Webster, and
other historical figures here. The graveyard, established in 1796, is a good
place to try your hand at grave rubbing.

East Rock Park
East Park Rd. (Willow St. Exit off I-91); (203) 787-8142.
The best part of this park is its height—drive up and you'll get an aerial
view of the city, the harbor, and Long Island Sound. You'll also find an
arboretum, a rose garden, and nature trails. Picnicking, too.

West Rock Park/West Rock Nature Center
Wintergreen Ave.; (203) 787-8016. West Rock Park: daily, 9–sunset. Free.
Nature Center: Mon.–Sat., 9–4:15; Sun., noon–4:15. Free.
Lots of family fun here, including Judges Cave, hiking trails, and a small
zoo with native animals. West Rock Park surrounds West Rock, which is
428 feet high. The summit is reachable by hiking, biking, or car. Along the
ridge you'll enjoy excellent views of New Haven harbor and Long Island
Sound. The West Rock Nature Center has displays of birds, insects,

: animals. The center is surrounded by 40 acres of
re trails, ponds, and meadows.

Park

, (203) 787-8016. Memorial Day–Labor Day.
k and beach have a special attraction: a turn-of-the-
century carouse. ou'll also find playground equipment, picnic tables, and
lots of happy kids splashing in the ocean.

Fort Nathan Hale
Woodward Ave. (Exit 50 off I-95 North); (203) 787-8790.
This reconstructed civilian fort gives kids a chance to play soldier with
reasonable authenticity. Located on the eastern shore of New Haven harbor,
the Fort has bunkers, gun emplacements, breastworks—even a Civil War-
era drawbridge that really works. Young patriots will have a great time
defending the fort against British warships.

Boat Cruises
If you want to see the area by sea, you have several options. Take a one-
hour tour of New Haven harbor or venture into Long Island Sound on a
longer trip. Cruises depart from Long Wharf Dock, New Haven; moonlight
cruises (live bands and dancing) are also available. Contact Liberty Belle
Cruise Lines (Long Wharf Dock, Exit 46 off I-95; (203) 562-4163). You can
also take a 40-minute narrated cruise among the 27 tiny Thimble Islands in
Long Island Sound. Depart from Stony Creek Dock in Branford. Call Vol-
singa III Cruises, (203) 481-4841.

Sleeping Giant State Park
Rte. 10, Hamden; (203) 566-2304.
Two miles of mountaintop form the outline of a "sleeping giant" along the
skyline. The park is a popular hiking area, with a 25-mile network of nature
trails. A 1.5 mile trail leads to a stone lookout tower on the peak of Mount
Carmel, offering great views of Long Island Sound. Rock climbing and
stream fishing, too.

Wharton Brook State Park
Rte. 5 (2 miles south of Wallingford); (203) 566-2304.
Quiet and peaceful, this park is a pleasant out-of-the-city escape. Fish,
swim, or enjoy a picnic here in relative solitude. Ice skating in winter.

Restaurants

Louis' Lunch
263 Crown St. (3 miles downtown from I-95); (203) 562-5507. Sept.–July, Mon.–Fri., noon–4; closed Aug.
Burger lovers in your group? Take them to the place where America's first hamburger patty was slapped on a bun in 1898 (the original broilers are still in use). Children's menu, too. Louis' also serves breakfast. Located in the theater district.

Chuck's
341 Whalley Ave.; (203) 776-6851. Daily, 6–8.
This Jewish deli is a favorite local spot for breakfast, lunch, or a low-key dinner. Chuck's specialty is a three-egg omelet stuffed with lox, onions, and cream cheese, with crispy home fries on the side. While that may not appeal to the youngsters in your party, the potato pancakes or cheese blintzes probably will.

Litchfield Hills Area

The village of Litchfield could be a movie set entitled "Quaint 18th-Century New England Town." It has the requisite white clapboard homes, a town green, and even some celebrities (albeit non-living ones): Ethan Allen, Harriet Beecher Stowe, and Aaron Burr's brother-in-law, Judge Tapping Deeve, who founded the country's first law school here.

If your children consider the excitement of a picturesque colonial village on par with a trip to a plumbing supply store, not to worry. The surrounding area is rich with possibilities for family fun. Northwestern Connecticut is studded with state parks where you can camp, fish, hike, swim, ride horseback, and picnic. Round out your visit with a museum, take in the action at Lime Rock race track, and stop at a local picking farm to load up on fresh produce.

White Memorial Foundation
Rte. 202 (just west of Litchfield); (203) 567-0015. Conservation Center

In most of New England's state parks, hiking trails become cross-country ski trails when the snow falls.

open Tues.–Sat., 9–5; Sun., 11–5. Adults, $1; 6–12, 50¢. Sanctuary open all year.

This 4,000-acre wildlife sanctuary, including half the shoreline of Bantam Lake and the Bantam River, features 35 miles of hiking trails. Take a guided tour or set your own pace, with time out for a picnic along the way. Bantam Lake is great for swimming, or rent a rowboat or canoe at Point Folly Marine. Be sure to visit the Conservation Center near the entrance. It has lots of kid-appeal, including a working beehive, an aquarium with turtles, and snakes, fish, stuffed hawks, and owls on display.

American Indian Archaeological Institute

Rte. 199 (Rte. 47 junction), Washington; (203) 868-0518. Mon.–Sat., 10–5; Sun., noon–5. Adults, $2; 6–18, $1.

If your children harbor any Western-movie notions about Native Americans, this museum will open their eyes. Local Indian history is illustrated through a collection of artifacts spanning 12,000 years. Most appealing to kids is a recreated Onondaga Indian long-house, filled with household objects and appearing as though the family will return home any minute. Dinosaur lovers will delight in the mastodon skeleton, unearthed in nearby Farmington. Walk along an Indian trail, visit a woodland encampment, and view a simulated archaeological site.

Lime Rock Park
Rte. 112, Lakeville; (203) 435-2571. Racing on most weekends, early May–early Oct. Call for schedule. Rates vary, $10 and up for adults; 12 and under, free.
If your kids love fast cars, lots of noise, and action, head to the track. Pro national and regional racing is held here. If you're bringing a small child, consider a regional race; they're shorter (30 minutes as opposed to 2.5 hours) and less crowded than other spectator events. Spectators are also welcome at Tuesday practice sessions. Your ticket entitles you to a walk around the paddock area, where drivers and crews are at work on their cars. You might even see Paul Newman or Tom Cruise.

Kent Falls State Park
Rte. 7, Kent; (203) 927-3029.
The most striking feature here is a 200-foot waterfall, a perfect setting for a picnic. Hiking trails, too.

Macedonia Brook State Park
Rte. 341, Kent; (203) 927-4100.
Beautiful and wild, this park is blessed with forests, mountainous terrain, a deep gorge, upper and lower falls, wildlife, and, of course, a brook. Great view of the Catskill and Taconic mountain ranges. Plenty of hiking trails, color-coded, including some along the Appalachian Trail. Fishing; cross-country skiing in winter.

Peoples State Forest
East River Rd., Barkhamsted; (203) 379-2469.
Great hiking here, with trails leading past caves and springs. Drop a line into the trout-stocked Farmington River, or look for beavers dam building in the marsh. Stop for a picnic among the 200-year-old white pines in Mathies Grove. Cross-country skiing in winter.

Black Rock State Park
Rte. 6 (north of Watertown); (203) 566-2304.
Here you can hike the scenic western highlands to Black Rock Pond, the park's focal point. Try your luck fishing for bass or rainbow trout, or go for

a dip in the pond. This is also a popular spot for collecting arrowheads. Cross-country skiing and ice skating are permitted in winter.

Burr Pond State Park
Rte. 8 (5 miles north of Torrington); (203) 566-2304.
Features here include trout-stocked Burr pond, a sandy beach, streams, rivers, and interesting rock formations. Swimming, boating, and fishing are permitted. A scenic path encircles the 88-acre pond. Easy cross-country skiing and ice skating in winter.

Topsmead State Forest
Rte. 118 (2 miles west of Rte. 8), Litchfield; (203) 567-5694.
The principal attraction here is an English Tudor-style cottage, the summer home of Edith Morton Chase. Miss Chase donated the 514-acre forest to the state of Connecticut upon her death in 1972. The cottage is open to visitors during the summer; call first to confirm schedule. The grounds include a 40-acre wildflower preserve and nature trail. Have a picnic at one of the tables, or spread a blanket wherever you choose. Cross-country skiing and snowshoeing in winter.

Haystack Mountain
Rte. 272 (1 mile north of Norfolk); (203) 566-2304.
Drive halfway up the mountain and enjoy the view, especially lovely during fall foliage season. From there, active types can hike the half-mile trail to the top of the mountain. At the summit, you'll see a 34-foot-high stone tower; climb it for dramatic vistas of Long Island Sound and the Berkshires.

Housatonic Meadows State Park
Rte. 7 (1 mile north of Cornwall Bridge), Sharon; (203) 566-2304.
If your group enjoys fly-fishing, the clear, cold Housatonic River is a great place to test your skills on trout and bass. A two-mile stretch of river is limited to fly-fishing. Enjoy a picnic under the tall pines on the riverbank. Hiking and canoeing, too.

Kent Falls
Rte. 7 (3 miles north of Kent).
This cascading waterfall draws thousands of visitors each year. Climb the stairs adjacent to the falls for great views at all levels. This is a favorite scene for professional and amateur photographers.

Lake Waramaug State Park
Lake Waramaug Rd. (Rte. 478) (5 miles north of New Preston), Kent; (203) 566-2304.
Picturesque, placid Lake Waramaug is a beautiful setting for a day or weekend of swimming, fishing, hiking, and picnicking. Ice skating in winter.

Mohawk Mountain State Park and Forest
Rte. 4, Cornwall; (203) 566-2304. Ski area, (203) 672-6100.
In summer or, even better, during peak fall color, drive to the mountaintop for enchanting views. An abandoned fire tower serves as a lookout. Plenty of hiking opportunities throughout the forest, with several loop trails and a section of the Appalachian Trail. Don't miss Black Spruce Bog, near forest headquarters, home of a unique community of insect-eating plants. Pond and stream fishing too. In winter, this is an active winter sports area. Cross-country ski on forest roads and trails, or join the downhill skiers at Mohawk Mountain ski area, a popular local resort.

Restaurants

Litchfield Food Company
West St. (across from Village Green), Litchfield; (203) 567-0448. Mon.–Sat., 9:30–5:30.
There are plenty of picturesque spots to enjoy a picnic in the Litchfield area, and this is a great place to pack your basket. You can select from a wide variety of gourmet take-out food. Not your ordinary fast-food picnic fare—instead, spread your blanket, open the basket, and feast on smoked salmon with capers, artichoke salad, duck à l'orange, and chocolate mousse balls. There are salads, pasta dishes, sandwiches, and soups to choose from.

Jonathan's
Rte. 47, Washington Depot; (203) 868-0509. Daily, 11:30–10:00; closed Wed. in winter.
Kids get first-class treatment at this casual family restaurant. The menu changes daily for children, as well as adults, making the most of seasonal fruits, vegetables, and fresh fish. The children's menu (under $5) might include roast turkey, a fresh fish dish, Jonathan's buffalo wings, grilled cheese, or a mini-steak. The adult's menu includes lots of fish dishes,

chicken, veal, and steaks. On nice days, sit outside on the deck and enjoy a view of the Shepaug River and surrounding countryside.

Deer Island Gate Restaurant
Rte. 209 (on Bantam Lake), Morris; (203) 567-0913. Wed.–Sat., 5–10; Sun. buffet, 1–7.
This is a large, casual restaurant with great views of Bantam Lake. The menu is ambitious, offering daily fish specials, steaks, pork, duck, chicken, lamb, and German dishes. Entrées range from about $10 to $19. There's no special children's menu, but they're happy to offer half-portions of most entrées for half price. Local folks love the Sunday German buffet.

Rhode Island

Providence Area

You might be tempted to pass by the Providence area, in a hurry to get to the more famous Rhode Island resorts of Newport, Narragansett, or Block Island. Yet this quiet, urban pocket, noted recently as one of the 10 best American cities to live in, has much to offer families. The biggest city in the smallest state boasts a revitalized downtown area with landscaped parks and waterfront brick walkways that are perfect for strolling along. Window shop along South Main Street, where historic colonial buildings have been authentically restored and now house unique boutiques, art galleries, and restaurants; visit the animals at the Roger Williams Park and Zoo; or let the kids run loose at the nearby Children's Museum.

Roger Williams Park and Zoo
Elmwood Ave. (off Interstate 95), Providence; (401) 785-9450. Zoo: May–Labor Day, daily, 10–5; winter, 10–4. Museum: Tues.–Fri., 10–4; Sat. and Sun., noon–5. Greenhouse: Sun.–Sat., 11–4. Adults, $2; under 12, $1. Park closes at 9 daily.

It's easy to spend a pleasant, busy day exploring this wonderland of parks, ponds, lakes, and winding waterways that cover more than 430 acres. But this isn't just a nature tour; there's plenty to do and see here. Start with the zoo, where you'll see polar bears, sea lions, zebras, llamas, and wolves, plus a host of exotic birds. The younger children will like the farmyard area and the miniature horses. At the Nature Center, you'll learn how animals and plants adapt to their environments as you view a series of exhibits, including a working beehive. The third oldest in the country, the zoo maintains its reputation as one of the best in New England.

Don't go home yet—there's lots more to see here. Rent a boat at the Dalrymple Boathouse and explore the park's connecting waterways. Visit the Natural History Museum and Planetarium; stroll through the

Miniature horses are a big hit at Roger Williams Park Zoo in downtown Providence.

greenhouse and gardens; catch the brass ring at the Park's carousel; or sit along the banks of Roosevelt Lake and listen to an outdoor concert.

The Children's Museum of Rhode Island

Pitcher-Goff Mansion, 58 Walcott St., Pawtucket; (401) 726-2590. Oct.–June, Sun.–Thurs., 1–5; Fri.–Sat., 10–5. July–Sept., Tues.–Sat., 10–5; Sun., 1–5. $2.50 per person; under 1, free.

This warm, lively museum, housed in a 19th-century Victorian mansion in nearby Pawtucket, is a place where children can touch, smell, draw, paint, explore, bounce, read, imagine, and learn. Join others for a make-believe tea party in Great Grandmother's kitchen; play hide-and-seek in a climbing maze of tunnels and platforms; or try your wits at the jigsaws in the Great Puzzle Room. The museum features a variety of hands-on, fun exhibits for the kid in all of us.

Slater Mill Historic Site

Roosevelt Ave., Pawtucket; (401) 725-8638. June–Labor Day, Tues.–Sat., 10–5; Sun., 1–5. March–May and Labor Day–Dec., Sat.–Sun. only, 1–5. Adults, $3; 6–14, $2.

Housed in a 19th-century Victorian mansion, the Children's Museum of Rhode Island offers plenty of hands-on activity.

This site is for older children who like the sounds of and are intrigued by the mechanisms of machinery. Billed as the birthplace of American industry, the site includes the Sylvanus Brown House (1758), an early skilled worker's home; the Wilkinson Mill (1810), which houses an authentic mid-19th-century machine shop; and a working, 16,000-pound waterwheel. The 90-minute tour includes demonstrations of early textile machinery, hand-spinning, and weaving.

Restaurants

The Arcade
65 Weybosset St., Providence. Mon.–Sat., 10–6; Thurs. 'til 8.
Located smack in downtown Providence, the Arcade (1828) was the first enclosed shopping center in the U.S. Inside you'll find a collection of eateries, offering everything from soup (Jen's Great Soups) to nuts (J. Phib's Candy and Gourmet Ice Cream). Whether your bunch likes Greek food, pizza, Chinese food, or burgers, you'll find it here. Find a table at Center Court and enjoy. Warning: Avoid weekday lunch hours. When the local business crowd rolls in, the Arcade gets mobbed.

Angelo's Civita Farnese
141 Atwells Ave., Providence; (401) 621-8171. Mon.–Sat., 11–8:30.
This comfortable family restaurant is located in the heart of "Little Italy." All your favorite pasta dishes are on the menu, available in half-size portions for kids. (That may not be necessary if you have a small child—regular portions are huge enough to share.) Mangia, mangia!

Worth a Trip

Southwick's Animal Farm
9 Southwick St. (off Rte. 16), Mendon, MA; (508) 883-9182. May–Sept., daily, 10–5. Limited hours, Apr. and Oct. Adults, $15.95; 3–15, $4.95.
Southwick's Wild Animal Farm, in the middle of 300 acres of quiet countryside, is home to New England's largest zoo. You'll see more than 500 animals, including giraffes, giant tortoises, lions, tigers, camels, zebras, monkeys, and more—100 species in all. Kids can feed and touch llamas,

deer, and other barnyard animals in the petting area; ride an elephant or pony on a safari; watch a circus performance; or learn all about animals at the Noah's Ark'ademy. If that's not enough to delight family members, there's a small collection of kiddie rides and a playground. Bring a picnic (there are refreshment stands, too) and make a fun-filled day of it.

Newport

America's First Resort.
Millionaire's Playground.
Queen of American Resorts.
The Yachting Capital of the World.

Visit Newport, and you'll soon understand why this island seaport town has been bequeathed with so many superlative titles. The city echoes its past: first as a 17th-century colonial town of merchants and traders; later as the summer resort of America's richest society members. You'll find the narrow streets surrounding its harbors to be lined with clapboard houses that were once home to sea captains and traders. You'll also see magnificent Gilded Age mansions hugging the shoreline, extravagant summer homes for the wealthy American aristocracy during the Industrial period.

Newport remains a prestigious East Coast resort—opulent sailing yachts and powerboats dot its harbors. The 17th-century mercantile harbor has turned into a contemporary center of fine restaurants, boutiques, and out-door cafes. The beauty of the island, with its dramatic views of Narragansett Bay and the Atlantic Ocean, remains.

Summer here is crowded and congested—great for people-watching, but you'll want to find time to venture beyond the town center. Tour one of the mansions, by all means, but take a drive to Fort Adams Park for a picnic, take a boat or sailing cruise, or walk the sand dunes at Second Beach for a pretty (and relaxing) view of this elegant coastal community.

Newport Mansions
Plan on seeing only one or two mansions. Children will quickly tire of the hour-long tours and the inevitable summer crowds that flock to see how the

Newport, the yachting capital of the world, has lots of places where young sailors can test their skills.

Vanderbilts, Belmonts, and Berwinds lived. You'll enjoy the tours most with older children (eight years and up), but if you're taking an infant or toddler, be prepared to carry them—most mansions are not stroller-accessible. Ten mansions are opened to the public. Here are three that families will enjoy the most:

□ The Breakers
Ochre Point Ave.; (401) 847-1000. May–Oct., daily, 10–5. Adults, $5.50; 6–11, $3.
The Breakers, built for Cornelius Vanderbilt, is the most palatial of the mansions. You'll marvel at this 70-room castle of marble, mosaics, alabaster, and mahogany. Included is a music room that was built in Europe and reconstructed here, a billiards room, a library, bathrooms that deliver both saltwater and fresh water, a magnificent double loggia with commanding ocean views, and a glittery, opulent dining room.

□ The Beechwood
Bellevue Ave.; (401) 846-3772. Late May–Oct., daily, 10–5. Adults, $5.25; 6–12, $4.

Children will enjoy the Beechwood. Instead of roped-off displays and historical tour guides, you'll be greeted by the Astors' staff of servants, who will show you around the house. You are the Astors' guests for their 10th anniversary ball. The Beechwood Theater Company re-enacts how life would have been at the Beechwood in the summer of 1891. If your children love make-believe (and what kids don't) you'll have fun here.

□ Hammersmith Farm
Ocean Dr. (adjacent to Fort Adams State Park); (401) 846-7346. Apr.–mid-Nov., daily, 10–5. Memorial Day–Labor Day, daily, 10–7. Adults, $5; 6–12, $2.
Hammersmith Farm, the Auchincloss family's summer cottage, is the only working farm left in Newport. The informal tour provides personal glimpses into the Kennedy family. When John Kennedy was in office, Hammersmith was often referred to as the "Summer White House." Its seaside location and gardens are beautiful, and the children will love visiting the miniature horses that graze in the fields. Consider combining a tour of Hammersmith Farm with a Viking Queen cruise. The hour-long narrated cruise goes through the harbor and bay to the private dock at Hammersmith. It's a nice water view of the yachting capital of the world, and a rather elegant way to arrive at Hammersmith.

Cliff Walk
Put the babies in the backpack and hold on to your toddler's hand for this dramatic walk overlooking the Atlantic Ocean. On this steep, picturesque walk, you'll see the rocky coastline at its best and pass by some of the Newport mansions. The three-mile trail runs from Memorial Boulevard and Eustis Avenue to Bailey's Beach. Walk it all or just part of it.

Fort Adams State Park
Ocean Dr.; (401) 847-2400. Year-round, 6–11. Free.
Built in 1824, the Fort was designed to accommodate 2,400 soldiers with 468 mounted cannons. It is not open for public viewing, but its park remains a great place for a picnic. The park has a small beach, fishing pier, barbecues, and picnic tables. Lots of room here for kids to run and play while you savor the oceanside setting.

The International Tennis Hall of Fame
194 Bellevue Ave.; (401) 846-4567. Apr.–Nov., daily, 10–5. Dec.–Mar., daily, 11–4. Adults, $4; 6–18, $2.

Tennis buffs will not want to miss this. Housed in the Newport Casino Building, it's billed as the birthplace of U.S. tennis tournaments. There are exhibits and displays of trophies, fashions, and equipment. Old Davis Cup films are shown in the 450-seat theater. It also boasts the only grass courts in the country open to the public.

Green Animals Topiary Gardens
Cory's Lane (off Rte. 114), Portsmouth; (401) 847-1000. May–Oct., daily, 10–5; Nov.–Apr., Sat.–Sun., 10–4. Adults, $5.50; 6–11, $2.50.
This maze of fun-loving, sculptured geometric figures and animal shapes is sure to delight young children and amaze adults. The gardens contain nearly 80 plant sculptures that have been lovingly pruned and shaped. The gardens are located in nearby Portsmouth. Drive yourself or take the Old Colony and Newport Railway, a 1930s train, from downtown Newport.

Sailing
Fort Adams State Park, Ocean Dr.; (401) 849-8385.
If you'd like to see Newport from the waterside, you can rent a sailboat from Newport Sailing Association. Sailboats, from 6 to 24 feet, are available by the hour or half day. Call ahead to reserve one during the busy summer weekends and for rate information.

□ Viking Queen
Goat Island Dock; (401) 847-6921. May–Oct., daily. Adults, $5; 12–16, $4; 5–11, $2. Call ahead for cruise times.
On a larger scale, the *Viking Queen* offers harbor and bay cruises.

Old Colony and Newport Railway
America's Cup Ave. (across from the Gateway). May–June and mid-Sept.–Dec., Sun., 1:30; July–Labor Day, daily, 1:30. Adults, $6; 14–17, $4; 2–14, $3; families, $15.
Board a vintage 1930's railway car for this eight-mile scenic trip to Portsmouth. The two-hour round trip includes a stopover at the Green Animals Topiary Gardens.

Norman Bird Sanctuary and Museum
583 Third Beach Rd., Middletown; (401) 846-2577. Year-round, daily, 9–5. Trail use: adults, $2; under 12, free. Museum is free.
This 450-acre refuge is a wonderful outdoors spot for families. Be sure to walk Hanging Rock Trail. This mile-long, gently sloping hike will take you to a dramatic rock formation overlooking the ocean. Before leaving the

sanctuary, stop in at the museum housed on the second floor of the large barn. You'll see lots of specimens of local birds and animals mounted on the walls, with explanations of their habitats and habits. Kids can crawl into the authentically-reconstructed New England wigwam made of bark.

Prescott Farm
West Main St. (off Rte. 114), Middletown; (401) 847-6230. Apr.–Dec., daily, 10–4.
At this historic site, Americans captured a British general in 1777. Today there's a collection of early colonial buildings here, including a general store, windmill, and guard house. The favorite part for most children is feeding the farm's ducks and goats and running around the pond and through the orchard.

Beaches
Kids might find that the best thing to do in Newport is to head for one of its sandy beaches. Besides swimming at Fort Adams State Park, you can ride the waves (or just dunk your toes) at First Beach (Memorial Boulevard, which runs from the Cliff Walk to Middletown), the three-mile long, sandy Second Beach (Sachuest Point Area in Middletown), and Third Beach (Sachuest Point Area on Sakonnet River).

Restaurants

Inn at Castle Hill
Ocean Dr.; (401) 849-3800.
If it's a sunny Sunday afternoon, don't miss the barbecue at this ocean bluff restaurant. It has the best view of any restaurant in town—a panorama of Narragansett Bay, Newport Harbor, and the Atlantic Ocean. You can sit on the grassy hill overlooking the water while listening to a live jazz band and awaiting barbecued chicken, hamburgers, and other favorites. Or children can feast on picnic food on the lawn while you dine on fresh fish delicacies at the more upscale dining rooms inside the Inn or outside on the terrace.

Newport Creamery
208 West Main St., 49 Long Wharf Mall, and 181 Bellevue Ave.; (401) 846-6332. Sun.–Thurs., 7–10; Fri.–Sat., 7–11.

This chain, located throughout the Newport area, is fine for a quick, inexpensive bite to eat. Best known for ice cream, these casual restaurants also offer sandwiches, hot dogs, and salads.

Bannister's Wharf

In the heart of downtown Newport, you'll find lively Bannister's Wharf. Sit outside under colorful umbrellas and order oysters on the half-shell, lobster rolls, fresh shrimp cocktail, or a bowl of chowder. You can get sandwiches, salads, hors d'oeuvres, and desserts from the outdoor cafés while you watch the harbor activity.

South County Beaches

From Narragansett Pier to Watch Hill, the southwestern coastline of Rhode Island is nearly one continuous stretch of beautiful white sand, offering beaches for every taste.

In South Kingstown, off Route 1, you'll find controversial Moonstone Beach, where bathing suits are optional. It's a small strip of sand for those who like to sunbathe and swim au naturel. The Charlestown Beach, at the edge of the Minigret National Wildlife Refuge, is popular with residents and visitors alike. You'll find it clean and spacious, with changing rooms, showers, and a small store for refreshments. If you'd like to get away from the ocean beach crowd, pack a picnic basket and head for the Minigret National Wildlife Refuge. You'll find peaceful walking trails to the small pond beach.

If peace and quiet are what you like in a beach, don't miss East Beach at the eastern edge of the Minigret Refuge. Considered one of the nicest beaches in the country, East Beach offers nearly three miles of white sand and lots of dunes to climb on. The kids will enjoy a walk over to Minigret Pond, where they can watch windsurfers sail the protected waters. There are no facilities at the beach, and the small parking lot fills up fast (before 9) on weekends, so get going early. Right next door to East Beach you'll find Blue Shutters Beach. (In fact, many East Beach-goers walk here for refreshments and facilities.) You'll find nearly four miles of clean sand, plus lifeguards, bathhouses, concessions, and lots of other families.

People-watchers and crowd-lovers congregate at busy Misquamicut Beach, where the air is filled with the smell of suntan lotion and the sound of boom boxes. This is a blanket-to-blanket, towel-to-towel sea of sunbathers. Kids will enjoy the food stands and activities surrounding the beach, including roller skating, mini-golf, rides, and games. In direct contrast is Watch Hill, a quiet Victorian town on the western border of the state. Watch Hill Beach is small and rarely crowded, with showers, changing rooms, and a cluster of restaurants and shops nearby. For years kids have enjoyed the beach's Flying Horse Carousel, where they try to grab the brass ring to win a free ride.

Block Island

If your description of the perfect getaway includes words like "serene" and "relaxing," and if your vision of the perfect place includes windswept dunes and sandy beaches, consider Block Island. Many visitors appreciate it most for what it doesn't have; namely, traffic, fast-food restaurants, noisy nightlife, and cutesy boutiques.

There's plenty for a family to do on Block Island. It's just that, once you arrive here, you won't feel all that compelled to rush around and do them. The pace is slow and the pleasures are simple: building sandcastles on the beach, bicycling around the seven-mile-long island, clam digging, kite flying, sailing, and fishing along the beach are popular pursuits.

The ferry ride to the island will put you in the mood, as you watch Block Island slowly appear on the horizon. Look closely to see if you can spot the buoys marking the harbor entrance as you get closer to the port. Ferries leave from Point Judith and Newport, Rhode Island; New London, Connecticut; and Montauk, New York. Even if yours accepts cars, don't bother to bring one. The only proper way to do Block Island is on a bicycle. (In bad weather it's okay to take a taxi.)

Block Island is less pretentious than other New England island resorts, as well as less expensive. It's "less" of a lot of things, which makes it more attractive to families who want a relaxing beach vacation.

How to find the best fishing spots in New England rivers and streams? Look for cars parked along the riverbanks or, even better, stop at a bait shop and get the real scoop from the proprietor.

Mohegan Bluffs

These intriguing clay cliffs are to be found at the southern-most tip of the island, off Southeast Light Road. Climb up a path (there are several) to 200 feet, and gaze out over the Atlantic. To the left you'll see Saileast Light, a beacon to seafarers since 1874. Wooden stairs will take you back down to Mohegan Bluffs beach, which is secluded but pebbly.

Block Island State Beach/Crescent Beach

Off Corn Neck Rd.; (401) 466-2611.

Located along the eastern shore of the island, both of these sandy beaches are popular with families. The beaches are long and wide, with white sand that's perfect for castle building. Lifeguards are posted at some spots; picnic tables and bathhouses are available also.

Bicycling

Pedal around this seven-mile-long, 3.5-mile-wide island, and you'll see rolling hills festooned with wildflowers, windswept sand dunes, and Victorian buildings. You may also see Great Salt Pond, where you'll find New Harbor, mainly a pleasure boat basin. Old Harbor is the commercial wharf where most of the ferries dock. At the northern tip of the island, you'll see Settler's Rock and the North Light lighthouse (no longer operating) at Sandy Point.

You'll also see numerous freshwater ponds (there are 200 ponds on Block Island) and wildlife refuge areas. Bicycles may be rented at several shops, including Esta's at Old Harbor, (401) 466-2651, and Old Harbor Bike Shop, (401) 466-2651 (children's seats available).

Boating
Sailboats are available for rent at the Block Island Club, (401) 466-5939. Rowboats are available at Twin Maples, (401) 466-5547.

Fishing
Go fishing from the beach or take out a rowboat. Bait and tackle are available at Twin Maples on Beach Avenue; (401) 466-5547.

Shellfishing
A license is required for shellfishing: Obtain one at the Block Island Police Station on the corner of Beach and Ocean avenues.

Restaurants

Finn's
Water St.; (401) 466-2473. End of April–Columbus Day, 11:30–9 or 10.
Eat indoors or outdoors at Finn's and watch the ferries docking at Old Harbor. You can order anything from a $3 sandwich to a $20 dinner here, all day, so kids can choose fun food while adults enjoy a leisurely meal. Number one kid's choice here is the fish sandwich; adults rave about Finn's baked stuffed shrimp.

Ballard's
End of Water St.; (401) 466-2231. Memorial Day–Labor Day, 11:30–11.
Craving Italian food? Indulge the urge at this waterfront restaurant located at the Ballard Inn. In addition to Italian specialties, you'll find clams, mussels, steaks, and steamed lobster—the biggest seller. The children's menu includes fried clams, fish and chips, spaghetti, and something called a "clam steak." Eat out on the deck on Ballard's private beach or in the large dining room, where there's often a band playing in the evenings. Or pull up in a boat and a waiter will come to you.

Picnicking

Want to take a picnic to the bluffs or the beach? Many delis and restaurants offer food to go. Our favorite: Humphrey's on Water Street, where you'll find a variety of sandwiches and hot foods—including good clam cakes—to take out. Call (401) 466-5155.

Tourist Information

Call or write to the following offices for detailed information on area attractions and events:

Connecticut

Department of Economic Development, 210 Washington Street, Hartford 06106.
Toll-free number: New England except Connecticut, 1-800-282-6863.
Southeastern Connecticut Tourism District, P.O. Box 89, 27 Masonic Street, New London 06320; (203) 244-2206/2357.

Maine

Maine Publicity Bureau, Inc., P.O. Box 157, Yarmouth 04096; (207) 846-0833.

Massachusetts

Massachusetts Office of Travel and Tourism, 100 Cambridge Street, Boston 02202; (617) 727-3201. Toll-free number for a Free Spirit of Massachusetts vacation kit and calendar of events: 1-800-632-8038.

For Boston:
Greater Boston Convention & Visitors Bureau, Prudential Plaza, P.O. Box 490, Boston 02199; (617) 536-4100.

For Cape Cod:
Cape Cod Chamber of Commerce, Mid-Cape Highway, Hyannis 02601; (508) 362-3225.

For Nantucket Island:
Nantucket Island Chamber of Commerce, Nantucket 02554;
   (508) 228-1700.

For the Berkshires
Berkshire Visitors Bureau, Box SG, The Common, Pittsfield 01201; (413)
   443-9186 or 1-800-237-5747.

**For the North Shore, Merrimack River Valley, and Concord and
Lexington:**
North of Boston Tourist Council, P.O. Box 3031, Peabody 01960;
   (617) 532-1449.
Northern Middlesex Convention and Visitors Bureau, 45 Palmer Street,
   Lowell 01852; (508) 937-9300.

New Hampshire

Office of Vacation Travel, P.O. Box 856, Concord 03301; (603) 271-2666.

Rhode Island

Rhode Island Tourism Department, 7 Jackson Walkway, Providence 02903;
   in-state, (401) 277-2601; outside Rhode Island, 1-800-556-2484.

Vermont

State Chamber of Commerce, Box 37, Montpelier 05602; (802) 223-3443,
   (802) 229-0154.
Vermont Travel Division, 134 State Street, Montpelier 05602;
   (802) 828-3236.

Annual Events

Connecticut

April
Connecticut Storytelling Festival, Connecticut College, New London;
(203) 447-7738.
Hockanum River Canoe Race, Vernon to East Hartford; (203) 742-6296.

May
Clown Town, Rockville; (203) 875-4322.
Artisan's Demonstration Day, Hicks-Sterns Family Museum, Tolland;
(203) 875-7552.
Webb-Deane-Stevens Museum Festival, Wethersfield; (203) 529-0612.
Lobster Fest, Mystic Seaport, Mystic; (203) 572-0711.
Return of the Pterosaurus, Dinosaur State Park, Rocky Hill;
(203) 529-8423.

June
Bluegrass Festival, Strawberry Park Campground, Preston; (203) 886-1994.
Saint Andrew Annual Feast, 515 Chapel St., New Haven; (203) 865-9846.
Bass and Catfish Tournament, Riverside Park, Hartford; (203) 293-0131.
Train and Miniature Show, 71 Hilliard St., Manchester; (203) 646-0610.
Sea Music Festival, Mystic Seaport, Mystic; (203) 572-0711.

July
Round Hill Highland Scottish Games, Norwalk; (203) 853-4228.
Riverfest, Hartford and East Hartford; (203) 728-3089.
Hartford Festival of Jazz, Bushnell Park, Hartford; (203) 280-0170;
July–Aug.
Deep River Muster/Parade of Ancient Fife & Drum Corps, Deep River;
(203) 669-8062.
Niantic Arts & Crafts Show/Lobster Fest, Niantic; (203) 739-7641.
Sail Festival, City Pier, New London; (203) 443-8331.
Blessing of the Fleet, Town Dock, Stonington; (203) 535-3150.
International Food Festival, Captain's Walk, New London; (203) 444-1879.

Antique & Classic Boat Rendezvous, Mystic Seaport, Mystic;
(203) 572-0711.
Antique Doll Show, Benton Homestead, Tolland; (203) 875-7559.
Summer Lawn Concert for Children, Hicks-Sterns Museum, Tolland;
(203) 875-7552.

August

Quinnehtukqut Rendezvous and Heritage Festival, Haddam Meadows State
Park, Haddam; (203) 282-1404.
River Front Festival, Riverside Park, Hartford; (203) 293-0131.
Country Western Jamboree, Strawberry Park Campground, Preston;
(203) 572-0711.
Outdoor Art Festival, Downtown Mystic; (203) 572-9578.
International Whaleboat Race, Mystic Seaport, Mystic; (203) 572-0711.
Summer Lawn Concert, Hicks-Sterns Museum, Tolland; (203) 875-7552.
Connecticut River Powwow and Rendezvous, Portland; (203) 487-0036.

September

Feast Fest (area restaurants' food festival), Main St., Manchester;
(203) 646-2223.
International Dance Festival, Olde Mistick Village, Mystic; (203) 536-4941.
Wapping Fair, Rye State Park, South Windsor; (203) 644-1513.

October

Harvest Celebration Weekend, South Windsor; (203) 528-2396.

December

Victorian Christmas Open House, Hicks-Sterns Museum, Tolland;
(203) 875-7552.
Holiday Open House at Cheney Homestead, Manchester; (203) 643-5239.

Maine

February

Caribou Winter Carnival, Caribou; (207) 498-6156.

March
Moosehead Region Sled Dog Races, Greenville; (207) 695-2702.
Rangeley Lake Sled Dog Races, Rangeley; (207) 864-5364.
Maine Maple Sunday, statewide; (207) 289-3491.

April
Fisherman's Festival, Boothbay Harbor; (207) 633-4008.

June
Old Port Festival, Portland; (207) 722-6828.
Great Kennebec River Whatever Week and Race, Augusta; (207) 623-4559.
Maine Storyteller's Festival, Rockport; (207) 773-4909.

July
Canada/USA Festival, Ocean Park; (207) 934-5034.
Windjammer Days, Boothbay Harbor; (207) 633-2353.
Oyster Festival, Damariscotta; (207) 563-3175.
Deering Oaks Family Festival, Portland; (207) 772-2811.
Yarmouth Clam Festival, Yarmouth; (207) 846-3984.
Maine Potato Blossom Festival, Fort Fairfield; (207) 472-3381.

August
Maine Lobster Festival, Rockland; (207) 596-0376.
Down East Jazz Festival, Rockport; (207) 594-7374.

September
Blue Grass Festival, Brunswick; (207) 725-6009.
International Seaplane Fly-In, Greenville; (207) 695-2702.

Massachusetts

January
Winter Carnival, Holyoke Heritage State Park, Holyoke; (413) 534-1723.

February
Washington's Birthday Celebration, Old Sturbridge Village, Sturbridge;
   (508) 347-3362.

March
Saint Patrick's Day Parade, South Boston; (617) 268-8525.
Saint Patrick's Day Parade, Holyoke; (413) 534-3376.

April
Boston Marathon, Boston; (617) 435-4303.
Reenactment of the Battle of Lexington and Concord, Lexington Green, Lexington; (617) 862-1450.
Reenactment of Paul Revere's ride, Hanover St., Boston; (617) 536-4100.
Patriot's Day Parade, City Hall to North End, Boston; (617) 742-3877.

May
Art Newbury Street, Boston; (617) 267-9416.
Salem Seaport Festival, Salem Common, Salem; (508) 462-1333.
Sheep Shearing Festival, Old North Andover Common, Andover; (508) 686-0191.
New England Street Performer's Festival, Faneuil Hall Marketplace, Boston; (617) 523-1300.

June
Saint Anthony's Festival, North End, Boston; (617) 523-2110.
International Dory Races, State Fish Pier, Gloucester; (508) 281-2695.
Bunker Hill Weekend, Charlestown Navy Yard, Charlestown; (617) 242-5642.
Saint Peter's Fiesta/Blessing of the Fleet, Saint Peter's Square, Gloucester; (508) 775-9100.
Soup & Chowder Festival, Provincetown; (508) 487-2313.

July
Boston Harborfest, Boston Harbor area and Harbor Islands; (617) 227-1528.
Harbor Islands Children's Fest, Boston Harbor Island State Park; (617) 740-1605.
Edgartown Regatta, Martha's Vineyard; (508) 627-4364.
National Folk Festival, Court Square, Springfield; (413) 787-6622.
Mashpee Wampanoag Powwow, Mashpee; (508) 477-0208.
Boston Chowder Fest, City Hall Plaza, Boston; (617) 227-1528.
Massachusetts Art and Craft Summerfest, Fairgrounds, Topsfield; (508) 887-2212.
Fishtown Horribles Parade, Gloucester; (508) 283-1601.
Old Sturbridge Village Independence Day, Sturbridge; (508) 347-3362.

Barnstable County Fair, Fairgrounds, East Falmouth; (617) 563-3200.

Feast of the Blessed Sacrament (largest Portuguese feast in the U.S.), Madiera Field, New Bedford; (617) 992-6911.

August

Centre Street Festival, Waterfront, New Bedford; (617) 997-1250.

Gloucester Waterfront Festival, Gloucester Harbor; (508) 283-1601.

Teddy Bear Rally, Amherst Town Common, Amherst; (413) 253-9666.

Carnival, Provincetown; (508) 487-2313.

Festival of Shaker Crafts and Industries, Hancock Shaker Village, Pittsfield; (413) 443-0188.

August Moon Festival, Chinatown, Boston; (617) 542-2574.

Blessing of the Fleet/Tall Ships, Piers 3 and 4, New Bedford; (617) 997-1250.

September

Gloucester Schooner Festival, Gloucester; (508) 283-1601.

Newburyport Waterfront Festival, Newburyport; (508) 462-6680.

October

Topsfield Fair, Fairgrounds, Topsfield; (508) 887-2212.

Head of the Charles Regatta (rowing event), Charles River, Boston; (617) 536-4100.

Haunted Happenings (citywide Halloween festival), Salem; (508) 774-0004.

New Hampshire

May

Historic Preservation Week, Strawbery Banke, Portsmouth; (603) 433-1100.

Memorial Day Celebration, Seashell Stage, Hampton Beach; (603) 926-8717.

Summer Kickoff Weekend, Funspot, Weirs Beach; (603) 366-4377.

Family Day, Main St., New Ipswich; (603) 227-3956.

June

Market Square Day, Portsmouth; (603) 431-5388.
Coach and Carriage Festival; (603) 432-7795.
International Children's Festival, Somersworth; (603) 692-5869.
Portsmouth Jazz Festival; (603) 436-7678.

July

Family Outdoor Discovery Day, White Lake State Park, Tamworth;
   (603) 271-3254.
Monadnock Summer Festival, Peterborough.
New Hampshire State Parks Week (family activities at many State Parks);
   (603) 271-3254.
Children's Day, N.H. Farm Museum, Milton; (603) 652-7840.

August

Children's Day, Strawbery Banke, Portsmouth; (603) 433-1100.
Children's Week, Hampton Beach State Park; (603) 926-8717.
Family Outdoor Discovery Day, Greenfield State Park; (603) 271-3254.
Attitash Equine Festival, Attitash Mountain; (603) 374-2374.
Lakes Region Fine Arts & Crafts Festival, Meredith; (603) 279-6121.

September

Labor Day Celebration, Francestown; (603) 547-2174.
Squam Lakes Apple Festival, Holderness; (603) 968-4494.
Apple Harvest Day, Dover; (603) 742-2218.

October

October-fest, Gunstock Recreation Area, Gilford; (603) 293-4341.
New Hampshire Wildlife Fest, Holderness; (603) 968-7194.
Fall Foliage Festival, Loon Mountain, Lincoln; (603) 745-8111.
Fall Festival, Strawbery Banke, Portsmouth; (603) 433-1100.
Family Halloween Party, Funspot, Weirs Beach; (603) 366-4377.

Rhode Island

May

Annual Sail Newport Sailing Festival, Newport; (401) 846-1983.

June
Narragansett Art Festival, Narragansett; (401) 789-4079.
Gospee Day Parade, Narragansett Parkway; (401) 781-1772.

July
Newport Music Festival, Fort Adams State Park, Newport; (401) 847-3709.
Black Ships Festival, Fort Adams State Park, Newport; (401) 846-2720.
South County Hot Air Balloon Festival, URI Athletic Fields, Kingston;
    (401) 783-1770.

August
Seafood Festival, Ninigret Park, Charlestown; (401) 364-4031.
Newport Jazz Festival, Fort Adams State Park, Newport; (401) 847-3700.
The Faire or Tales of the Knights of Revelry, The Monastery, Cumberland;
    (401) 333-9000.

September
Providence Waterfront Festival, Providence; (401) 941-6790.

Vermont

May
Spring Festival, Billings Farm and Museum, Woodstock; (802) 457-2355.
Recreational Water Sport Races, Jamaica State Park, Jamaica;
    (802) 824-8178.
Mayfest, Downtown Bennington; (802) 447-3311.
Arts & Crafts Festival, Bennington; (802) 442-9624.
Bennington County Horse Show, Hildene Meadowlands, Manchester;
    (802) 362-1788.

June
Annual Quechee Balloon Festival and Crafts Fair, Quechee;
    (802) 295-7900.
Lake Champlain International Fishing Derby, Lake Champlain;
    (802) 862-7777.
Discover Jazz Festival, Burlington; (802) 863-7992.
Kid's Summerfest, Fairbanks Museum, Saint Johnsbury; (802) 748-2372.

Hand-Milking Contest, Billings Farm & Museum, Woodstock; (802) 457-2355.

July
Yellow Barn Music Festival, Putney; (802) 387-6637; July–Aug.

Vermont Symphony Picnic Concert, Woodstock; (802) 457-3981.

Killington Showcase (music and dance), Killington Resort, Sherburne; (802) 422-3333; July–Aug.

Winter Games (ice skating, skiing, snowboarding), Church Street, Marketplace, Burlington; (802) 863-1648.

Woodstock Summer Festival and Craft Fair, Route 4, Woodstock; (802) 457-3981.

Vermont Hand Crafters Stowe Craft Fair, Stowe; (802) 388-0123.

Southern Vermont Craft Fair, Hildene Meadows, Manchester; (802) 362-1788.

Aquafest Summer Celebration, Gardner Park, Newport; (802) 334-7782.

Midsummer Festival of the Arts, State House Lawn, Montpelier; (802) 229-9408.

Killington Mountain Equestrian Festival, Sherburne; (802) 422-4302.

19th-Century Crafts Day, Billings Farm & Museum, Woodstock; (802) 457-2355.

A Fair Day on the Hill, S. Vermont Art Center, Manchester; (802) 362-1405.

August
Champlain Valley Festival, Kingsland Bay State Park, Ferrisburg; (802) 849-6968.

Great American Buskers Festival (comedy/vaudeville), downtown Burlington; (802) 864-8178.

Quechee Scottish Festival, Quechee Polo Field, Quechee; (802) 295-5351.

Bennington Battle Day Weekend, Bennington; (802) 447-3311.

Shelburne Craft Fair, Shelburne Farms, Shelburne; (802) 864-8178.

Children's Day, Billings Farm & Museum, S. Woodstock; (802) 457-2355.

September
Vermont State Fair, Rutland; (802) 775-5200.

Mad River Valley Craft Fair, Howard Bank Green, Waitsfield; (802) 496-3639.

December
Candlelight Tours, Hildene, Manchester Village; (802) 362-1788.

Going apple picking—and allowing
yourself several samples—is a great way
to spend an autumn day in New England.

Index

Photo Credits

Our heartfelt thanks to Greg Nikas for his special style and unlimited patience. Greg's photographs can be found on pages: cover, x, 5, 11, 23, 26, 33, 65, 141, 154, 173, 190.

George Bellerose/Appalachian Mountain Club: 47, 79, 125, 130, 195, 206, 216, 222. Courtesy of Museum of Science, Boston: 3; Courtesy of New England Aquarium: 7; Courtesy of Plimouth Plantation: 29; Courtesy of Edaville Railroad: 31; Robert S. Arnold/Old Sturbridge Village: 39; Bartlett Hendricks/Berkshire Visitor's Bureau: 42; Courtesy of Office of Travel & Tourism, Commonwealth of Massachusetts: 50, 235; Courtesy of Children's Museum of Maine: 72; Courtesy of Sugarloaf U.S.A.: 84; Courtesy of the Children's Museum of Portsmouth: 95; Courtesy of Science Center of New Hampshire: 104; Brad Hills/Fort at #4: 111; Brian McCarthy/Six Gun City: 116; Courtesy of Bretton Woods Ski Resort: 119; Bob Grant/Wildcat Ski Resort: 138; Courtesy of Santa's Land: 148; John Douglas, Flying Squirrel Graphics/Montshire Museum of Science: 157; John Smith/UVM Morgan Horse Farm: 165; Courtesy of Shelburne Museum: 166; Courtesy of Smugglers' Notch: 170, 176; Claire White-Peterson/Mystic Seaport: 181; Courtesy of Mystic Marinelife Aquarium: 183; Courtesy of Roger Williams Park Zoo: 212; John C. Meyers/Children's Museum of Rhode Island: 213.